MW01626389

PLAYBOY HELMUT NEWTON

PLAYBOY

HELMUT NEWTON

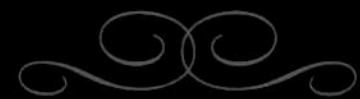

FOREWORD BY **HUGH M. HEFNER**

INTRODUCTION BY **WALTER ABISH**

AFTERWORD BY **GARY COLE**

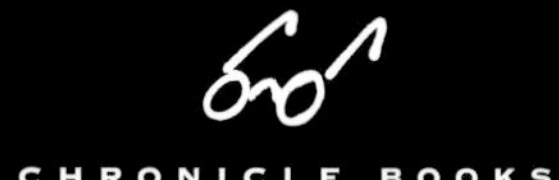

CHRONICLE BOOKS

Thanks to Bonnie Jean Kenny, Malina Lee, Mary O'Connor, Neil Olson, and Marcia Terrones.

Library of Congress Cataloging-in-Publication Data available.

ISBN: 0-8118-5065-X

Manufactured in Hong Kong

Designed by VSA Partners, Inc.

Distributed in Canada by Raincoast Books
9050 Shaughnessy Street
Vancouver, British Columbia V6P 6E5

10 9 8 7 6 5 4 3 2 1

Chronicle Books LLC
85 Second Street
San Francisco, California 94105

www.chroniclebooks.com

CONTENTS

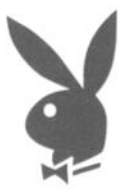

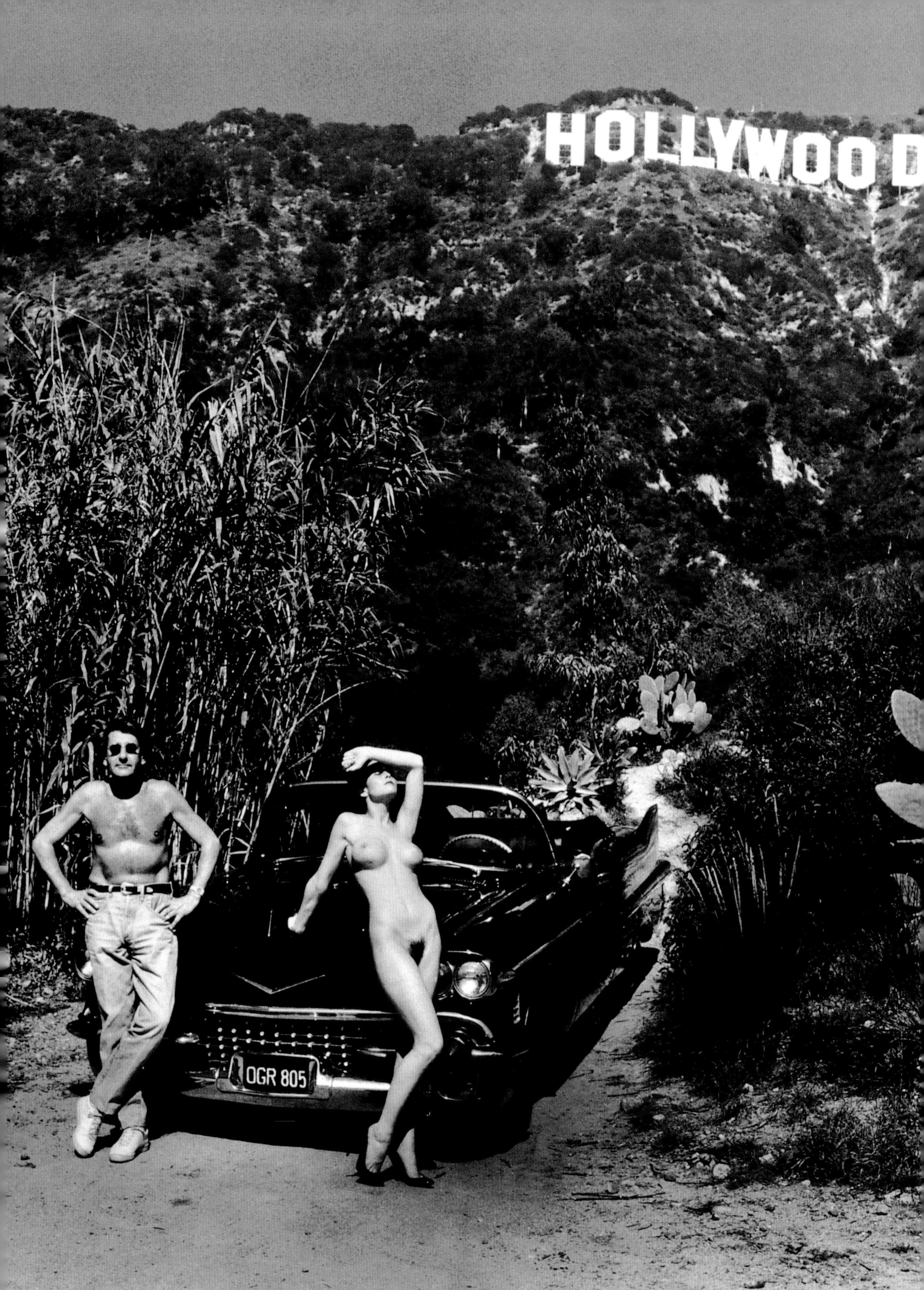
HOLLYWOOD
OGR 805

Helmut Newton was both a friend and a longtime contributor to *Playboy*. He and his wife, Alice Springs, visited the Playboy Mansion on a number of occasions for parties and movie nights. It was always fascinating to watch Helmut watch other people. He was constantly observing, often with that ironic detachment he used to particular advantage in his photographs. Of course, he found the Mansion fertile ground.

Helmut's influence on nude photography cannot be overstated. He used his fashion photographer's eye to make the erotic almost surrealistic. He could take a Playmate and put her in an alternate universe. Newton's camera turned Centerfolds into something curiously unsettling. His pictures were never simply erotic. They had an additional dimension that made a deep impression, creating a parable, a tableau vivant, not easily forgotten.

Newton had a delicious European sensibility. Many of his photos—of grand hotels, Riviera swimming pools, and mysterious salons—comment on a world far removed from our American psyche. But, like many Europeans, he was fascinated with the city of Los Angeles. As it exists in his photographs, it is a city of dreams, a strange place where naked women in high heels pick oranges from a tree. And, even though Helmut Newton was from Berlin, he comprehended that essence of Los Angeles. He knew it really is a city of dreams.

HUGH M. HEFNER

INTRODUCTION

The sexually provocative assignments that Helmut Newton undertook on behalf of *Playboy* are especially illuminating, given that the internationally renowned fashion photographer was unconstrained by the exacting dictates of the fashion world and, hence, able to seek out the erotic subjects dear to his heart to the fullest extent of the imagination.

Newton's far-reaching body of work includes portraits and cityscapes, but it is first and foremost identified with the feminine—highly sexual women acting as a lure. The poised, long-legged, interchangeably eye-catching models disclose independence and self-absorption as Newton positions them in a variety of settings to bring into play the make-believe central to his inspiration. His offhand remark that the camera is a barrier between himself and reality reveals the archetypal female who occupies so much of Newton's imagination to be an outcome of that variance. His photograph of the elegant costumed woman perched on a faux antique table, head tilted, calmly eyeing a nude who is her virtual replica, anticipates the likely interaction of control and submission. The luxurious Paris apartment, with its clinical, shiny metallic walls, the eighteenth-century painting, a copy as well, and the women's identical hairstyles sums up the staged mannerism that takes the place of a personal relationship. It comes as no surprise that Newton, the master of fantasy, after a near-fatal heart attack in 1972, was wheeled from the operating room clutching his tiny automatic Minolta as if it were a totem with the power to transform what was indeed a potent reality into one of his stimulating mise-en-scènes.

Inventing the unexpected, Newton, in a startling escalation, introduced bizarre props and mannequins to objectify the model. He even resorted to prosthetic devices in a further effort to encode and fetishize the alluring women, symbols in the ongoing narrative at the heart of each tableau. For their part, the men, young and docile or elderly and powerful, on the rare occasion when they make an appearance are more likely to participate as voyeurs—not pursuers.

In what is a personal commentary, Newton aims the camera at a mirror to frame the voyeuristic reflection of himself on a motel bed next to an artfully posed young nude. However, the camera Newton holds to his face obscures it. He is, in fact, playfully photographing his anonymity. No matter how near the women are to the men, the distance between them is fixed and irreducible. Thus, the woman enticingly parting her velour robe to expose herself to the white-haired man in the foreground, who, a cigar between his fingers, calmly appraises her, stays beyond reach. As she stands on the garden steps, gazing down at the man, her symmetrical features register nothing. A product of Newton's controlling imagination, her provocative stance substantiates her contradictory role.

Newton's depiction of the tall blonde whose only garment is a black cloak that she has draped over her dark-haired, blindfolded companion—a diminutive woman—as the two, in their high heels, preoccupied, as if on a mission, stride rapidly past a statue of a young man—may owe its composition to *The Story of O*, a book Newton admired. The tantalizing ambiguity—at first glance the minuscule woman could be mistaken for a shapely child—thrusts the viewer into a perverse reaction. It's as if Newton was intent on leading the observer into an emotional labyrinth.

It may not be possible to determine the degree to which Newton's formative years in Berlin, the city of his birth, influenced his particular photographic approach. To be German and a Jew in Berlin after Hitler's ascent to power was to experience an emotional divide—an instant drastic lesson in the paradox of everyday reality. Yet, doubtlessly, the city that until 1933 teemed with revolutionary concepts in the arts left its imprint on the budding photographer. The unfeeling female of his imagination is a familiar icon of the Berlin cabaret.

Given Newton's preoccupation with cool, self-contained women, it's noteworthy that women played such a supportive role in his career, beginning with his mother, whose encouragement and connections led to his apprenticeship with the fashion photographer Yva in 1936. Unlike her young trainee, who was smitten with her, Yva, who was Jewish, failed to heed Newton's example and flee Germany. She was sent to her death in Auschwitz a few years later.

Newton, who reached Australia by a circuitous route after being interned as an enemy alien, served in the army until the war's end, then opened his own photography studio. His meeting with and marriage to June Browne, an Australian-born actress who was to become a photographer under the name Alice Springs and his close collaborator, was providential. In quest of the success as a fashion photographer that had eluded him in Australia, Newton's return to Europe was the true beginning of his career. He and June moved to London, and then, when his already distinct, playful erotic fashion shots raised eyebrows, to Paris, the capital of fashion, which proved far more amenable to his imaginative vision and sensibility. In view of the favorable reception he was receiving in the French fashion magazines *Vogue* and *Elle*, and despite the language barrier, Newton, feeling at home in Paris, proceeded to expand the seductive, decadent allusions in his fashion photographs.

With the publication of *White Women* and *Sleepless Nights* in the seventies, and major gallery and museum exhibitions, Newton's sexually charged, fetishized point of view transfixed an audience unaccustomed to sexual defamiliarization.

In a lifetime of photographing a vast number of beguiling women, over and over again, in what Newton regarded as appropriate surroundings—shimmering swimming pools, opulent summer houses, luxurious apartments—his determination to capture their fundamental essence took on the characteristics of a quest. Albeit, given the deliberate compositional incongruities, it's at best an ambivalent quest. Nevertheless, the emblematic women Newton created as objects of wonder do satisfy a universal need, even a longing, that no amount of his ironic intimations could undo.

For the last twenty years Newton and his wife chose to live in a lavish existential no-man's-land, wintering at the Chateau Marmont in Los Angeles and spending the remainder of the year in Monte Carlo—each location, like his fashion photography, imparting an inviting artificiality.

In 2000, the retrospective exhibition of Helmut Newton's photographs at the Neue Nationalgalerie in Berlin on the occasion of his eightieth birthday signaled, in essence, a welcome greeting by the city of his youth and the beginning of a comprehensive summing-up of the fashion photographer's remarkable career. Shortly before his fatal car crash in Los Angeles, Helmut Newton carried out his long-contemplated decision to establish a foundation under his name that would permanently house and display his photographs in Berlin. For the celebrated photographer whose ashes have been laid to rest in the Friedenau cemetery in the vicinity of Marlene Dietrich's grave, it was to be a final symbolic and poignant reunion with the city he'd fled in 1938.

The widespread approval in Germany of Helmut Newton's perceived act of reconciliation was echoed in Chancellor Gerhard Schroeder's words: "His photos live on and, through them, Helmut will be remembered." It's clear that any conclusion about Newton's far-reaching achievement and the undoubted influence of his work must also take his choice of Berlin as his ultimate home into account. That this singular, purposeful figure in photography would end his life in this dramatic fashion is further evidence of his artistic constancy and resilience.

WALTER ABISH

200
MOTELS

Or, How I Spent My Summer Vacation

FEATURING

Kristine De Bell

August 1976

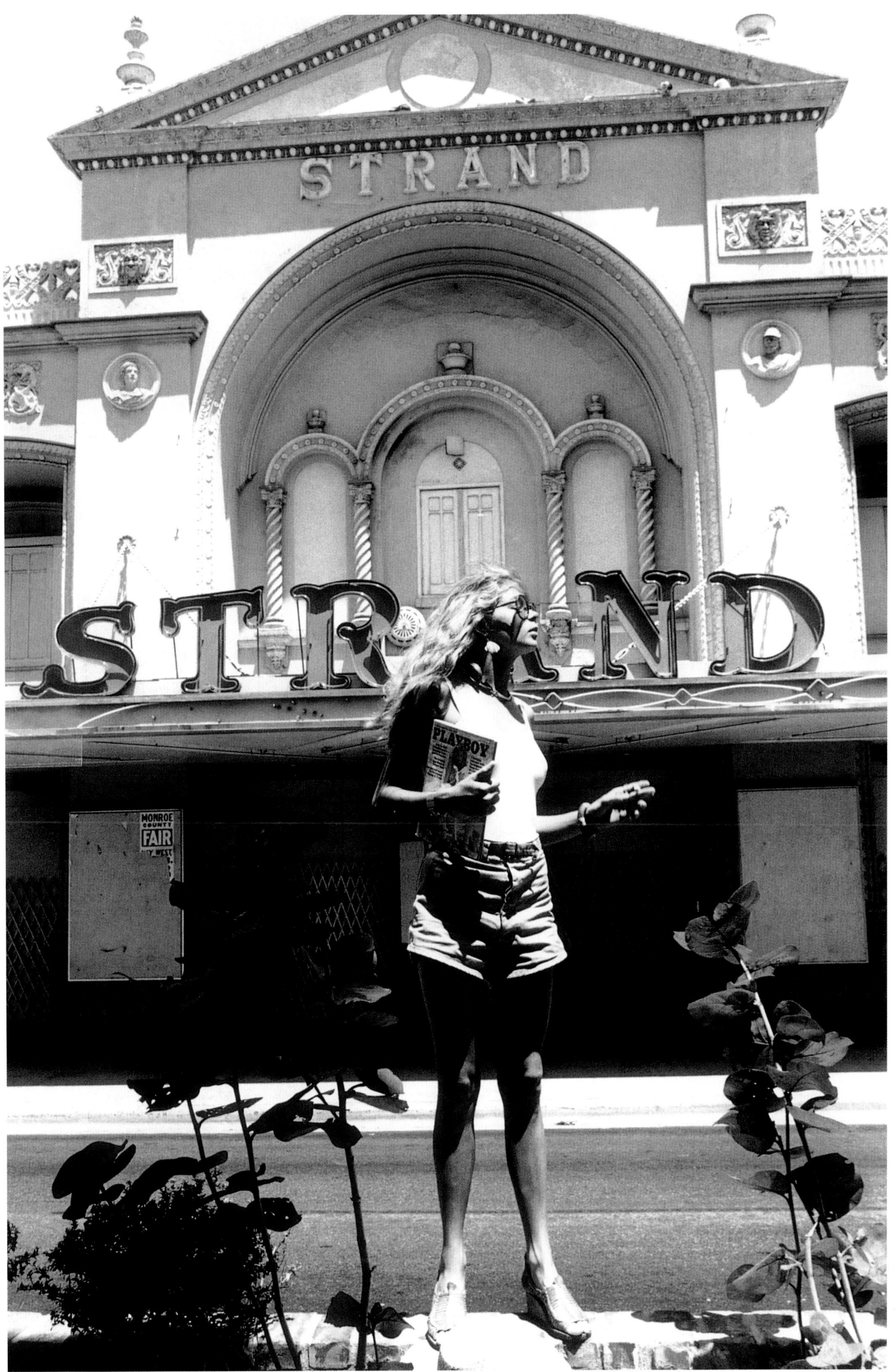
STRAND
PLAYBOY
MONROE
COUNTY
FAIR

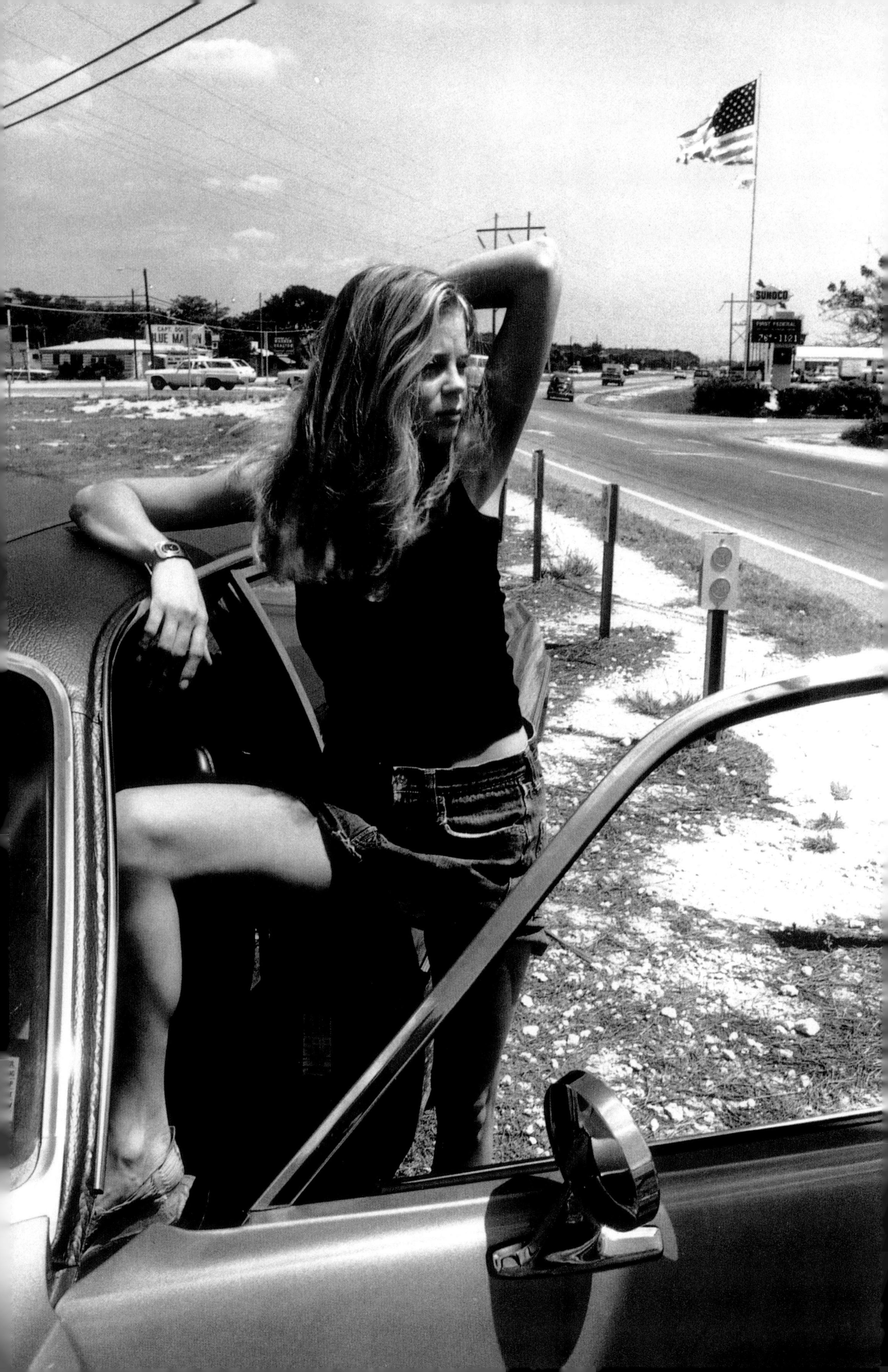
SUNOCO
FIRST FEDERAL

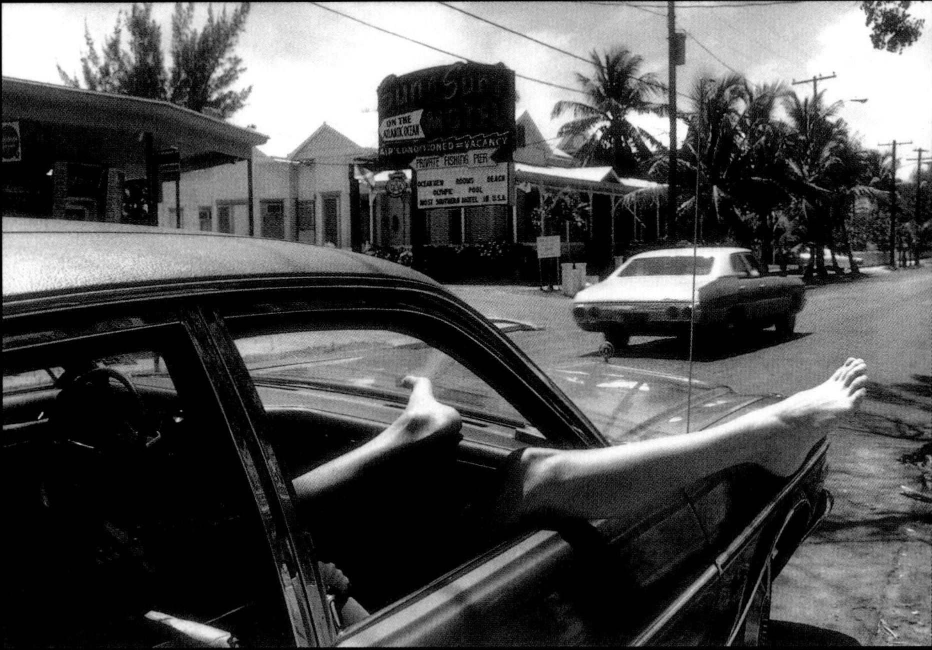

ON THE ATLANTIC OCEAN
AIR CONDITIONED = VACANCY
PRIVATE FISHING PIER
OCEANVIEW ROOMS BEACH
OLYMPIC POOL
MOST SOUTHERN MOTEL IN U.S.A.

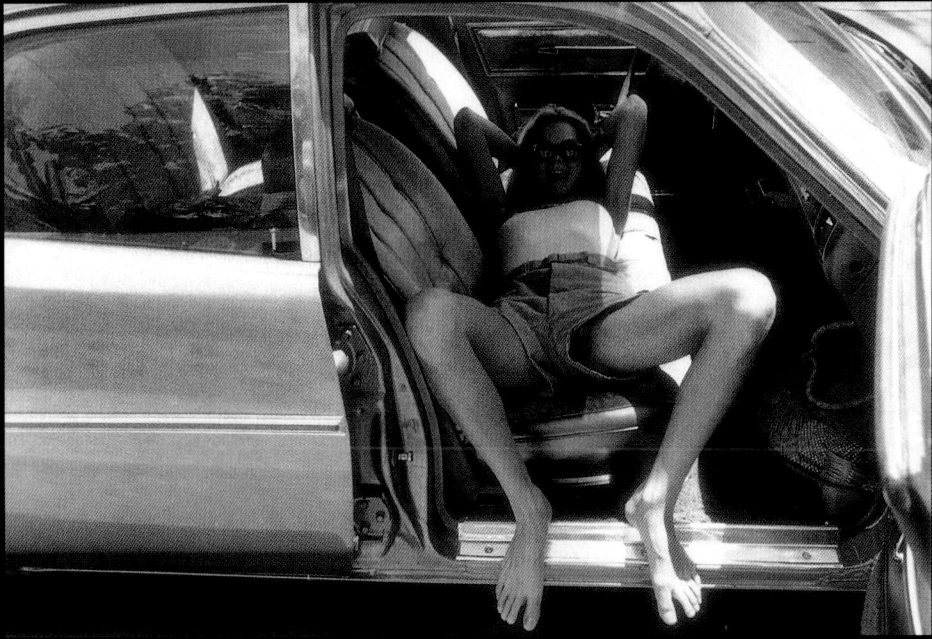

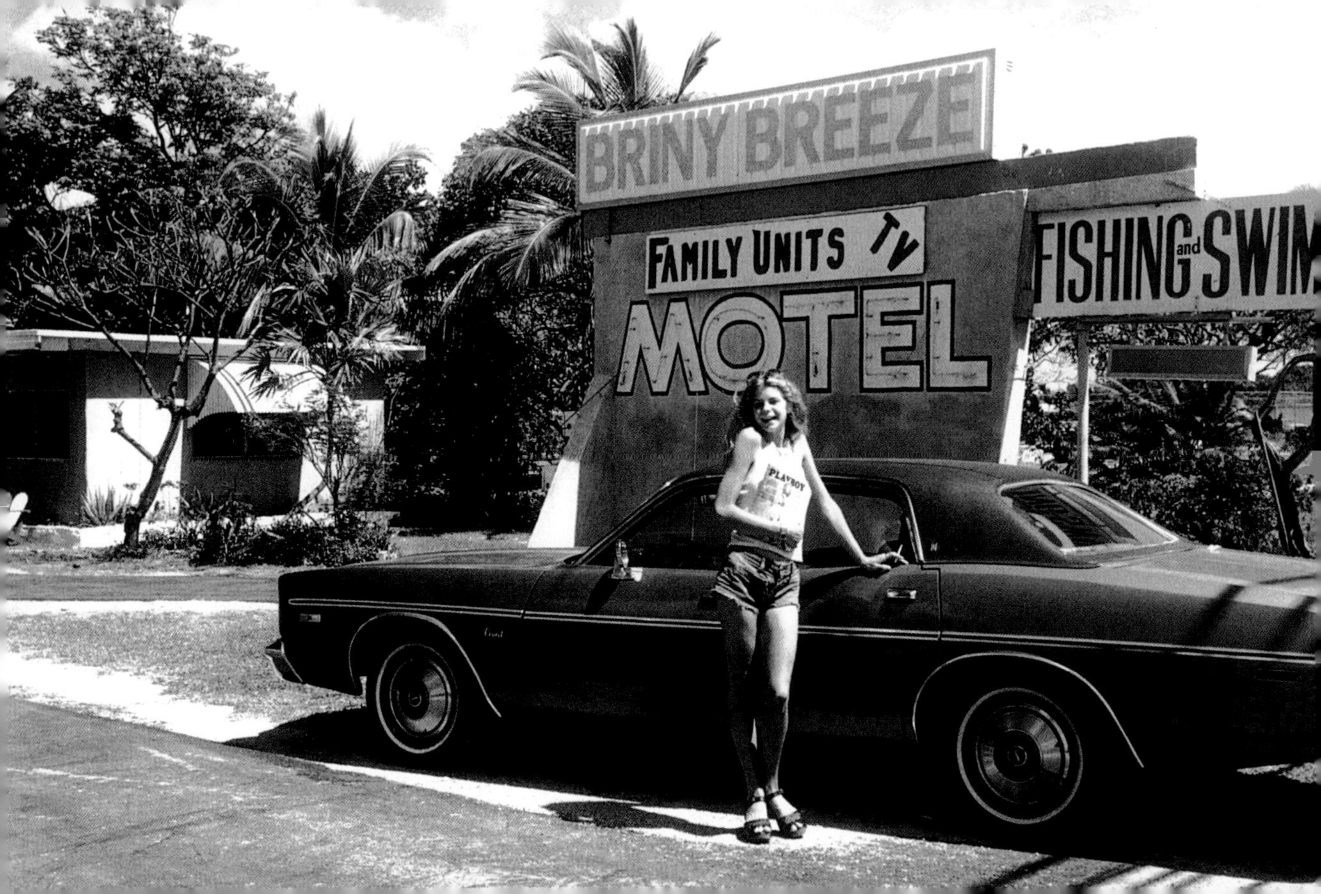
BRINY BREEZE
FAMILY UNITS TV
MOTEL
FISHING and SWIM
PLAYBOY

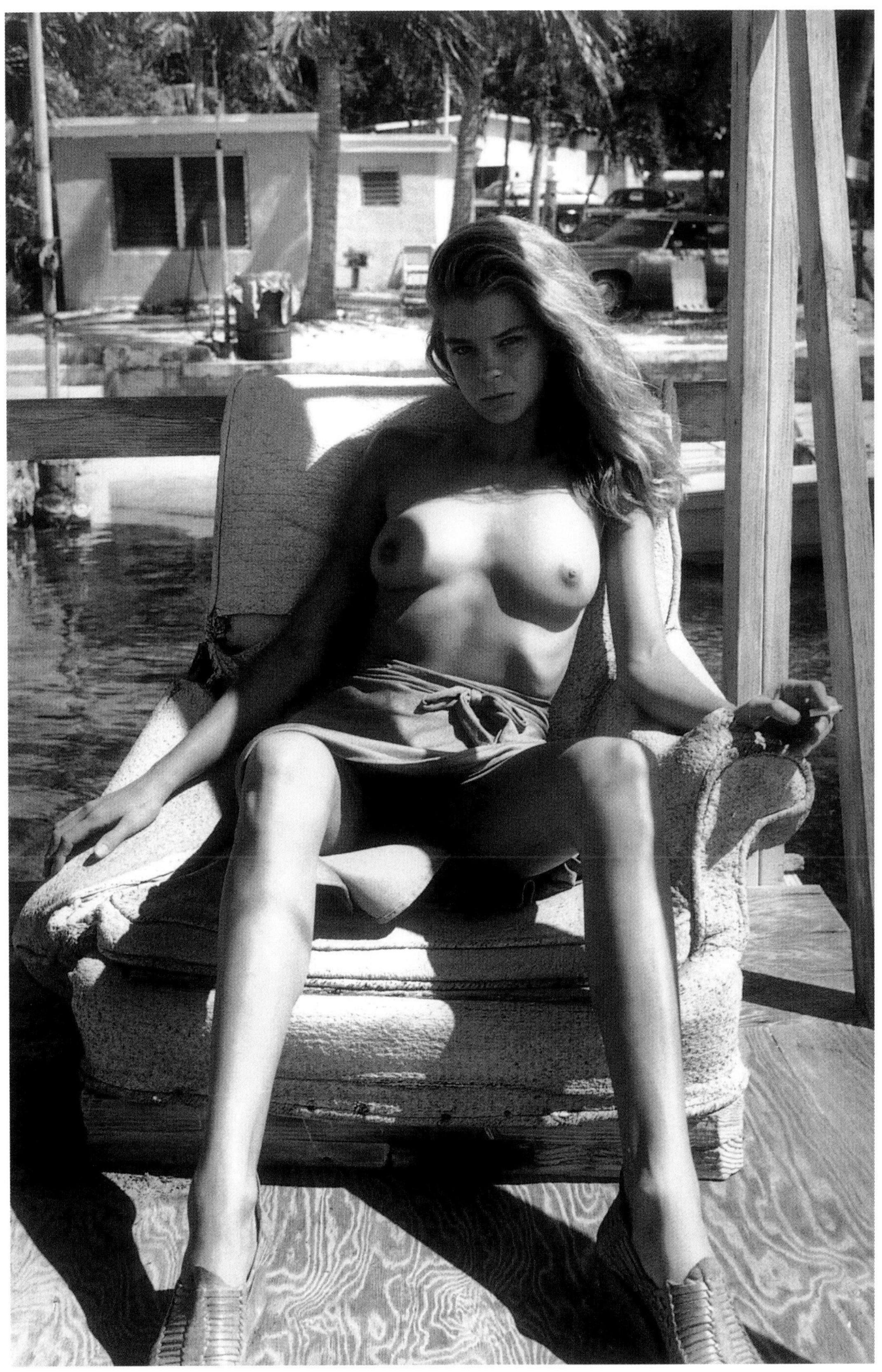

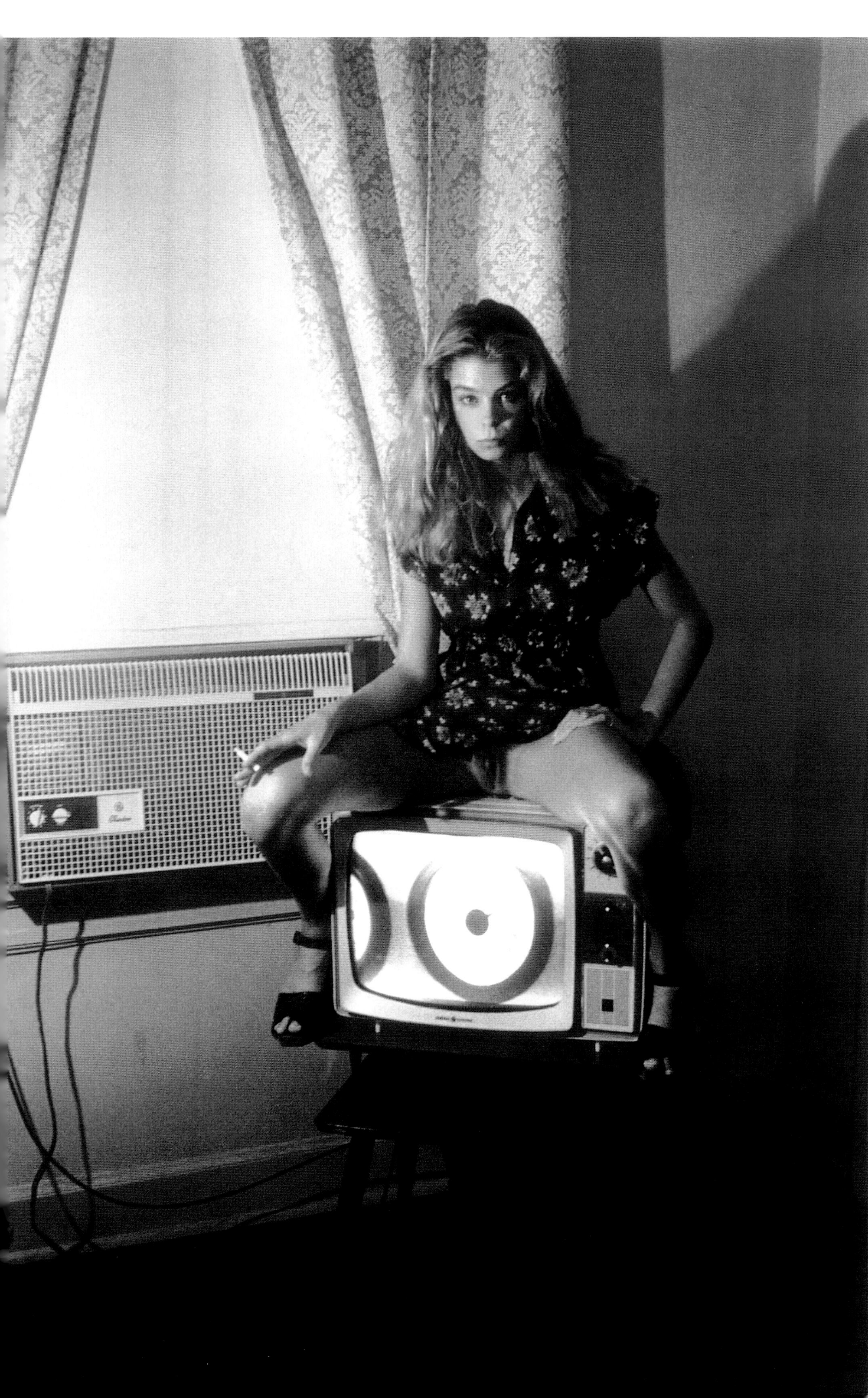

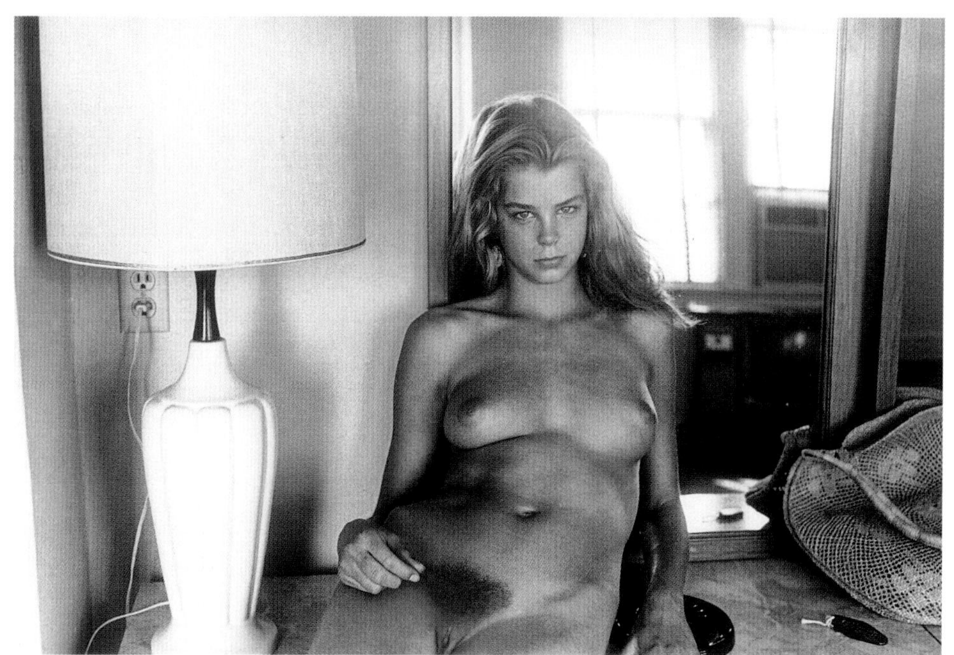

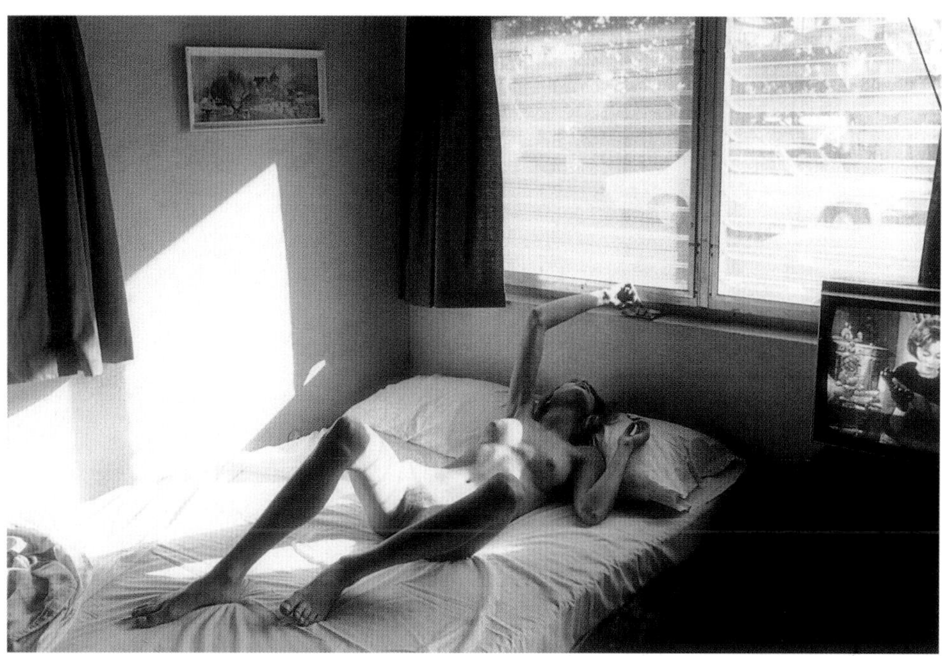

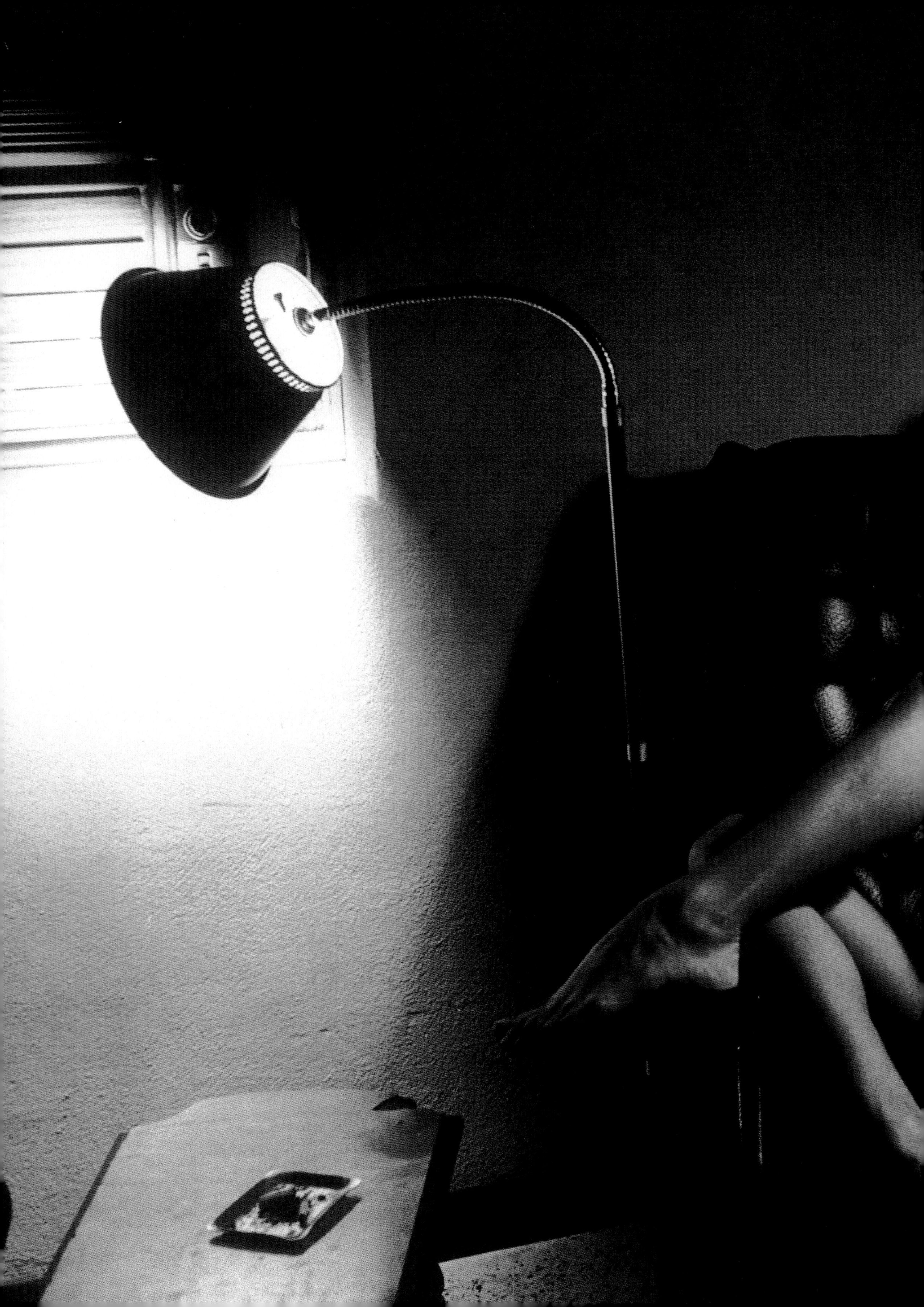

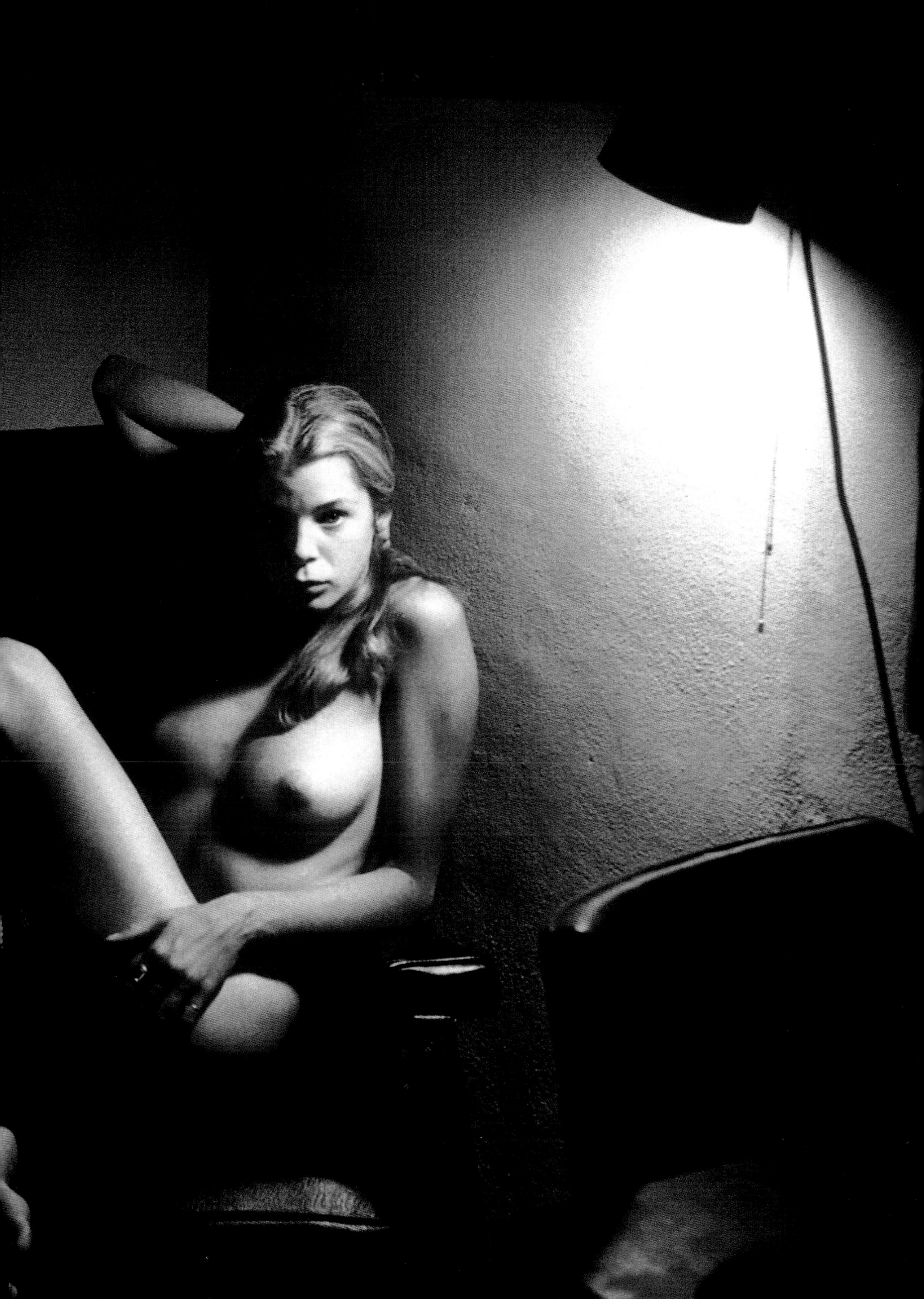

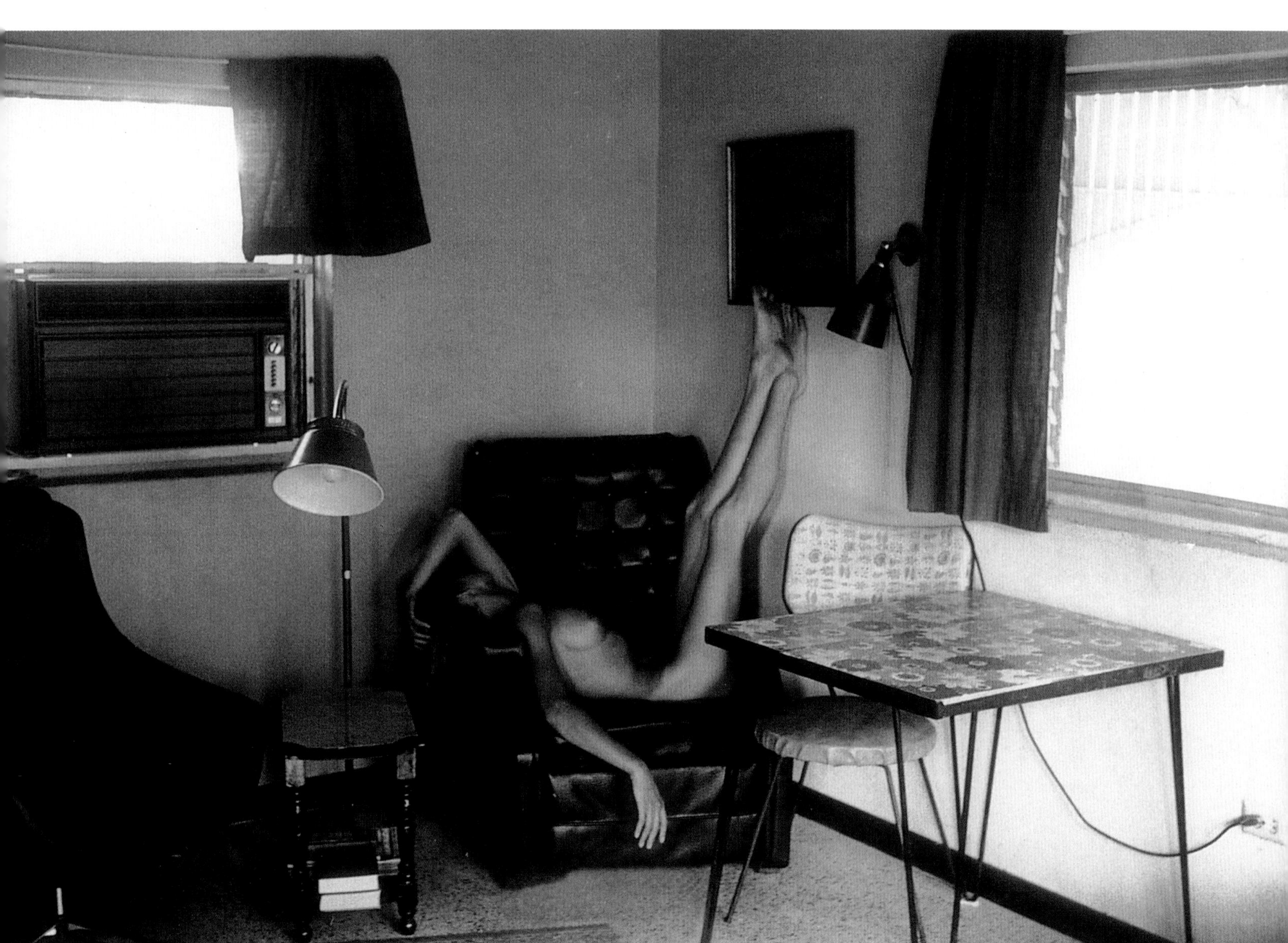

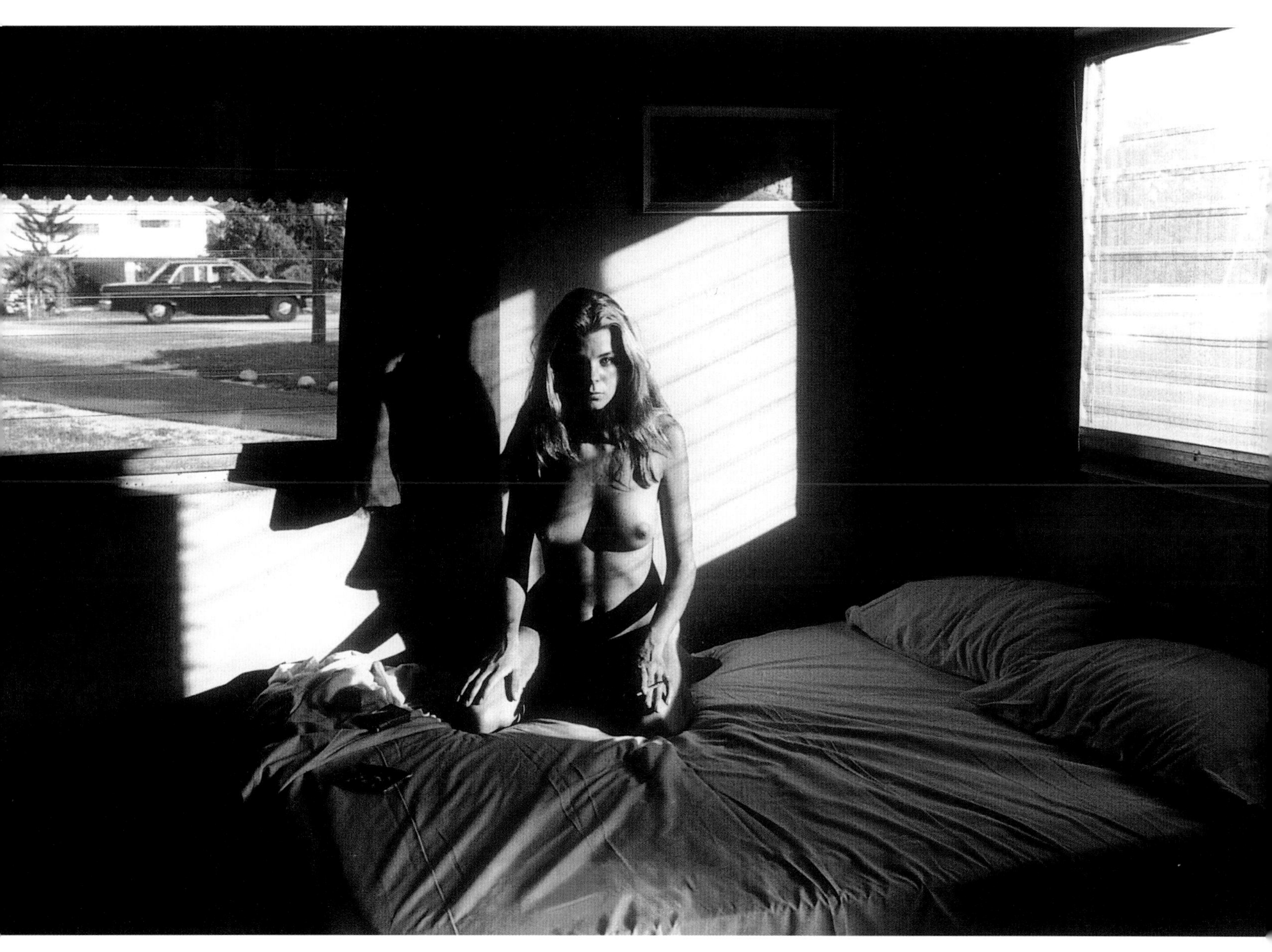

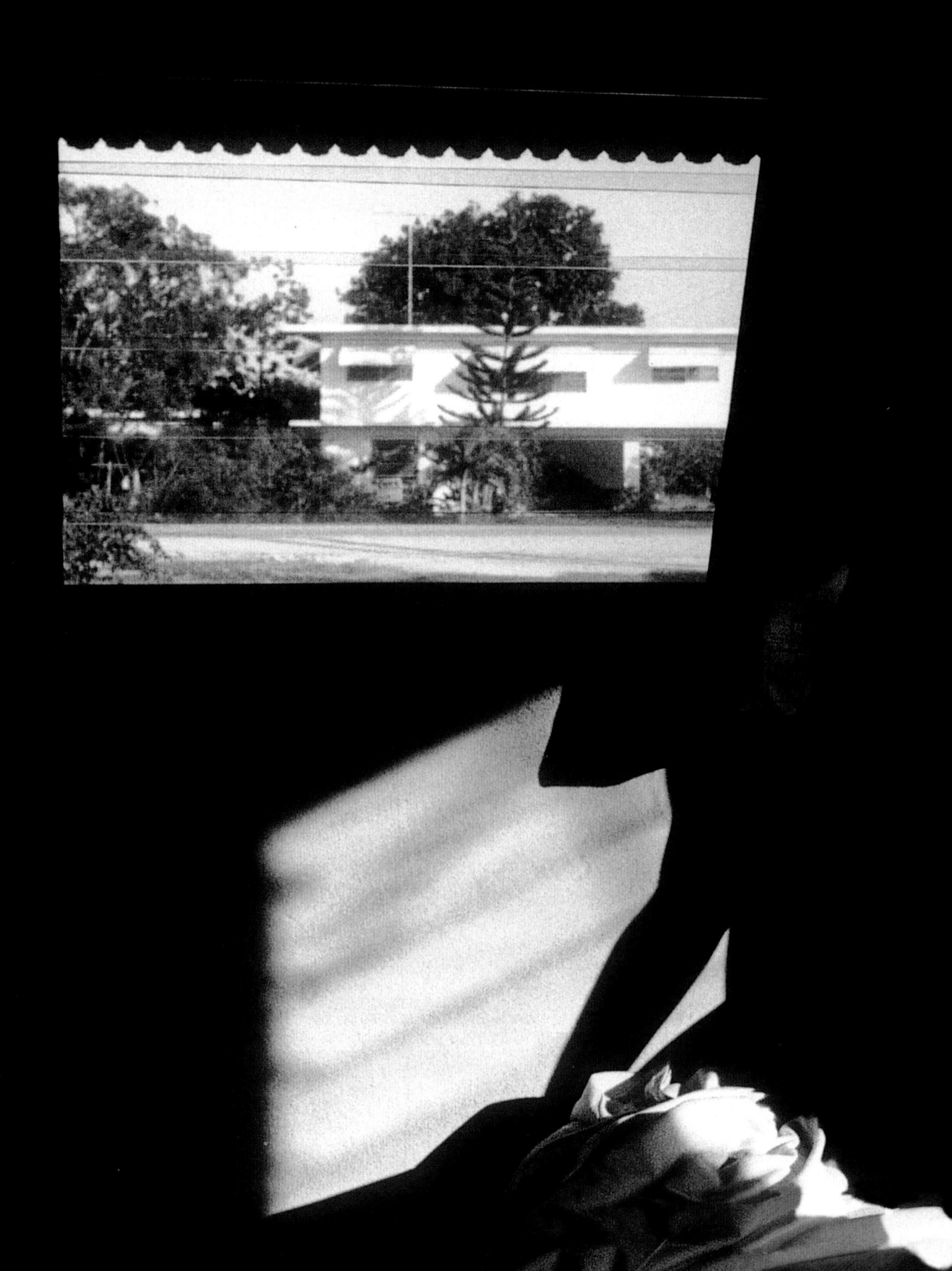

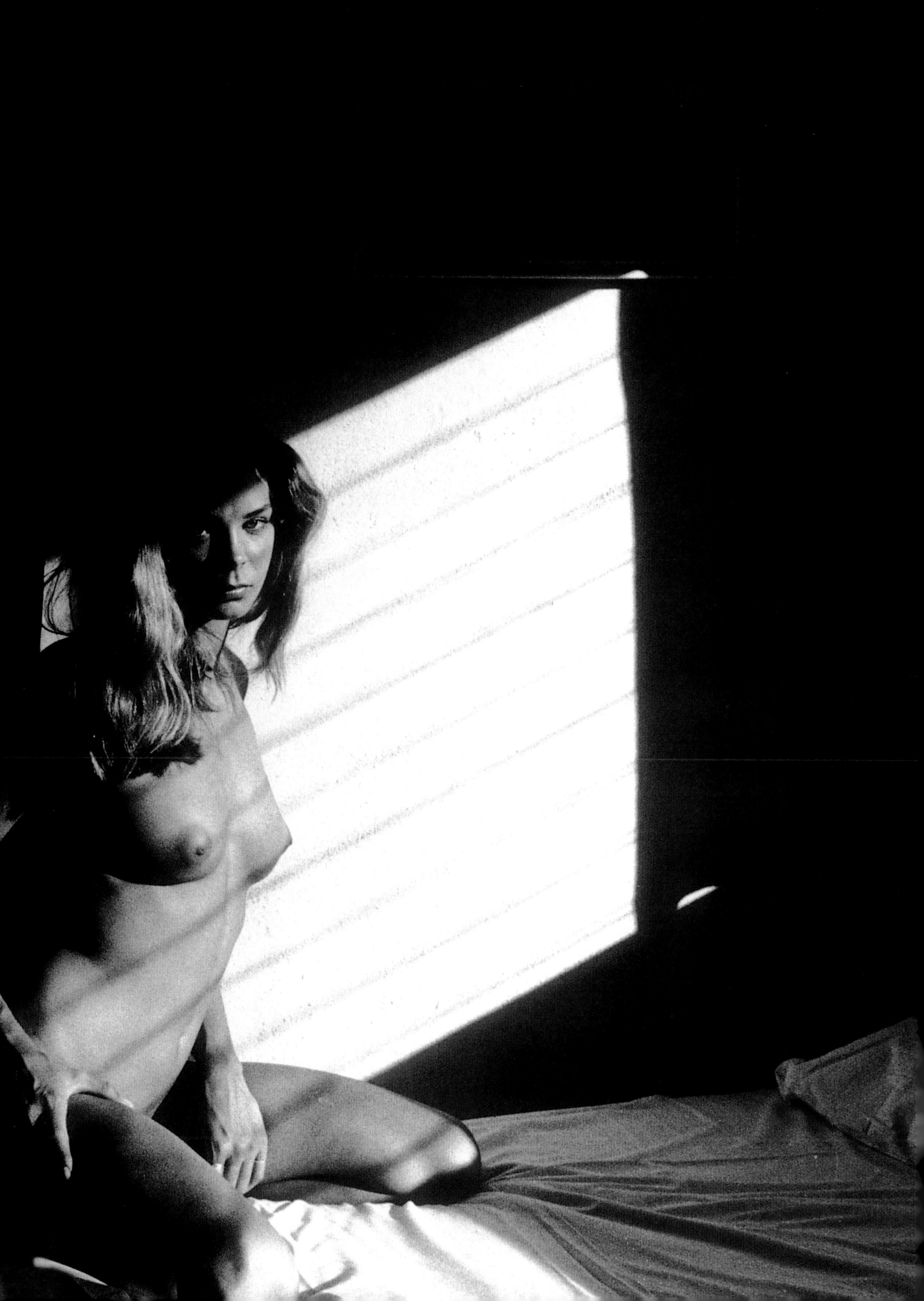

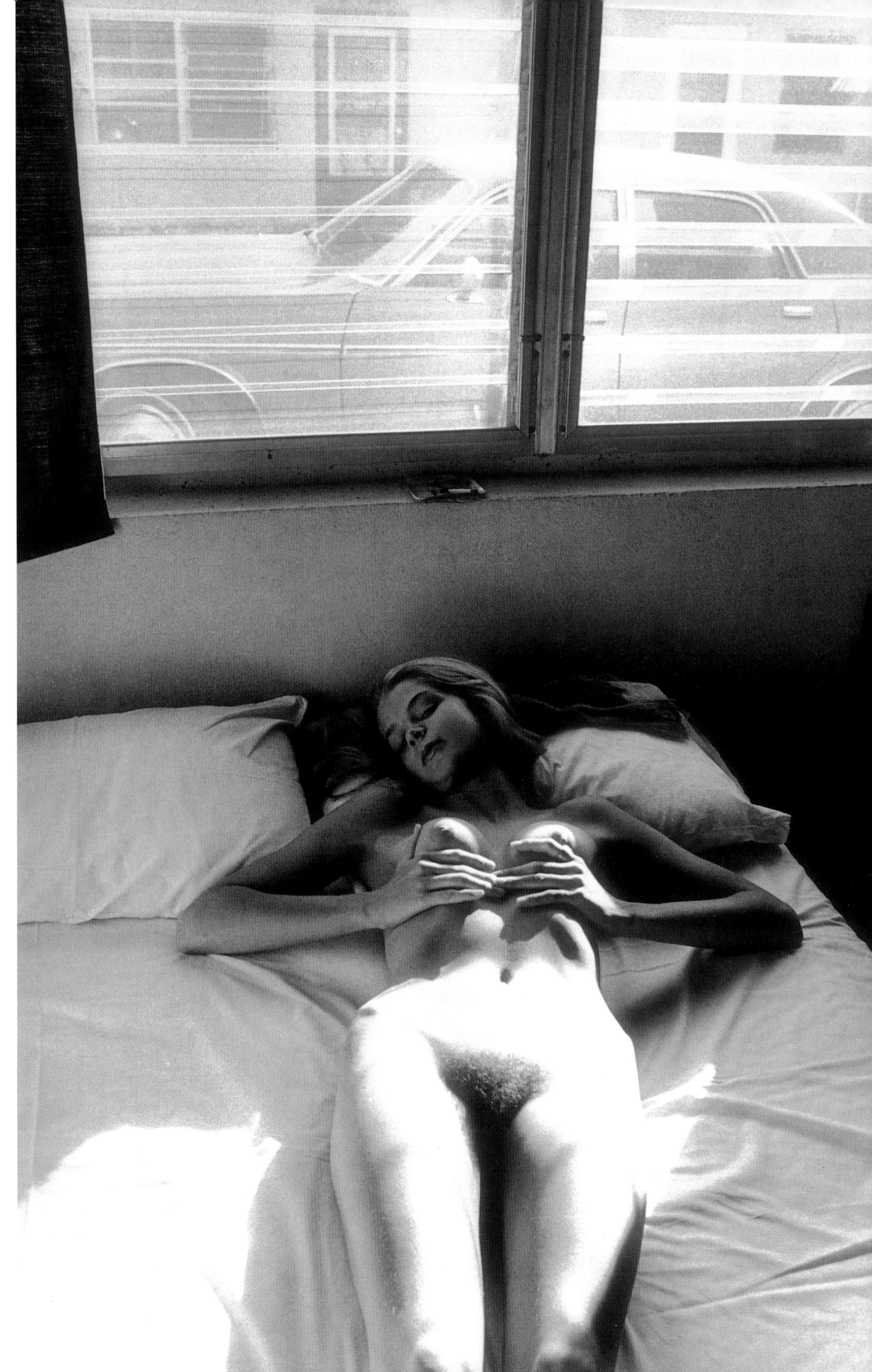

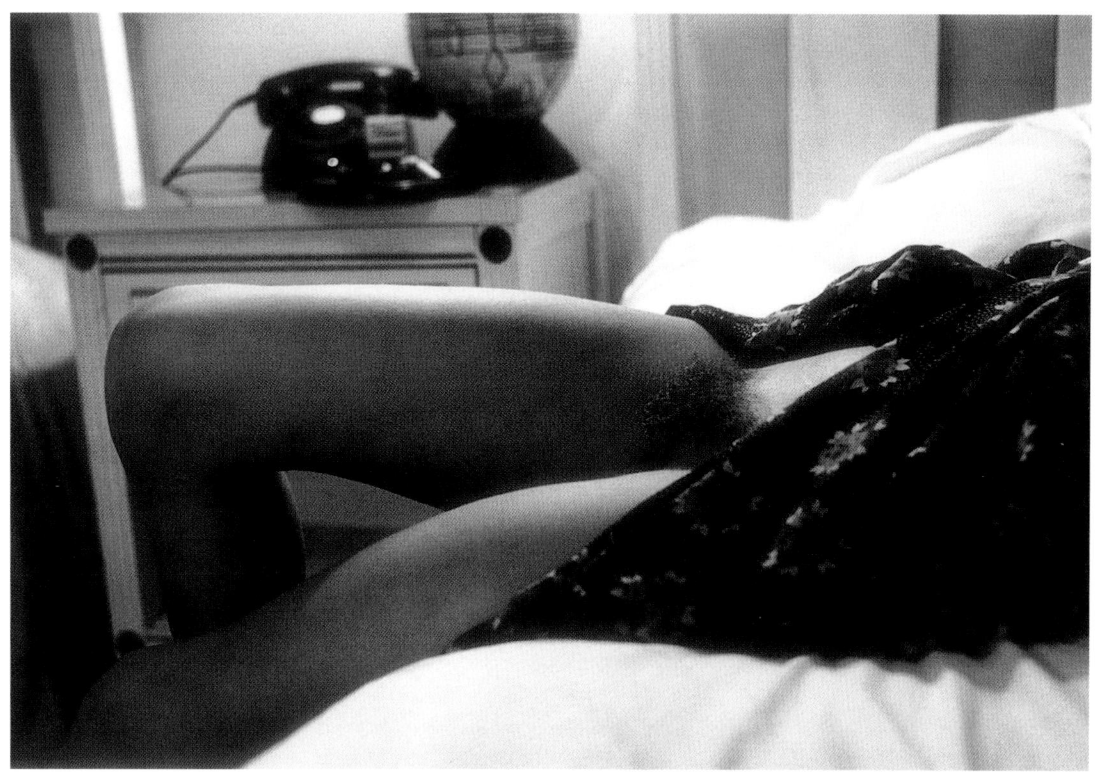

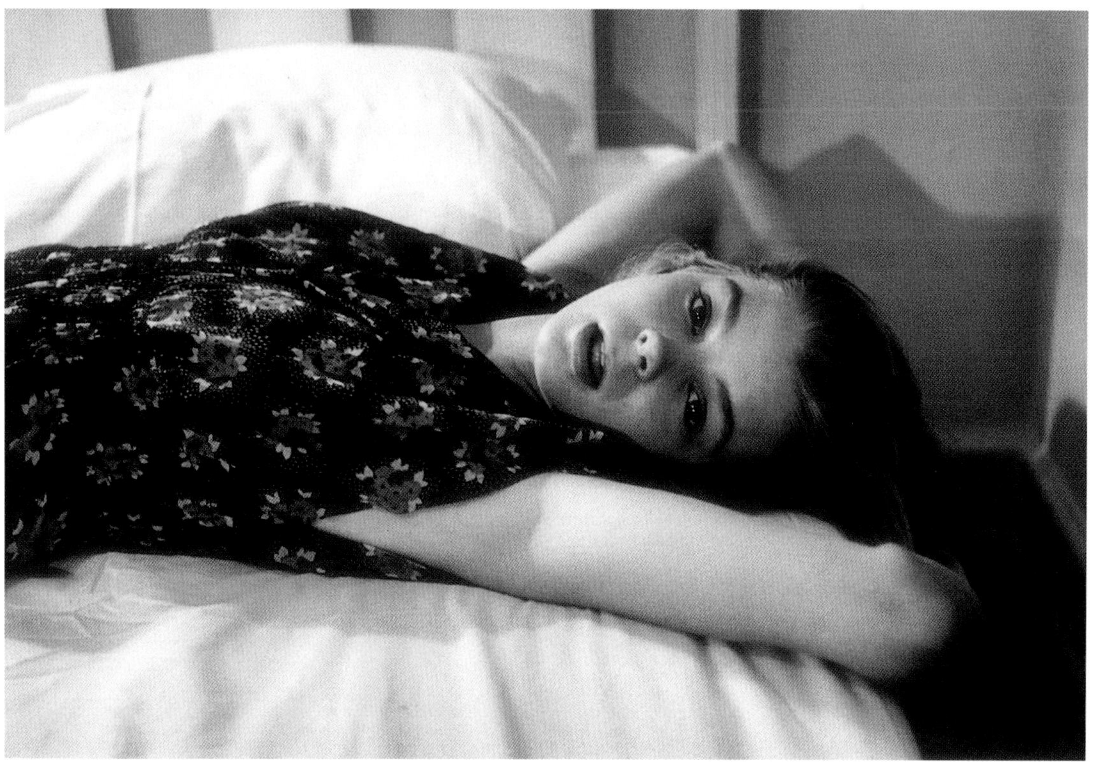

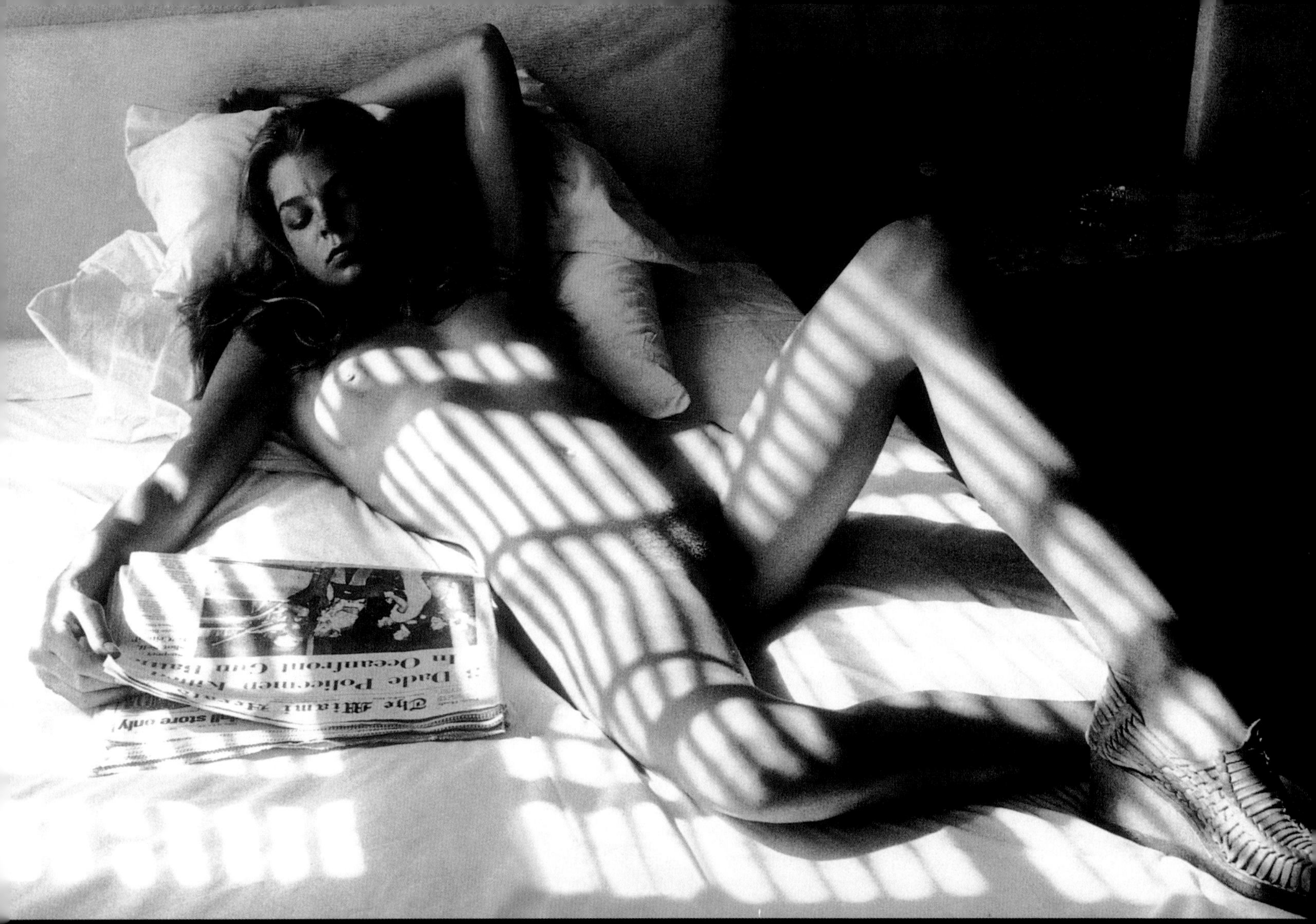

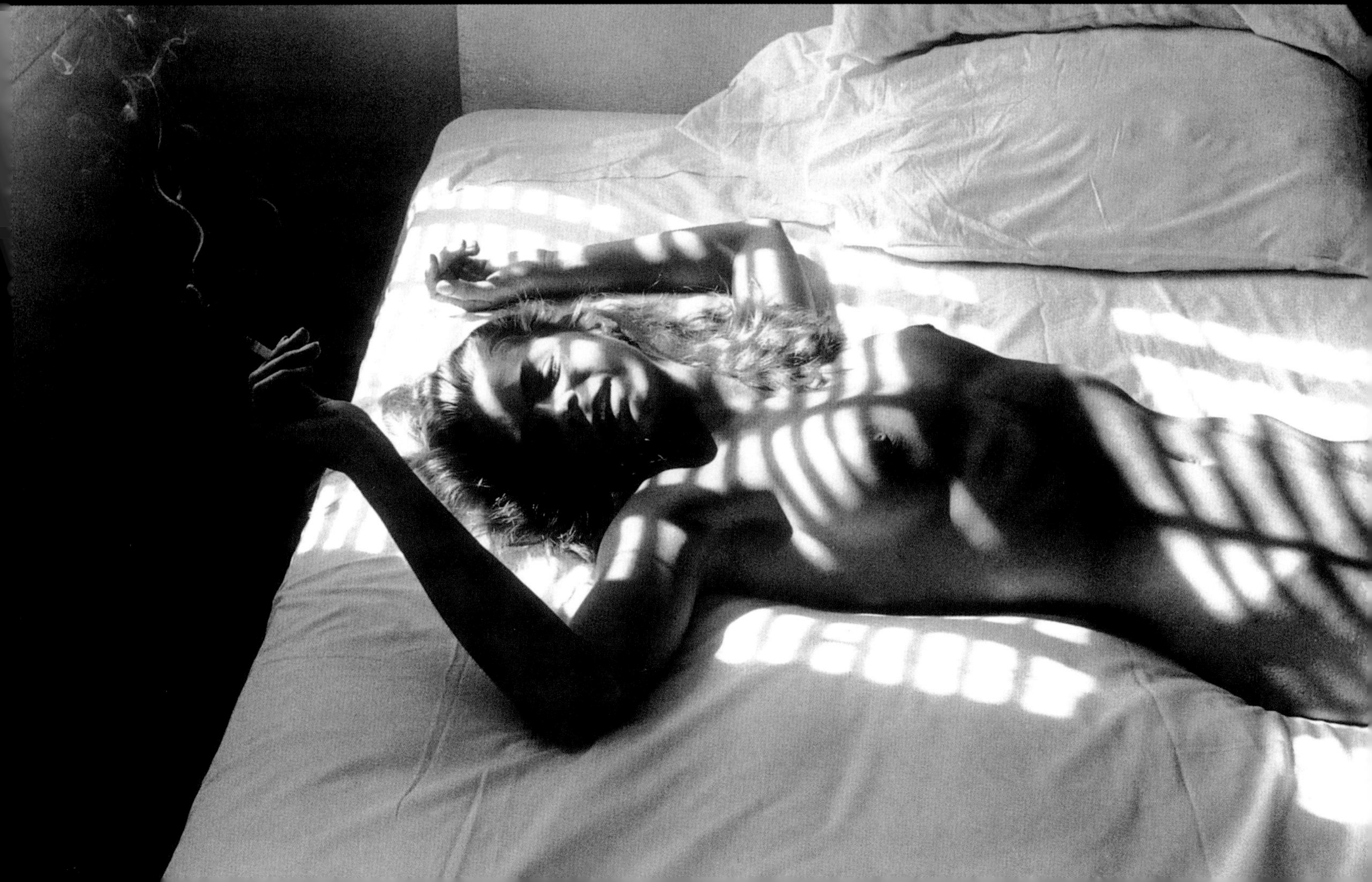

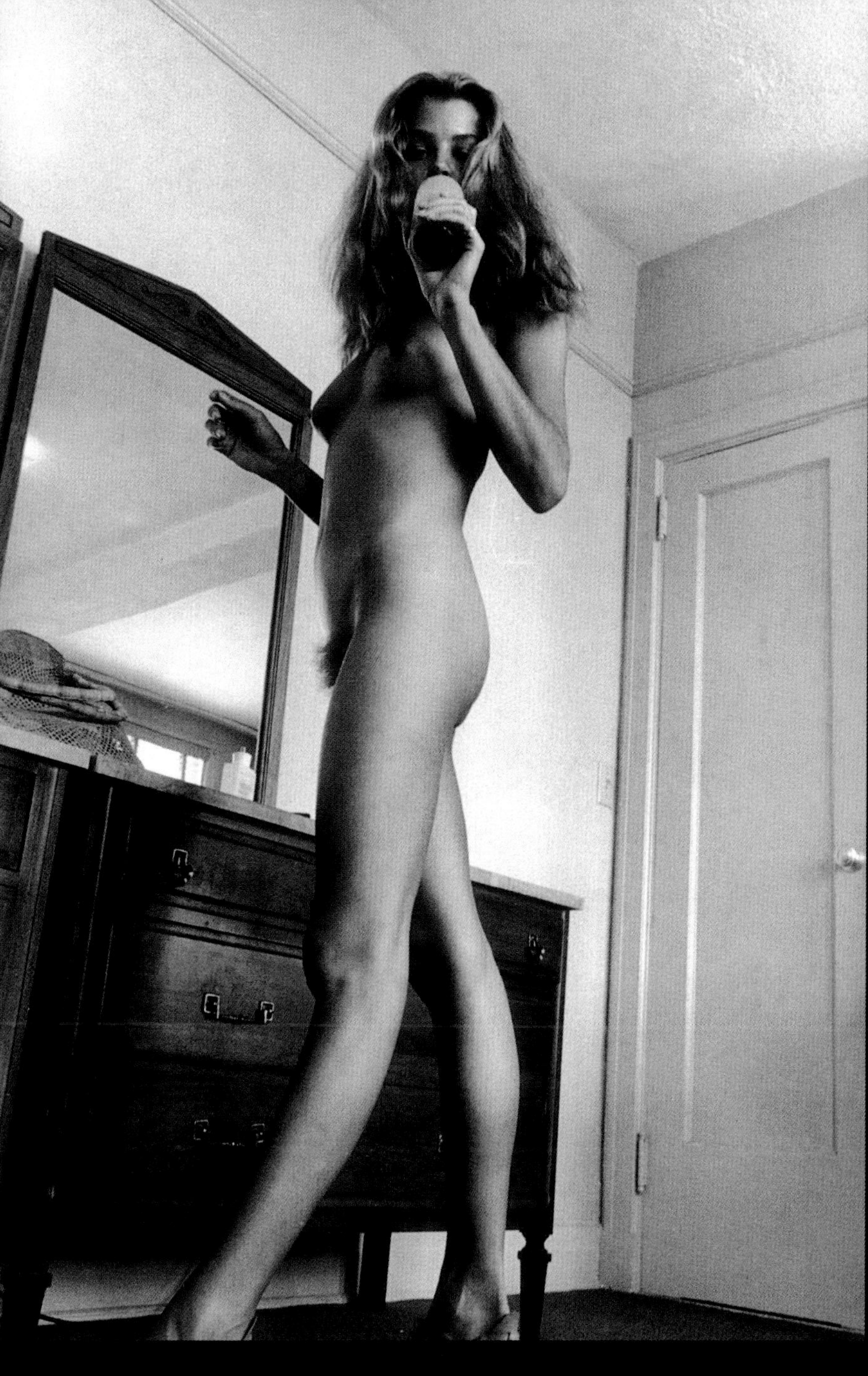

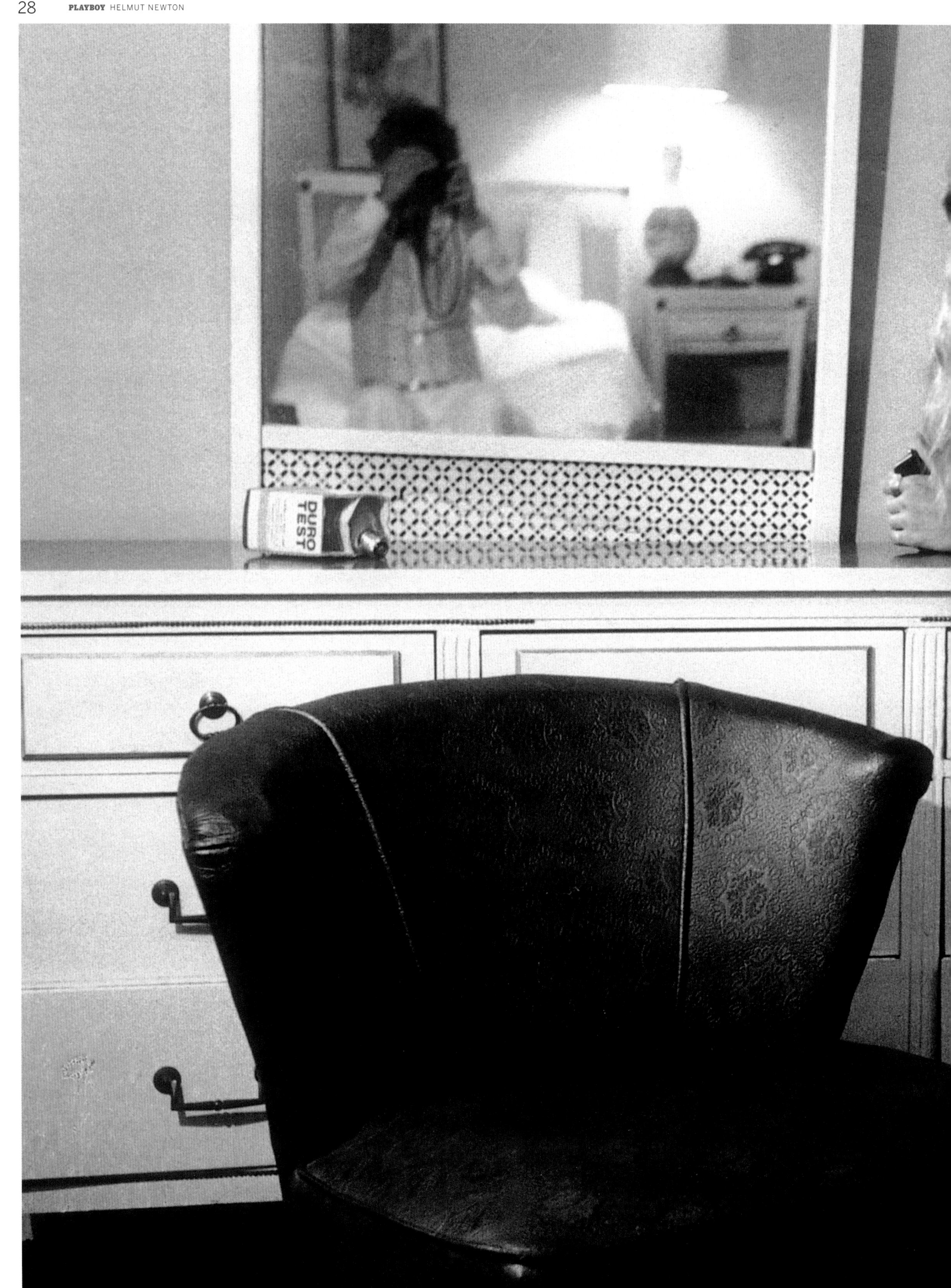
DURO
TEST

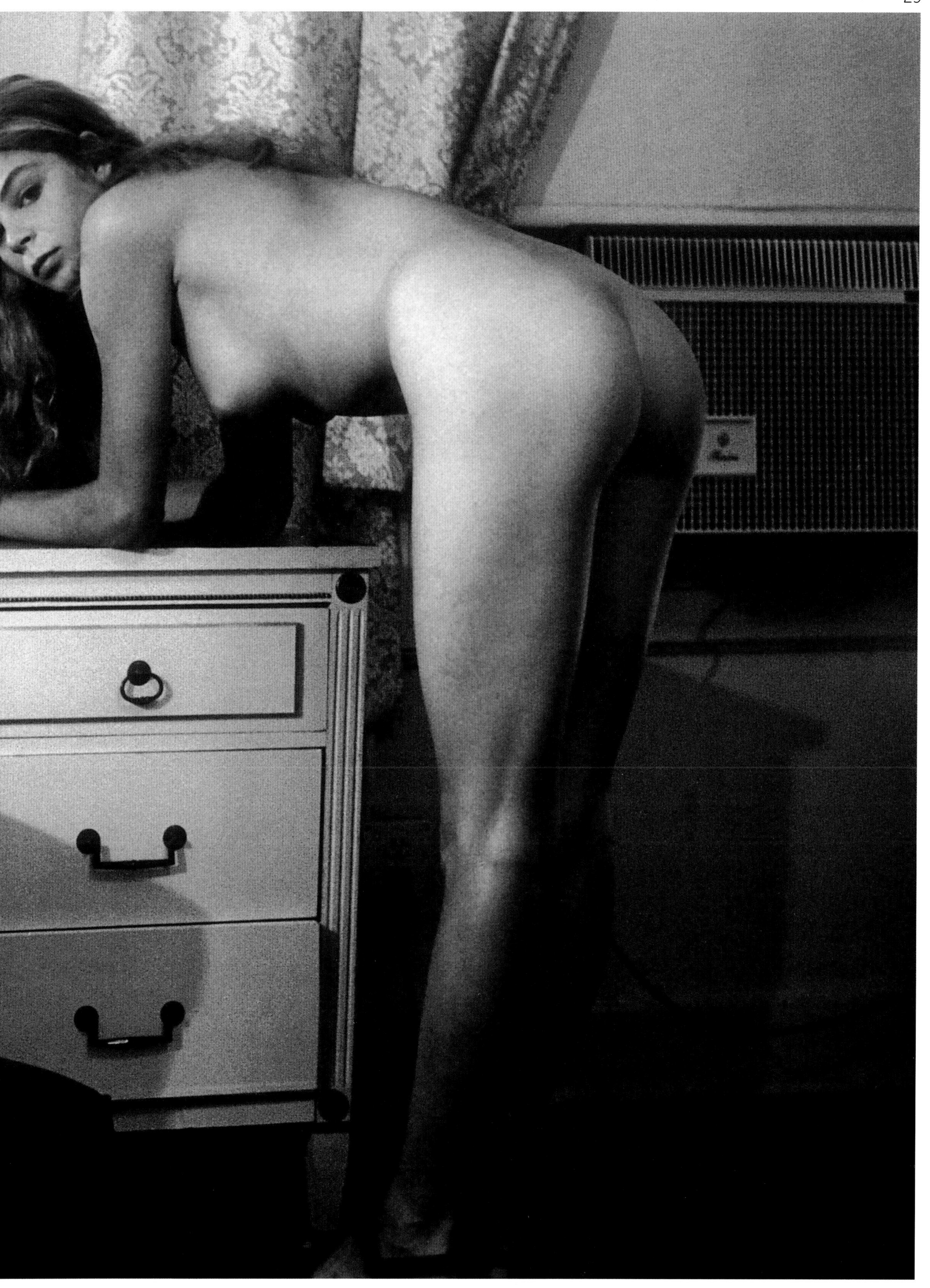

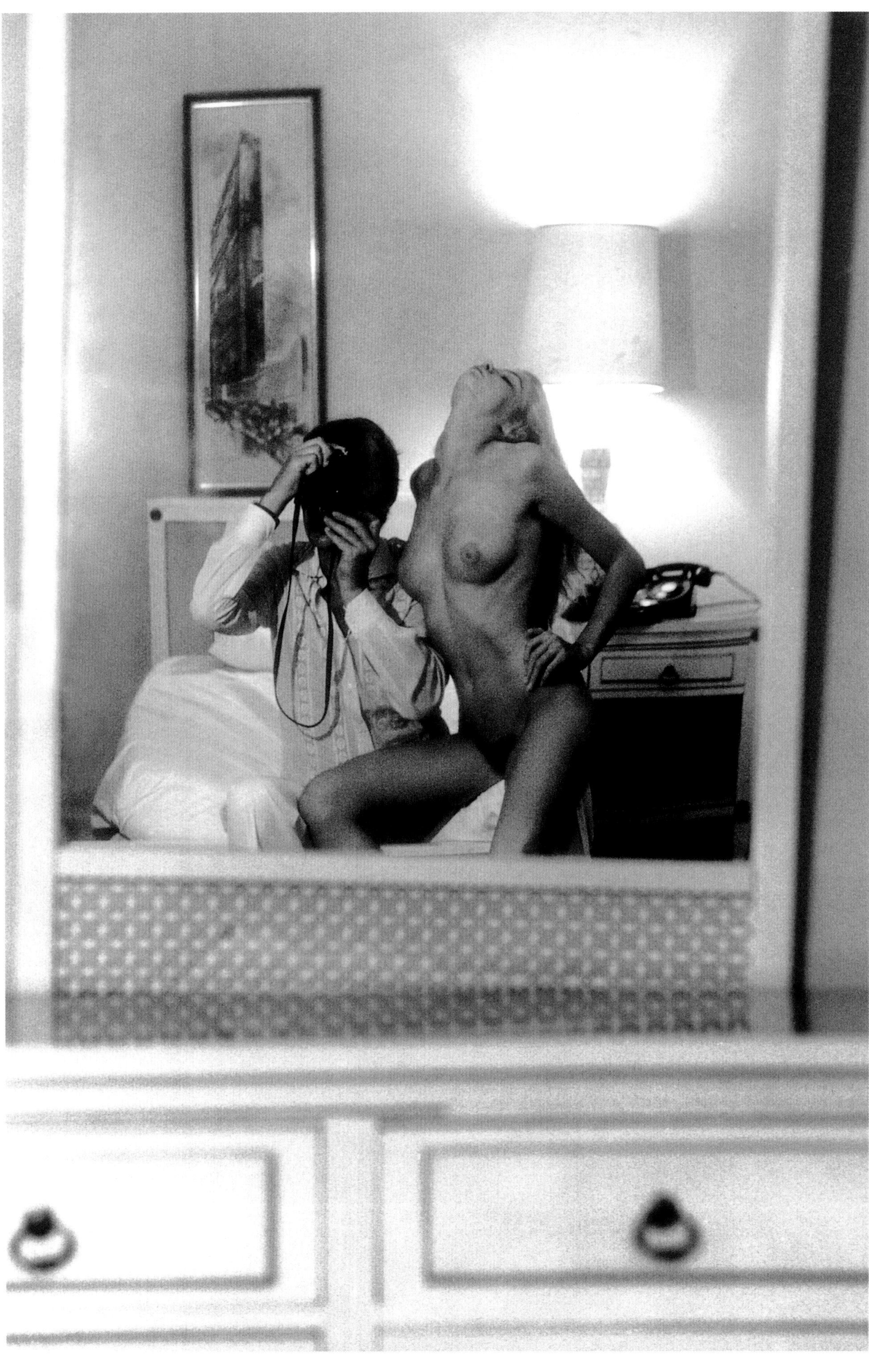

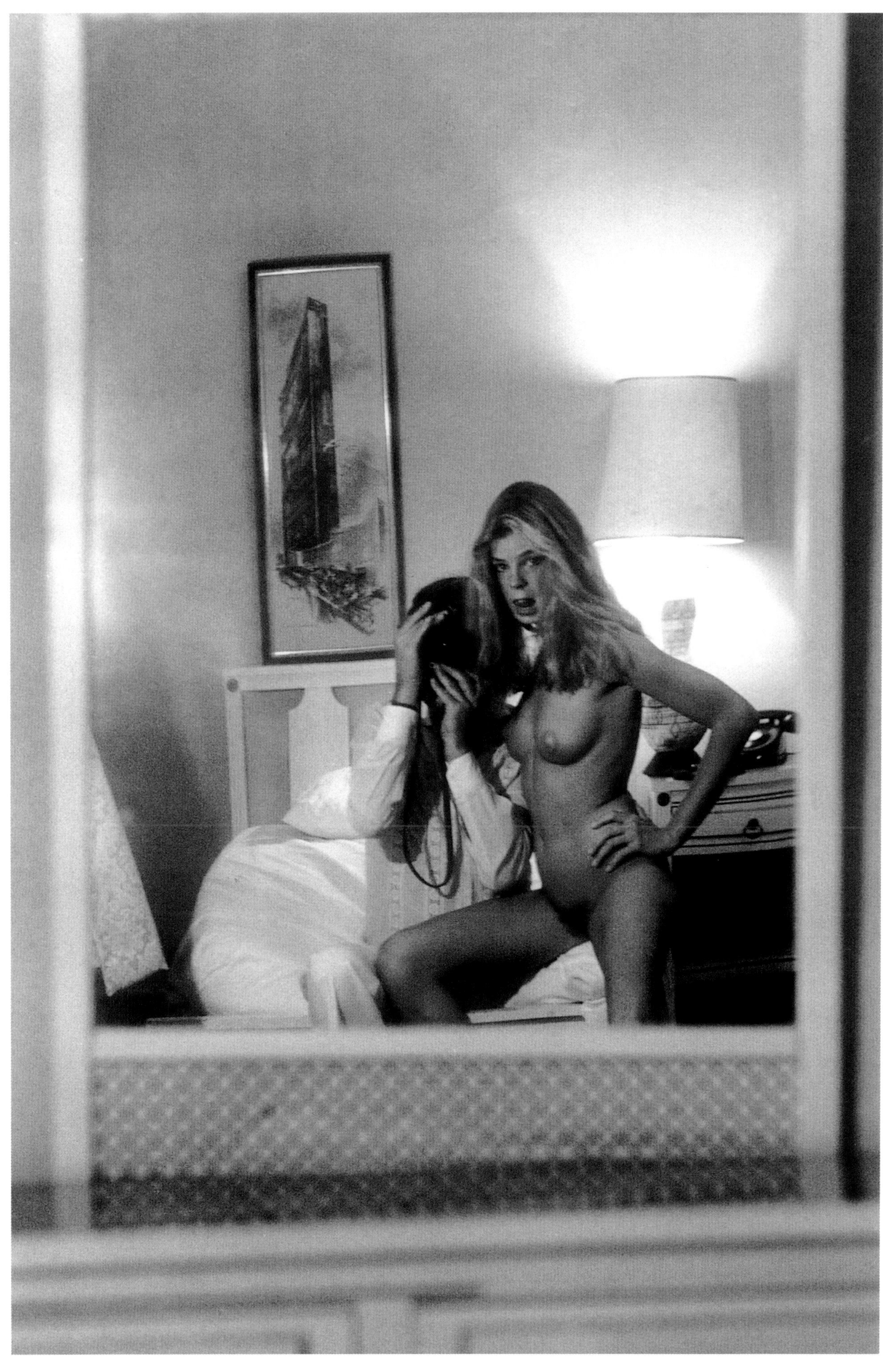

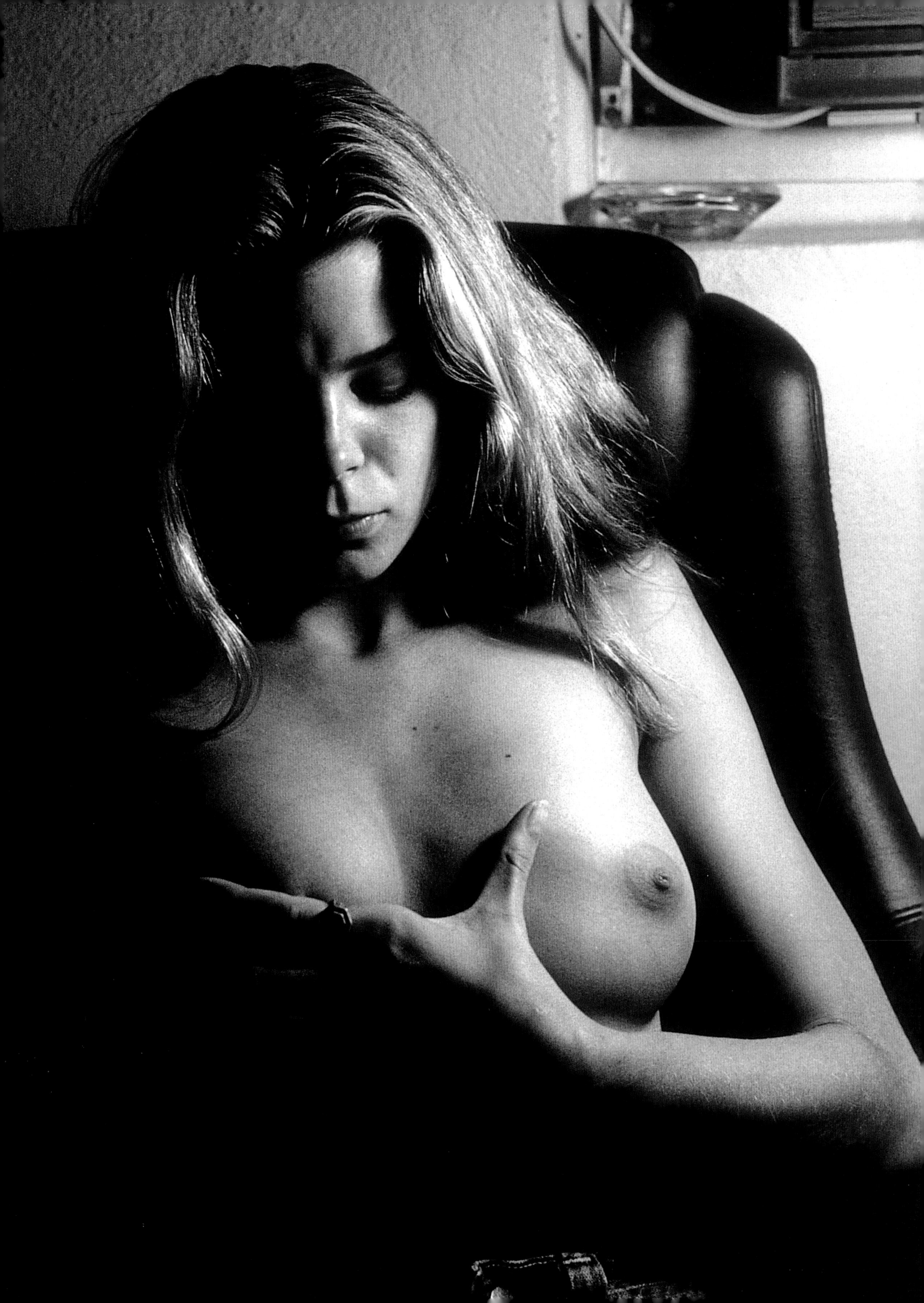

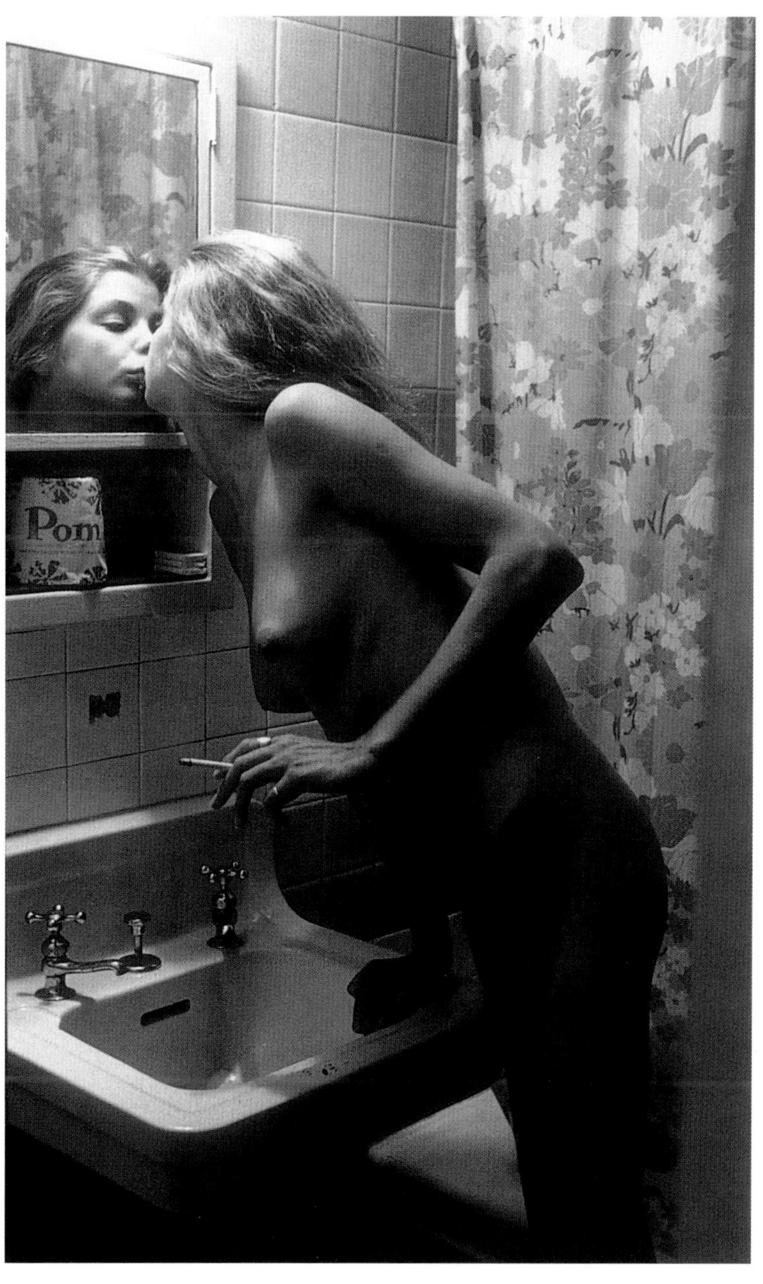
Pom

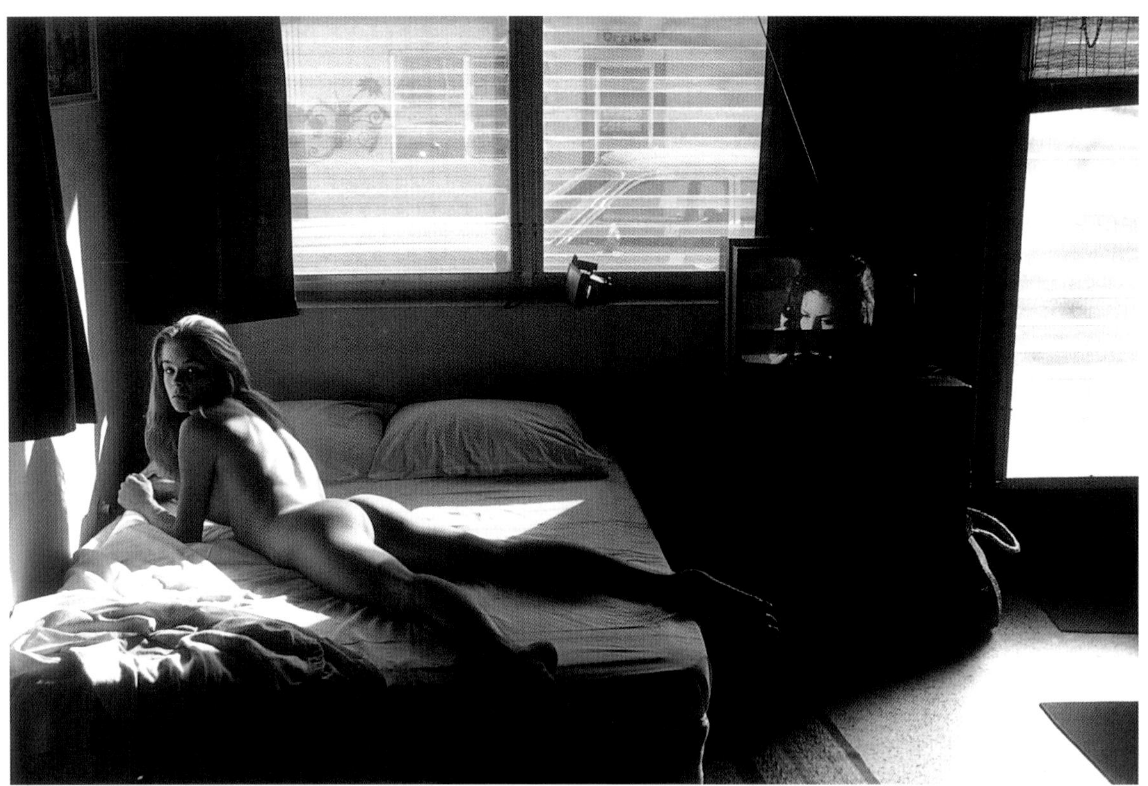

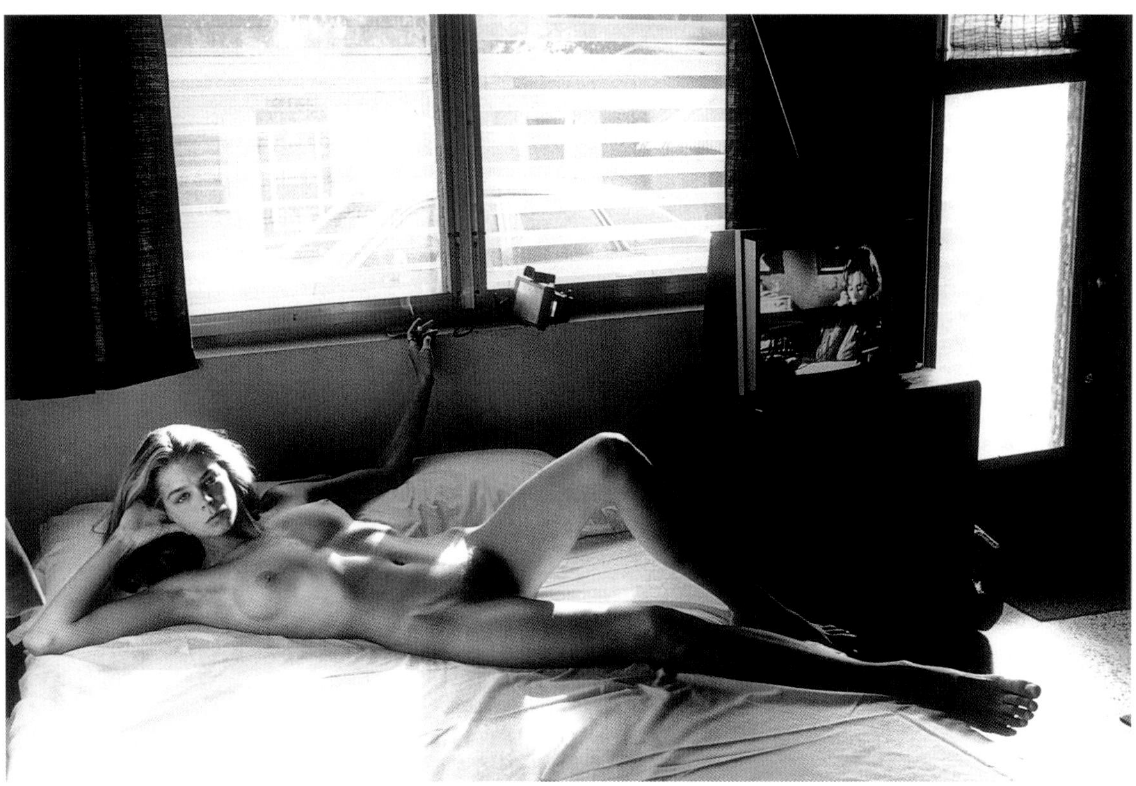

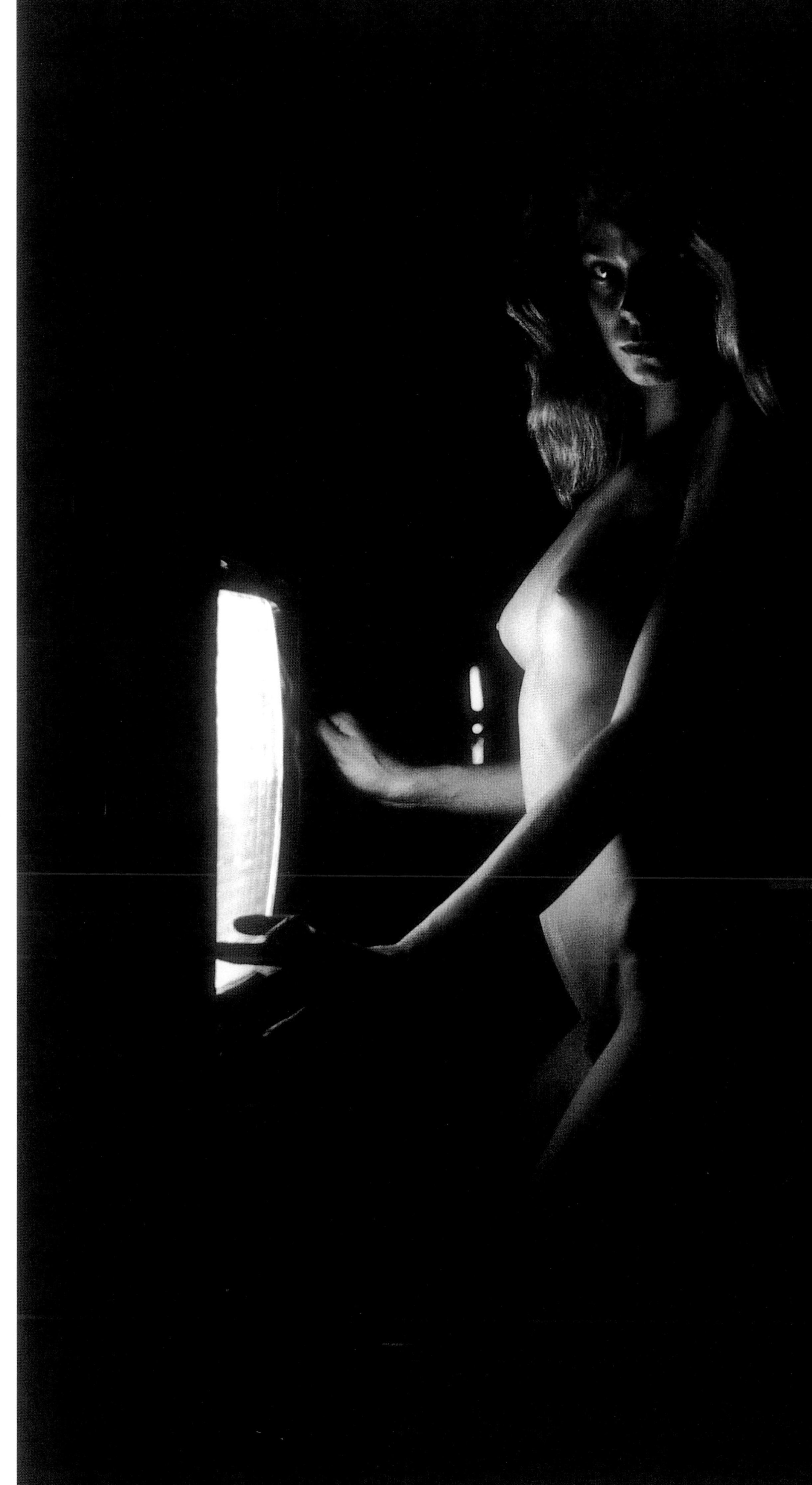

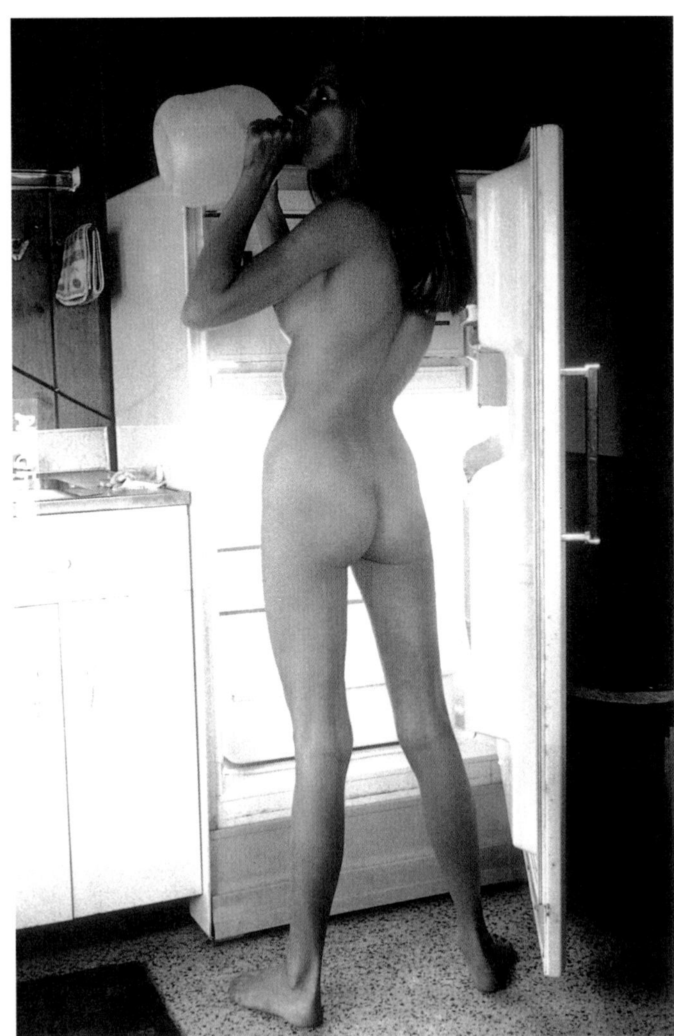

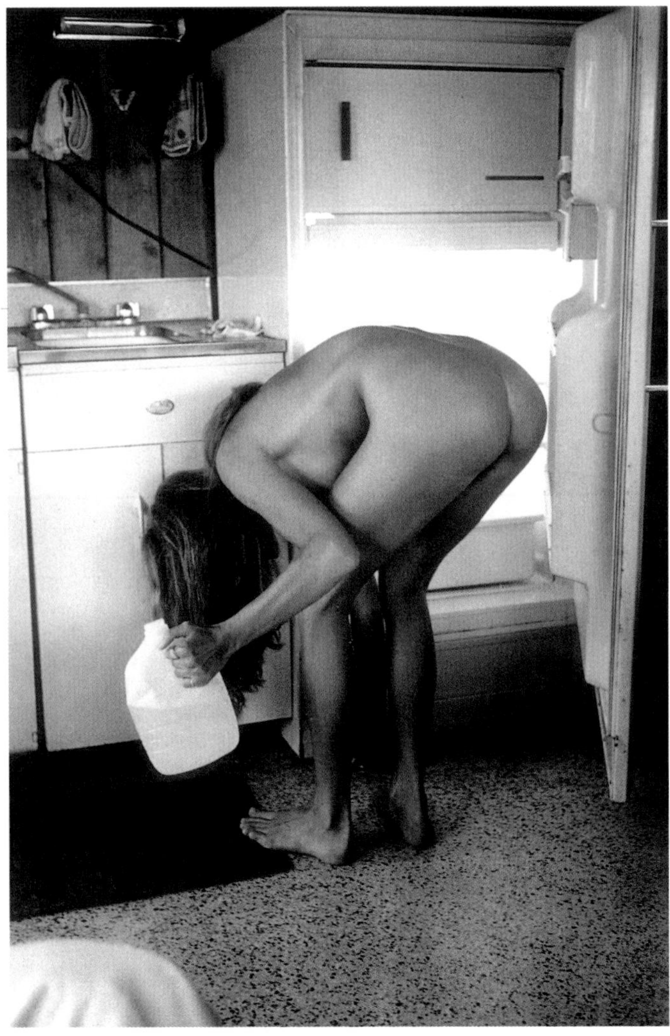

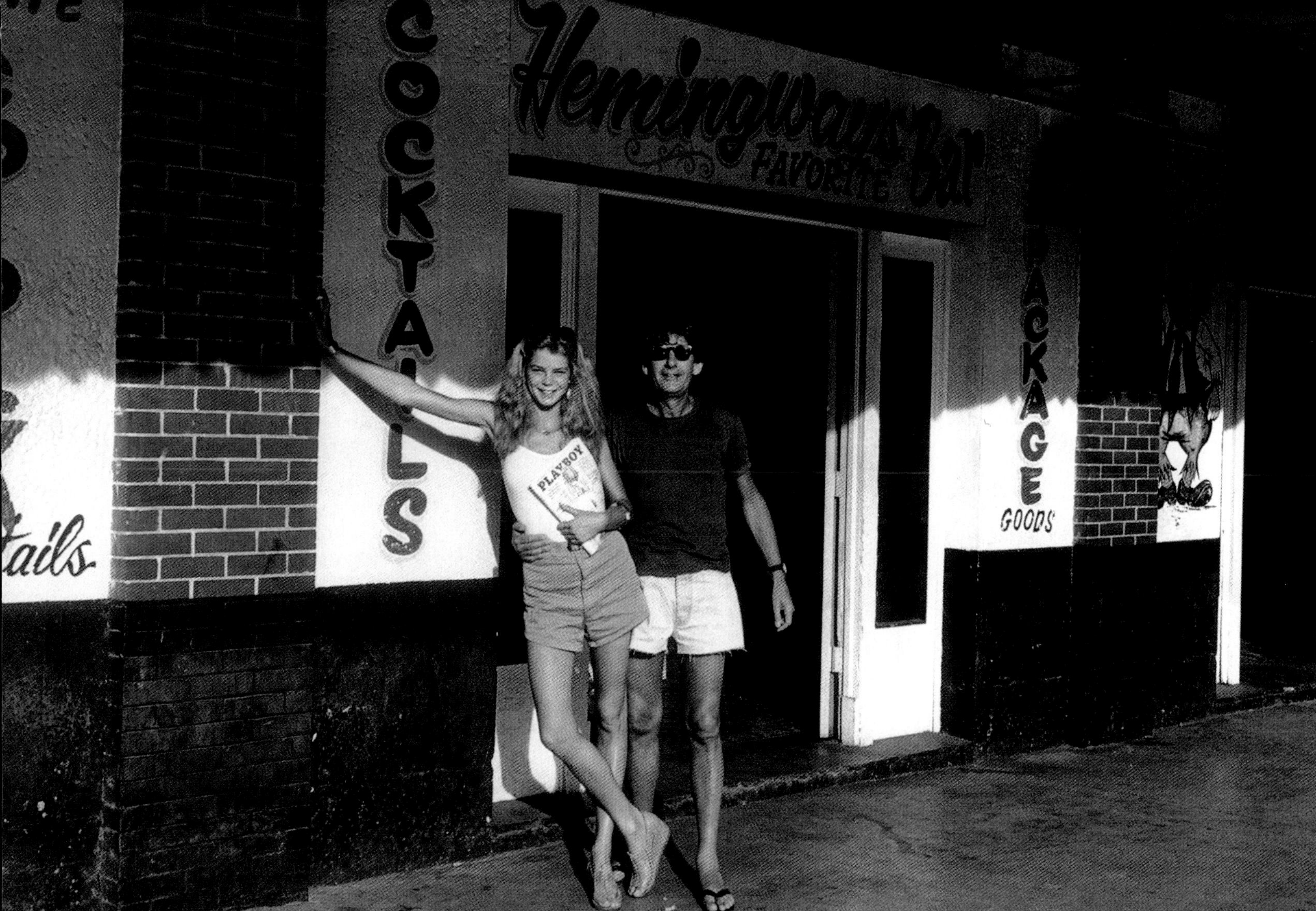

Hemingways
FAVORITE Bar
COCKTAILS
PACKAGE
GOODS
PLAYBOY
tails

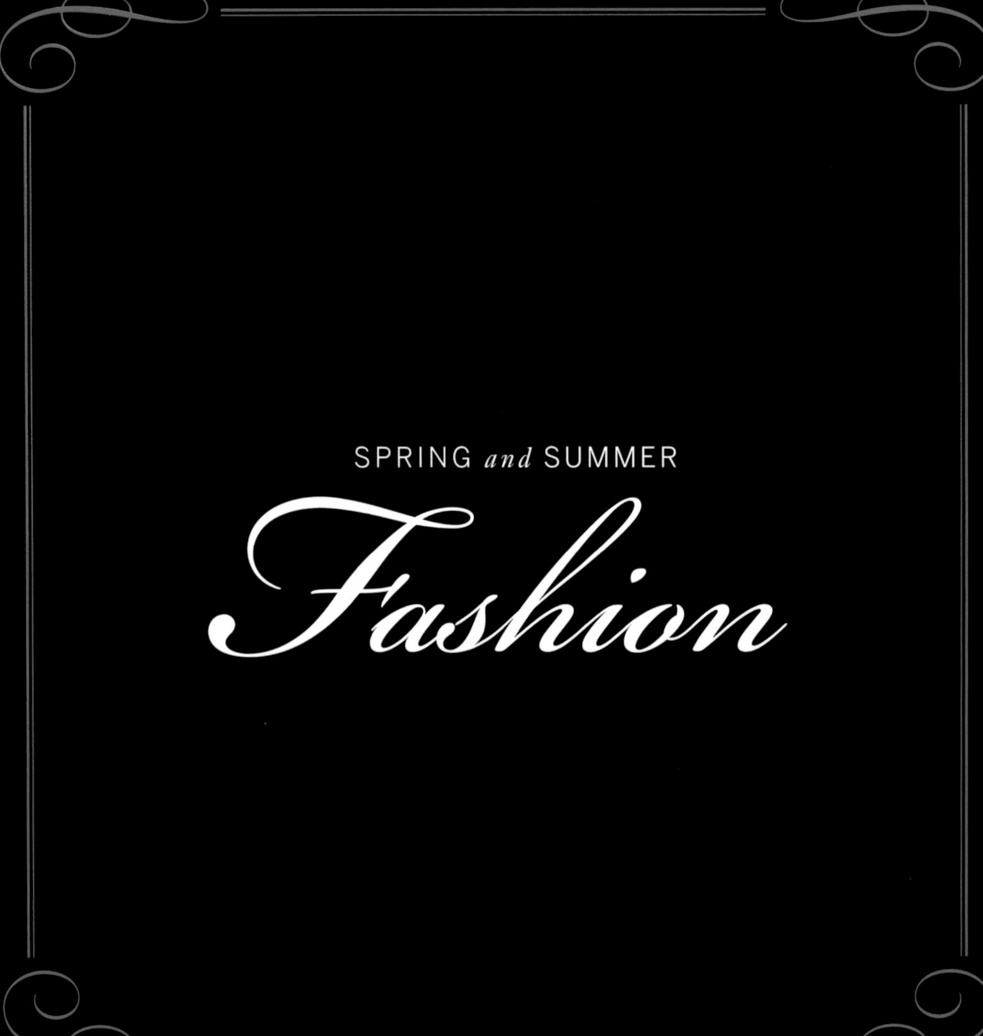

SPRING *and* SUMMER

Fashion

FEATURING

Mary Ella Rhodes

May 1977

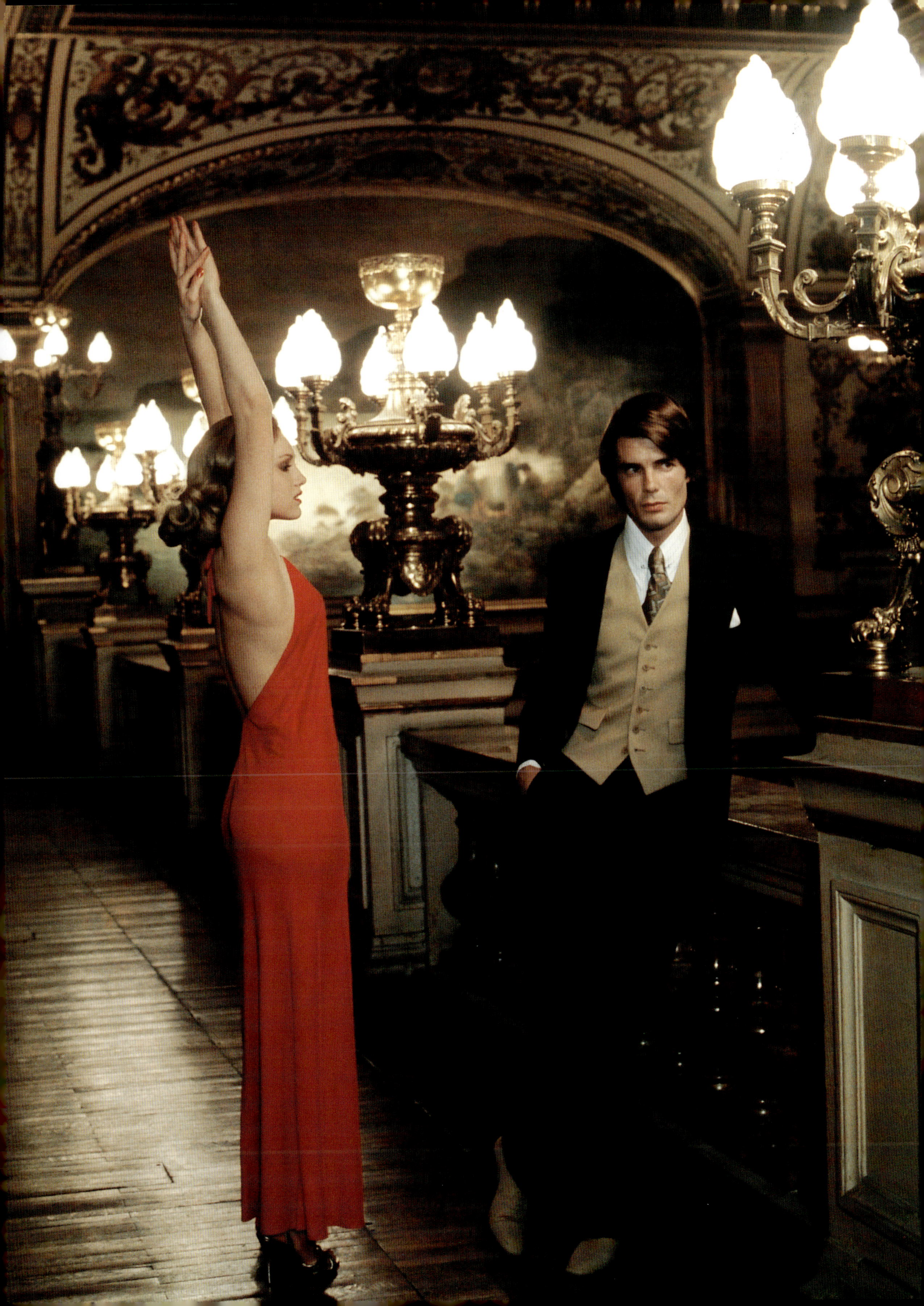

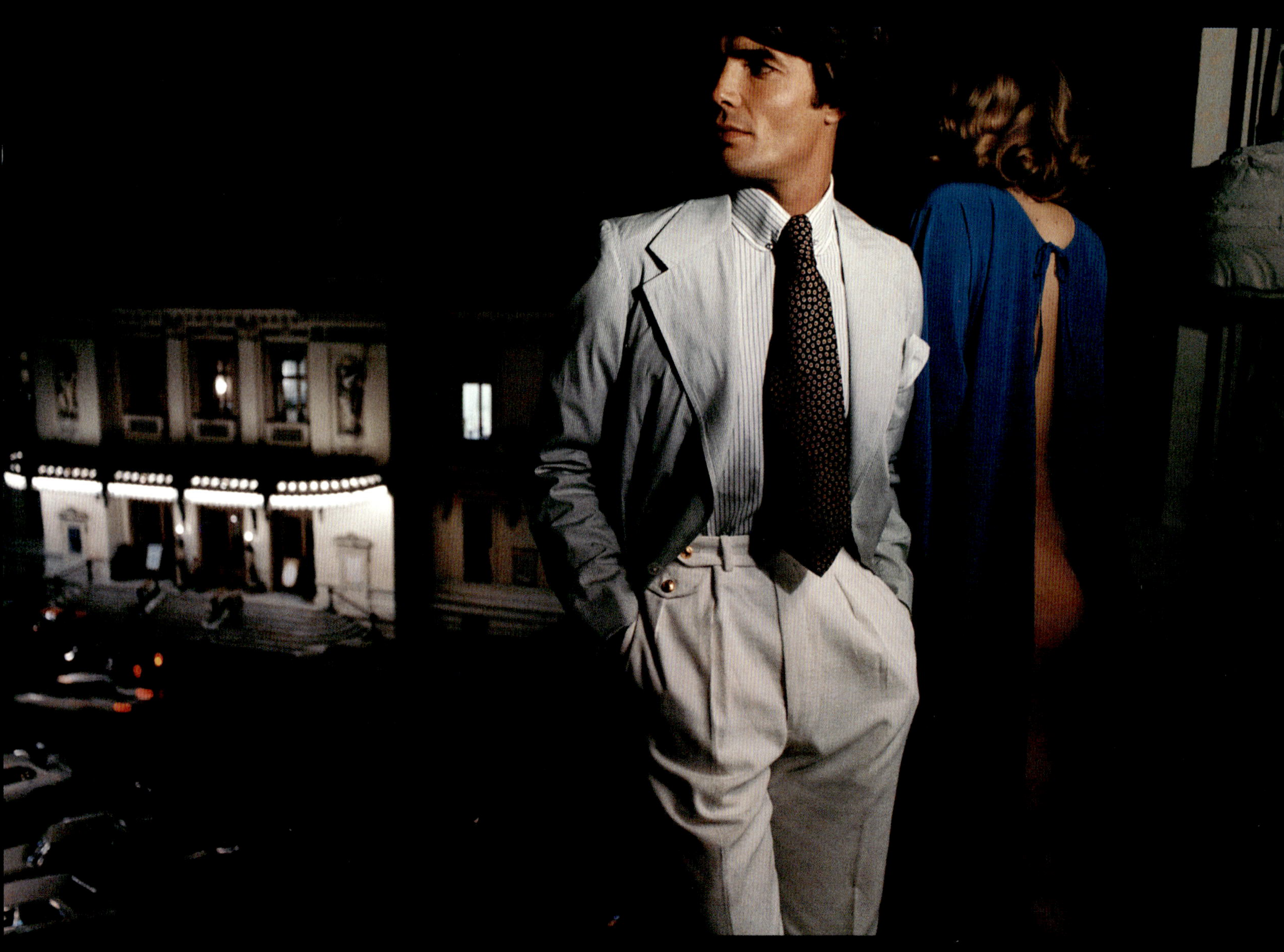

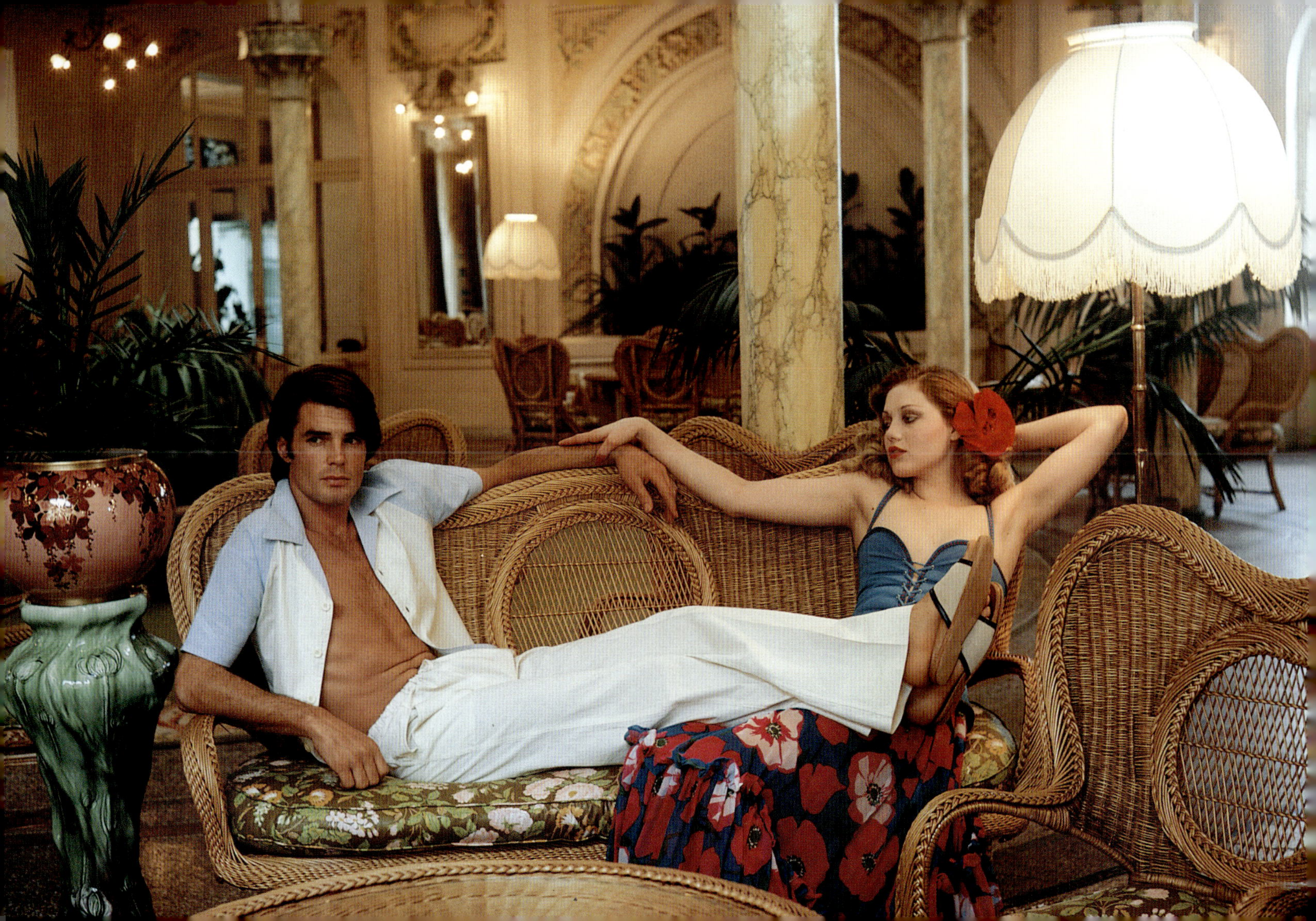

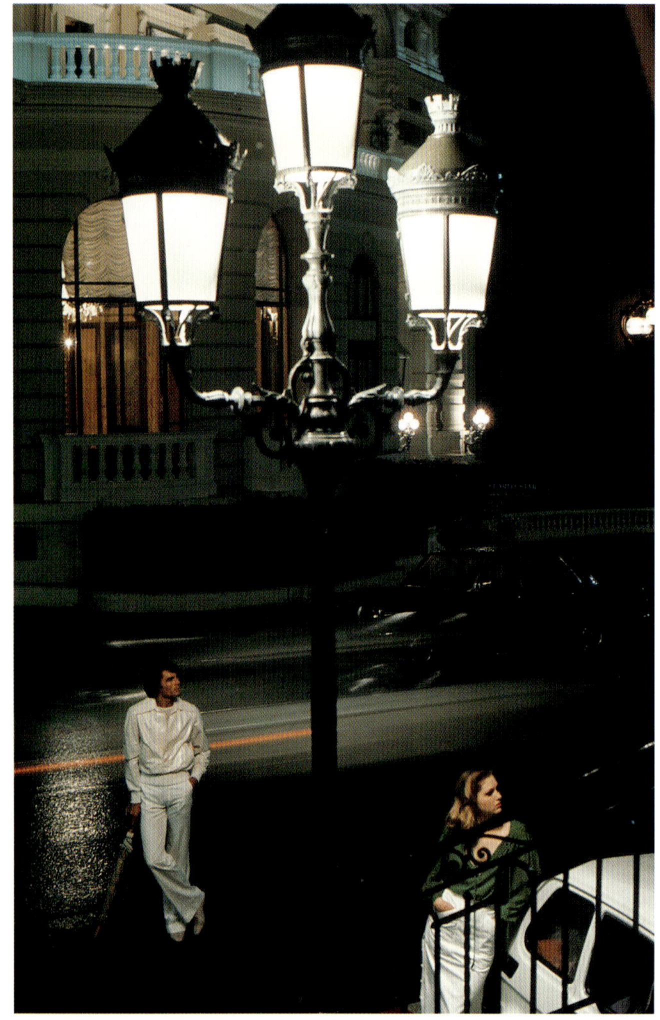

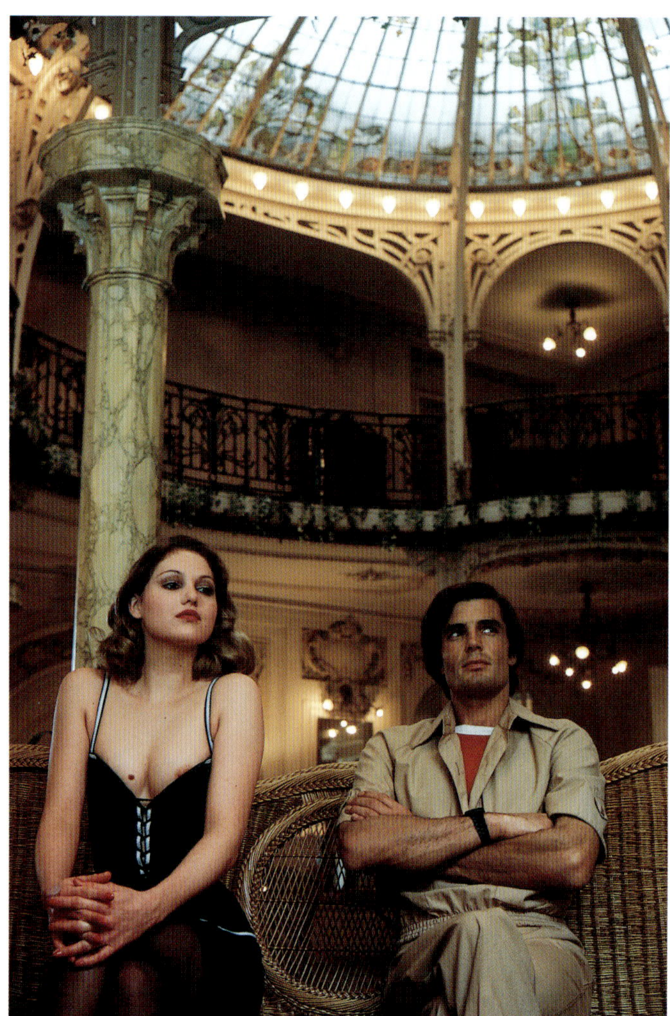

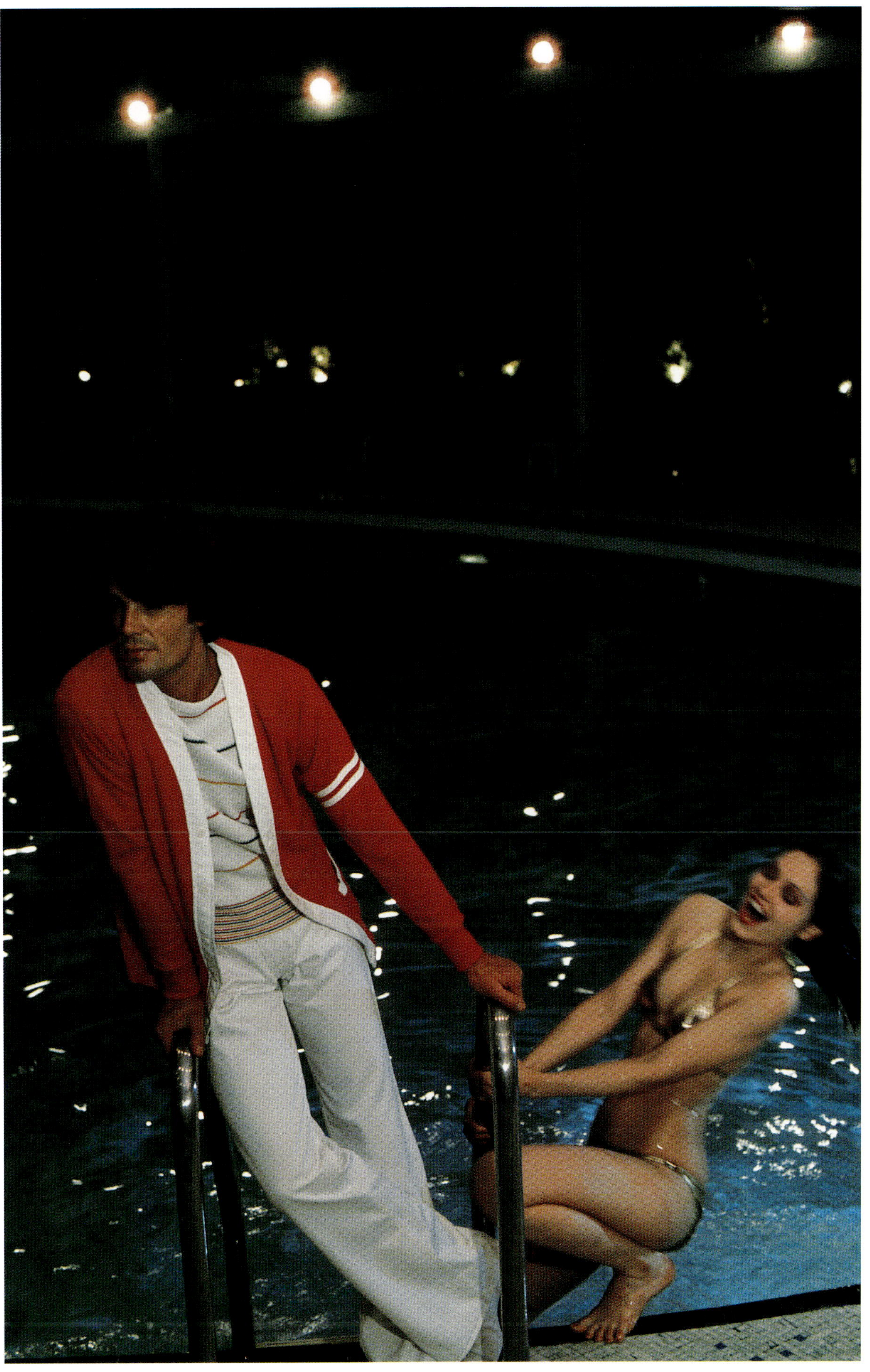

KINSKI *exposed*

FEATURING

Nastassia Kinski

May 1983

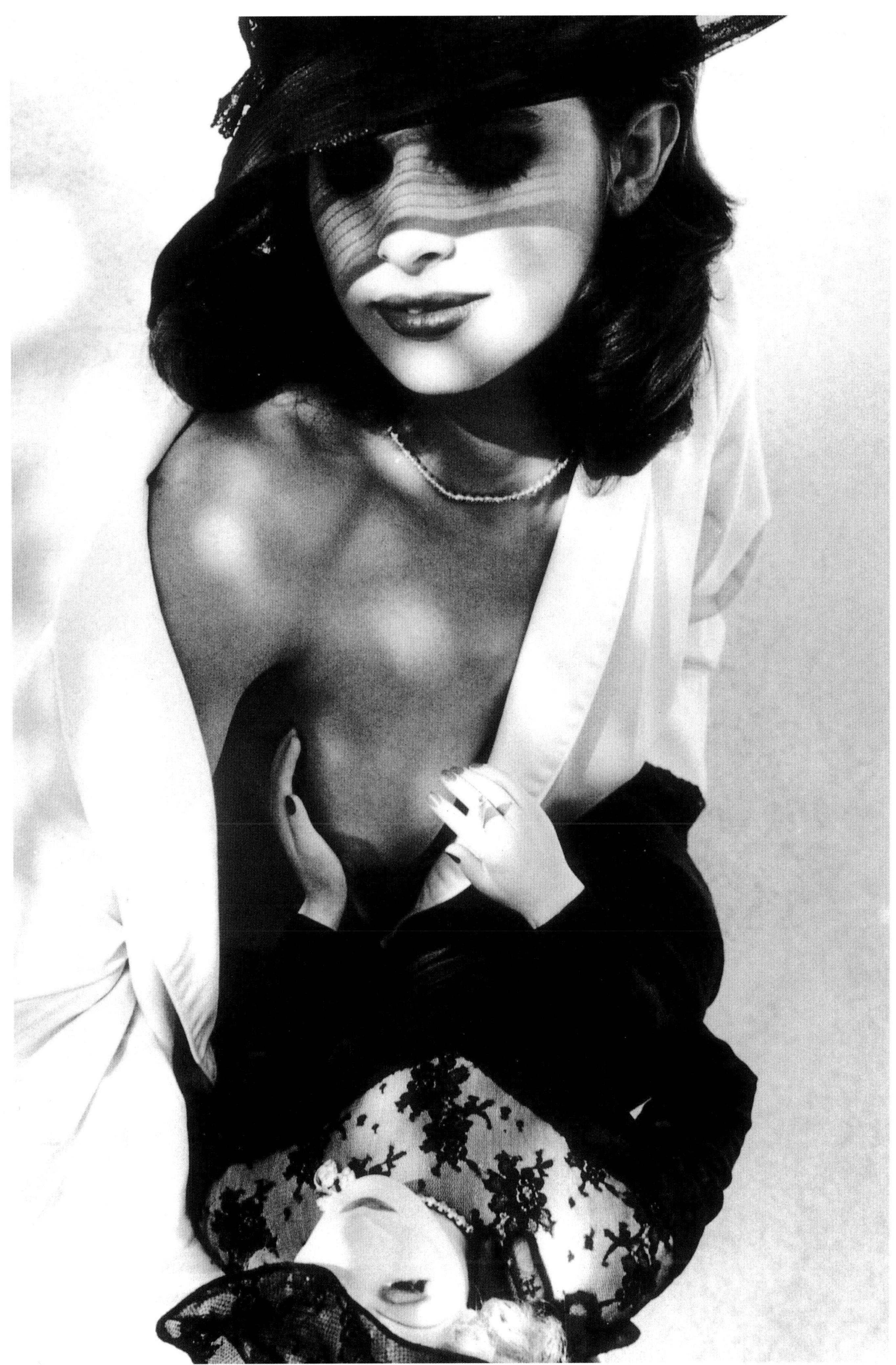

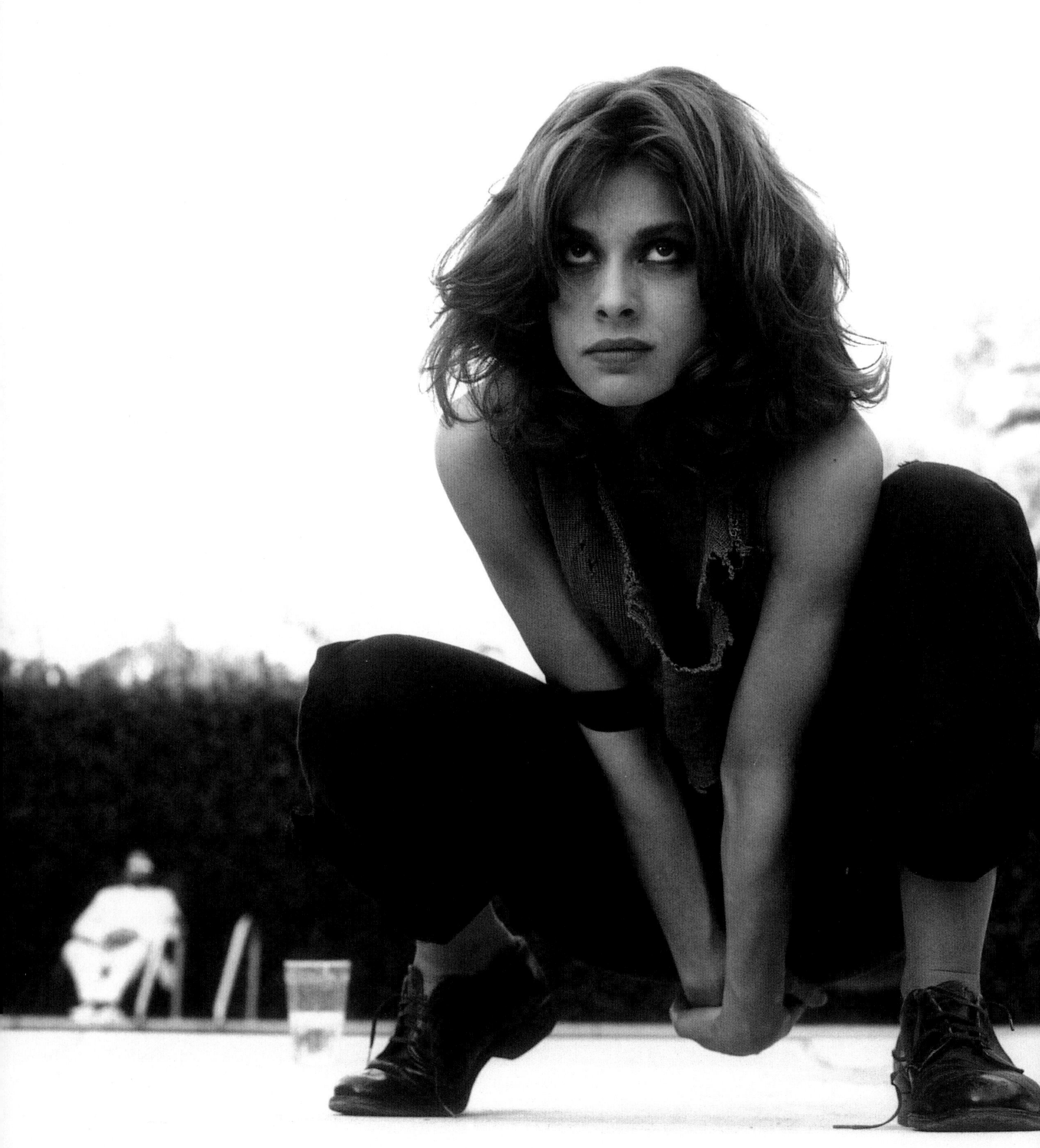

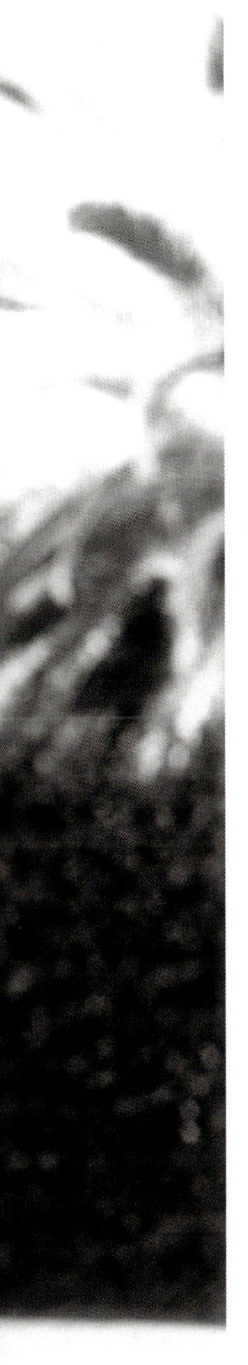

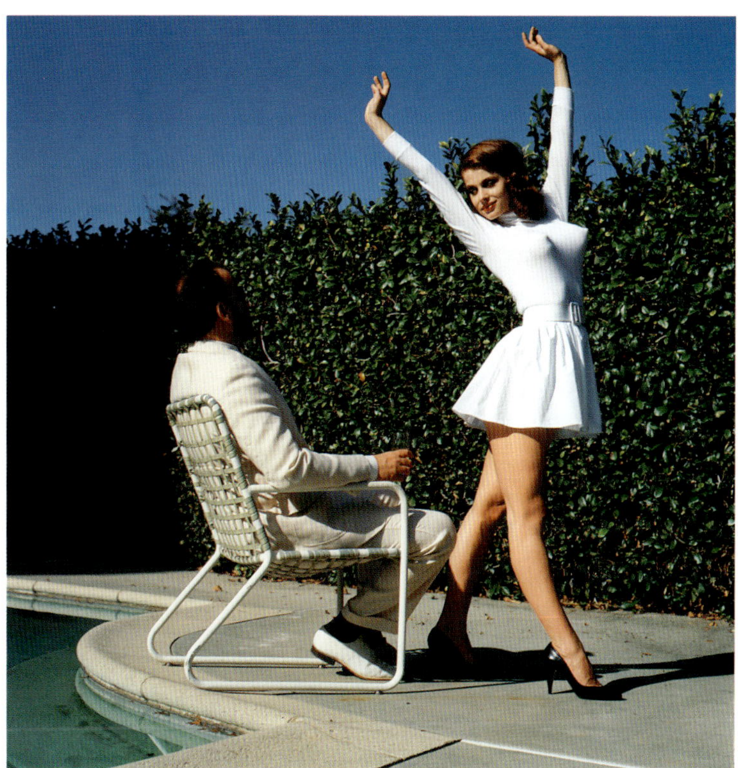

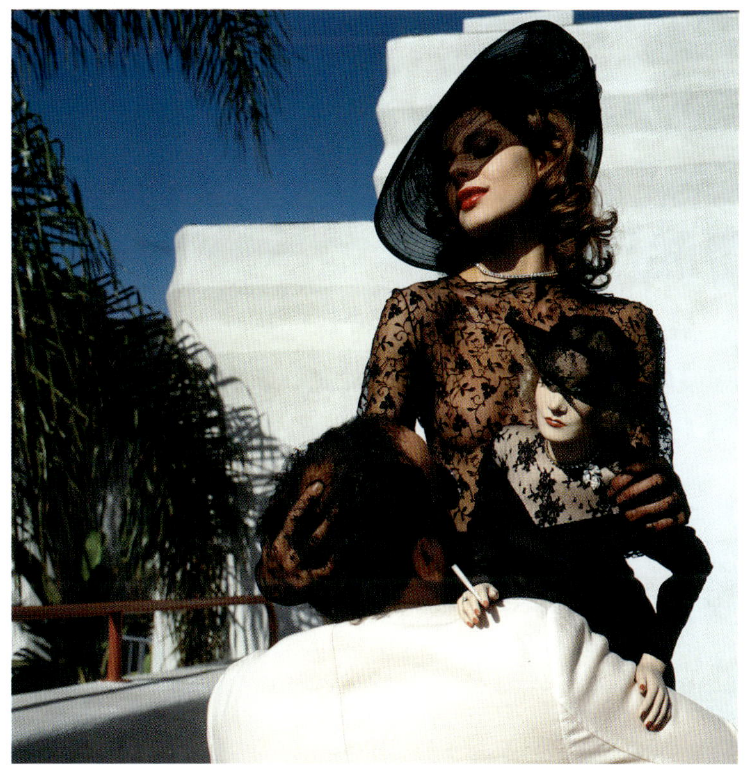

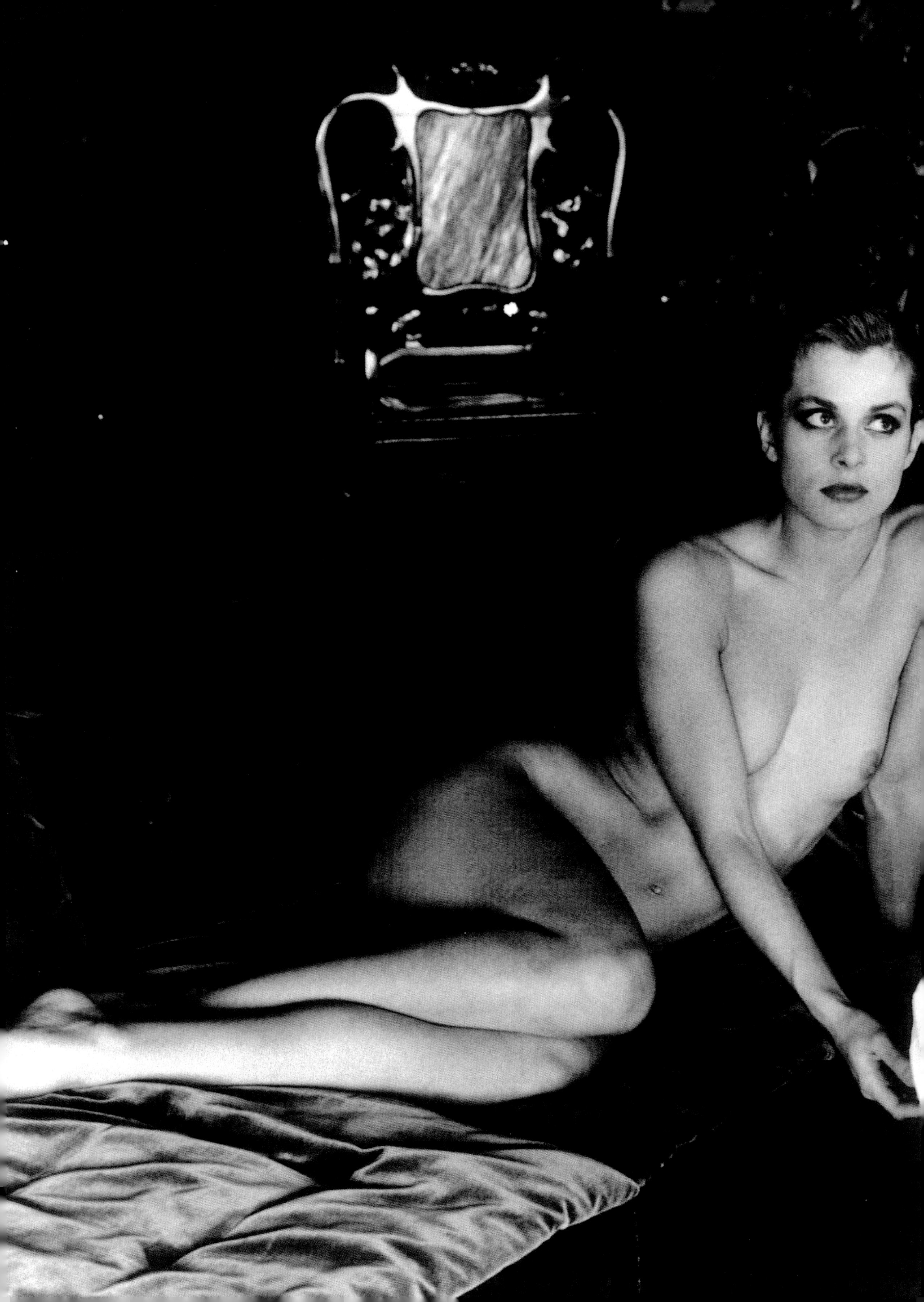

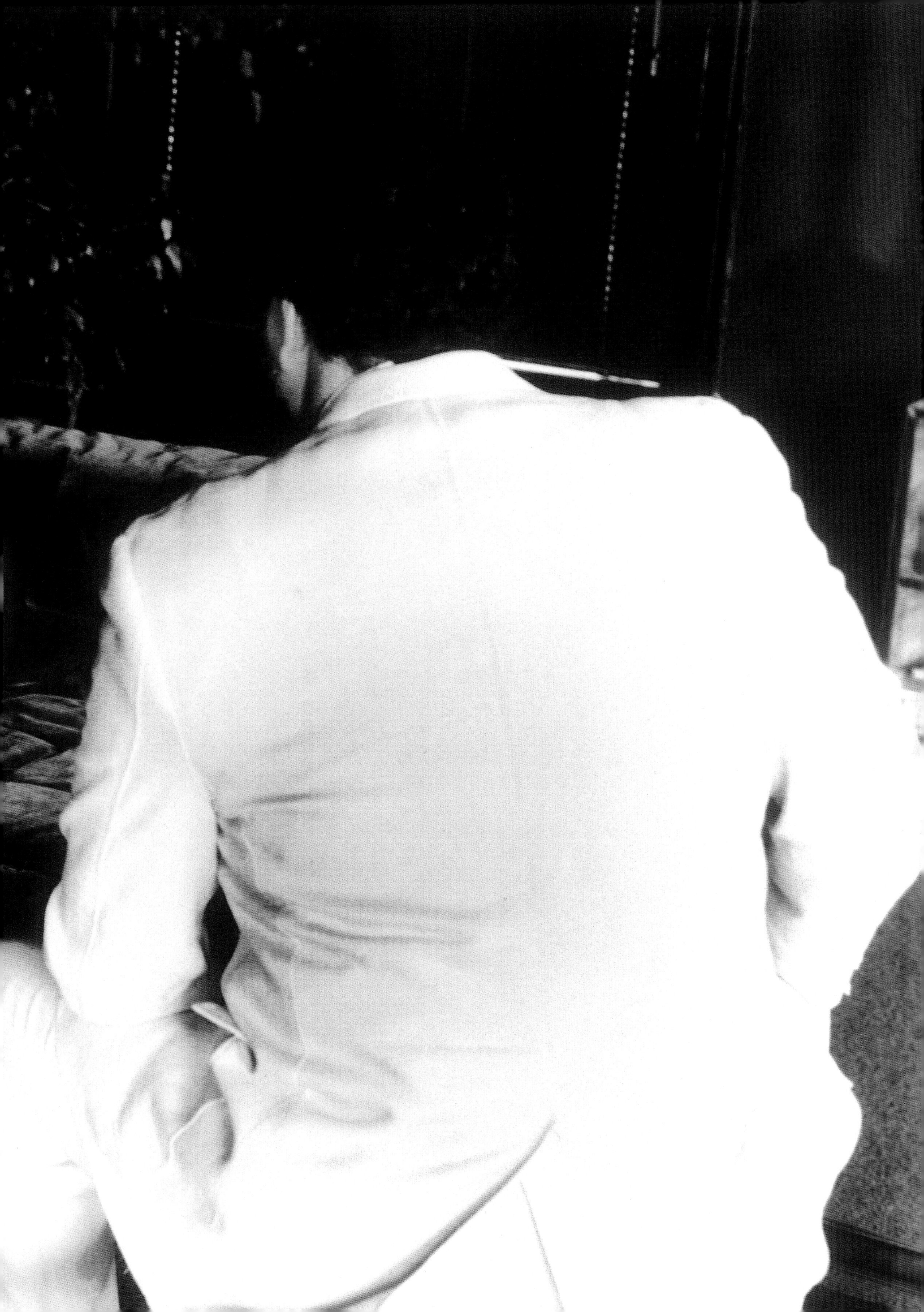

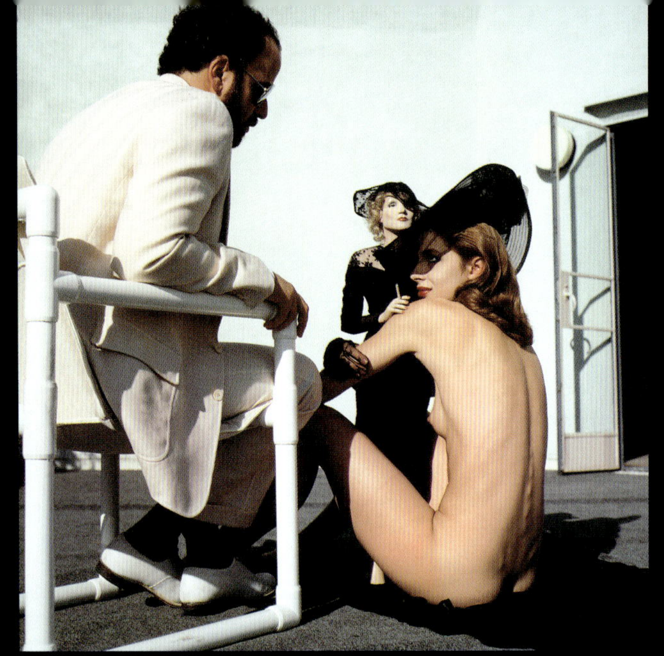

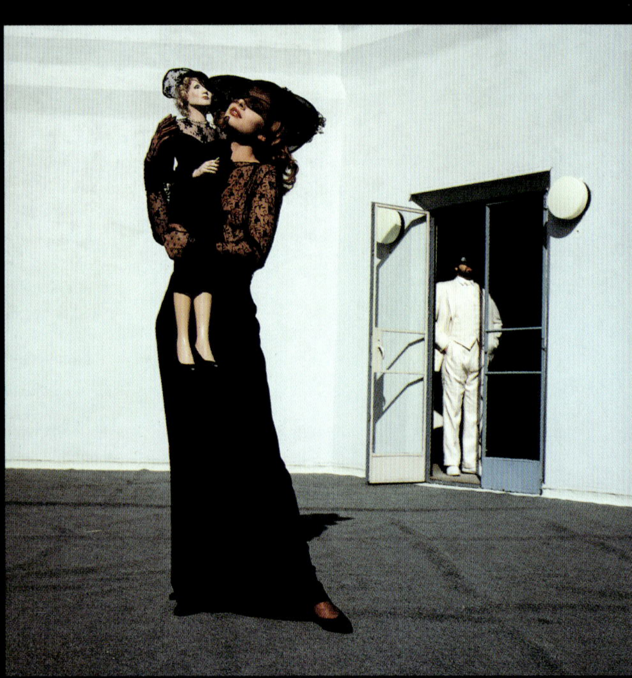

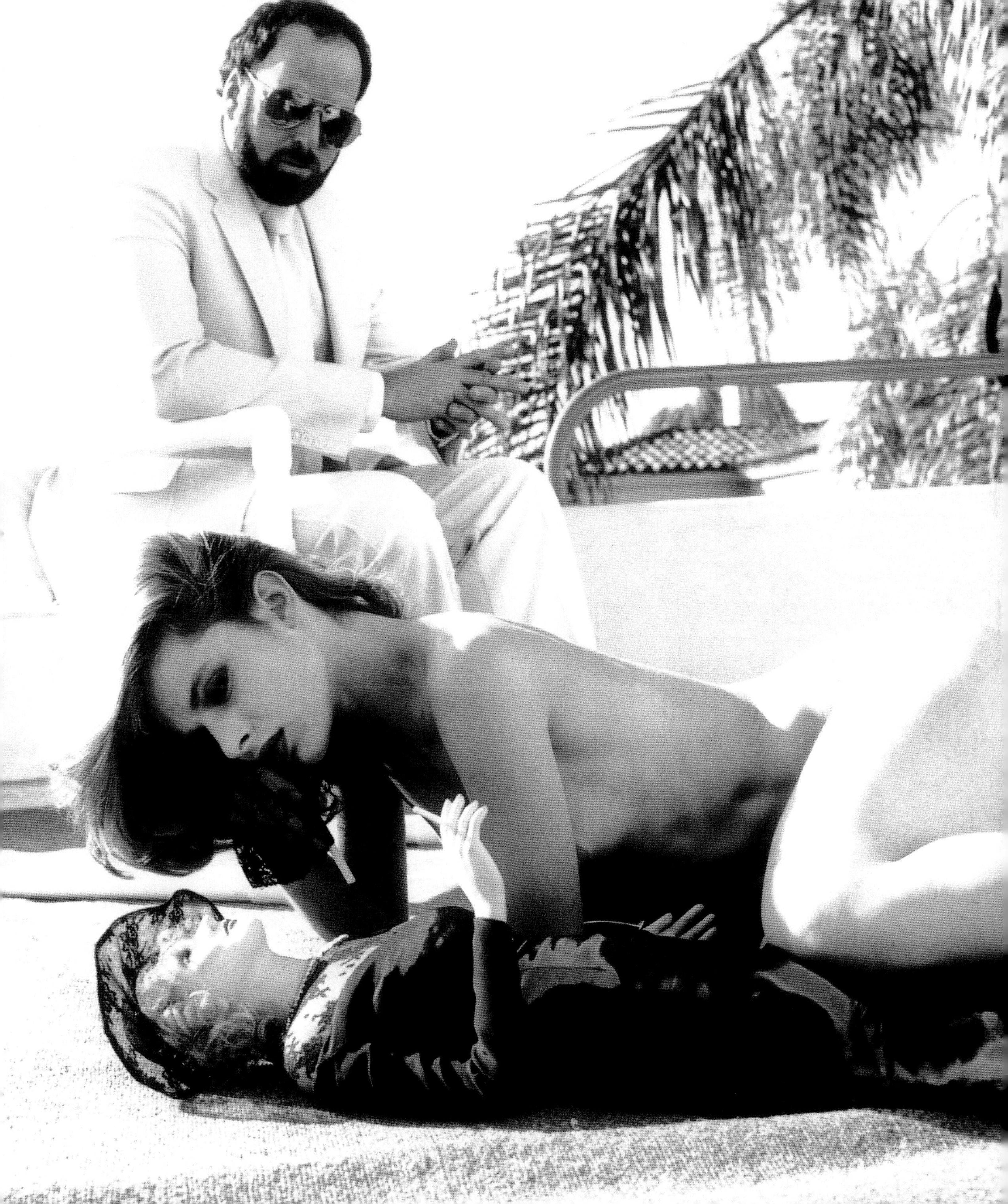

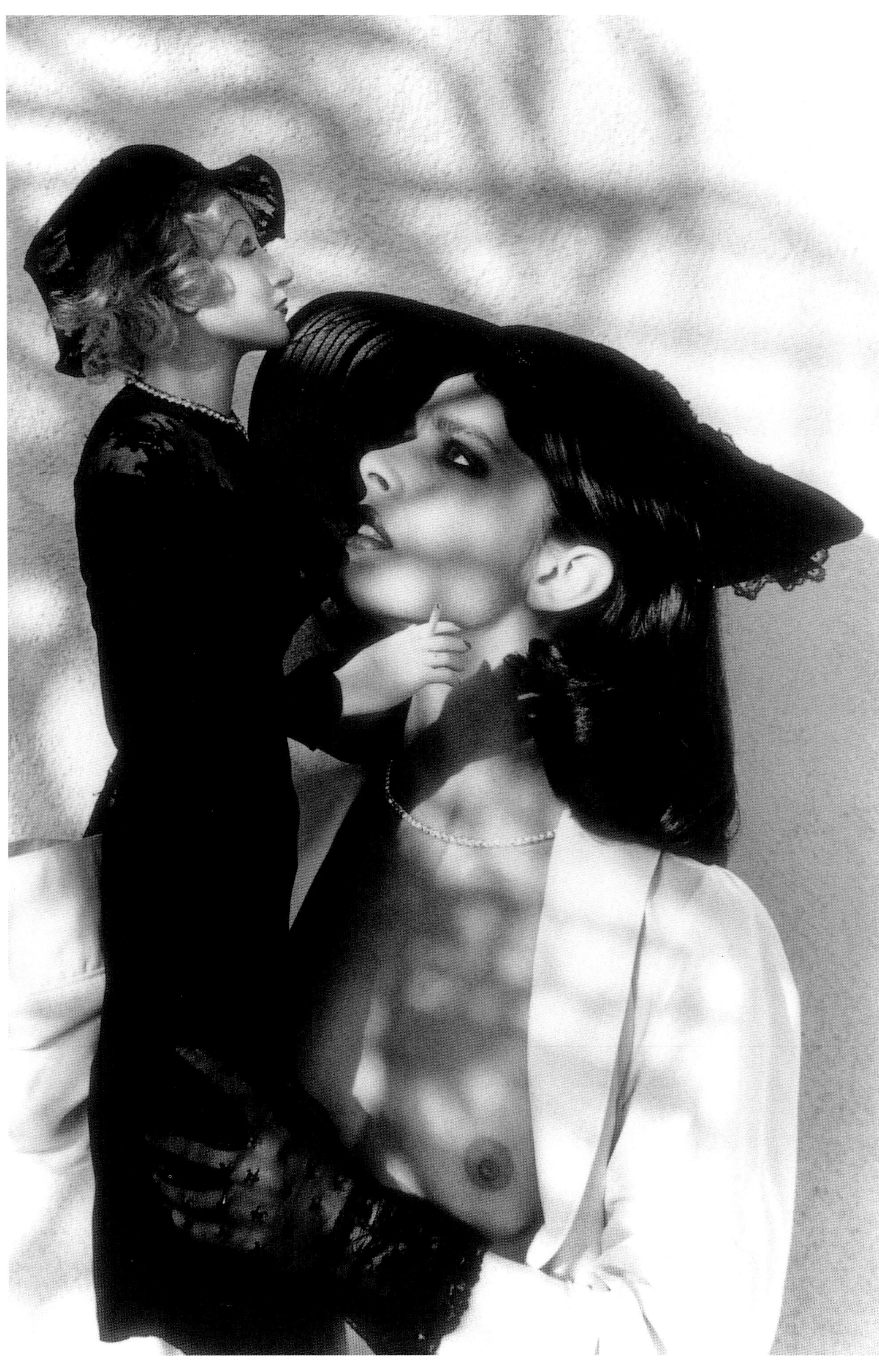

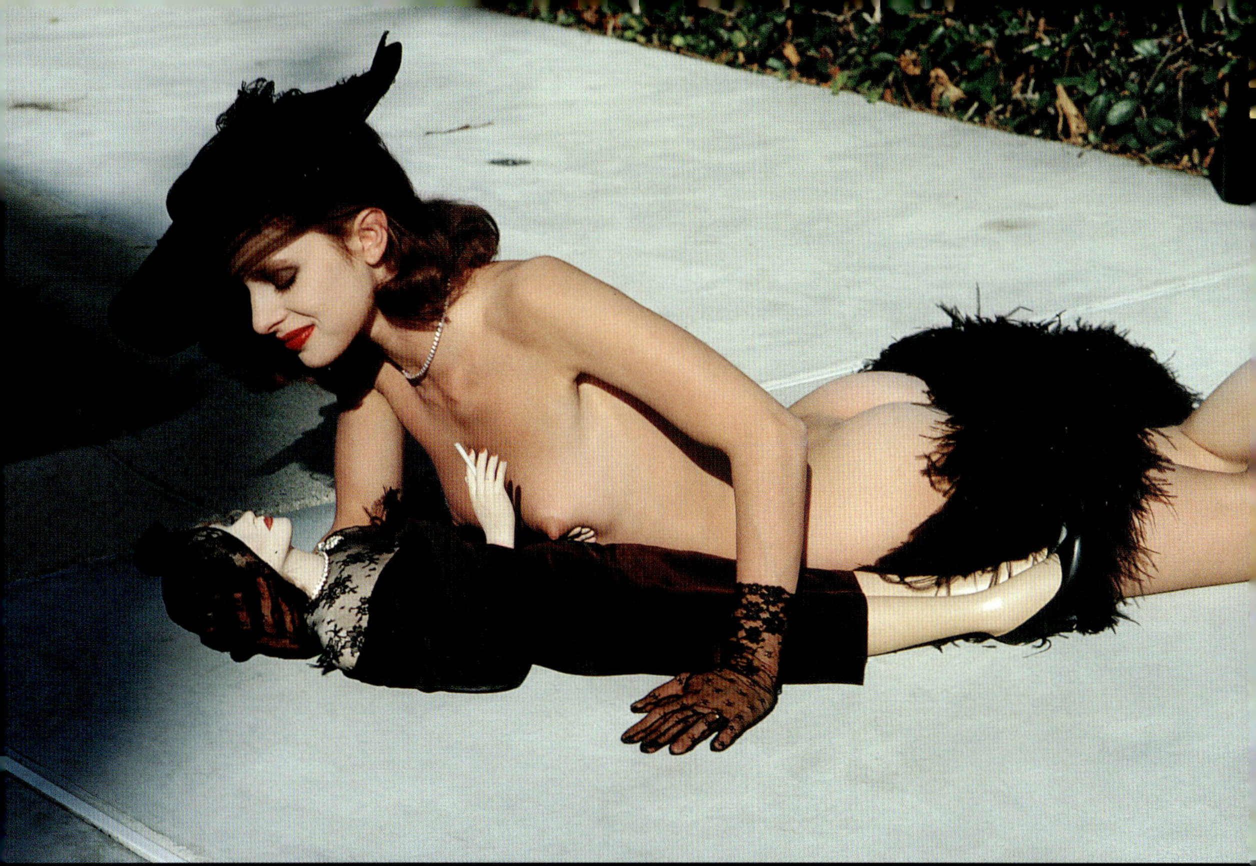

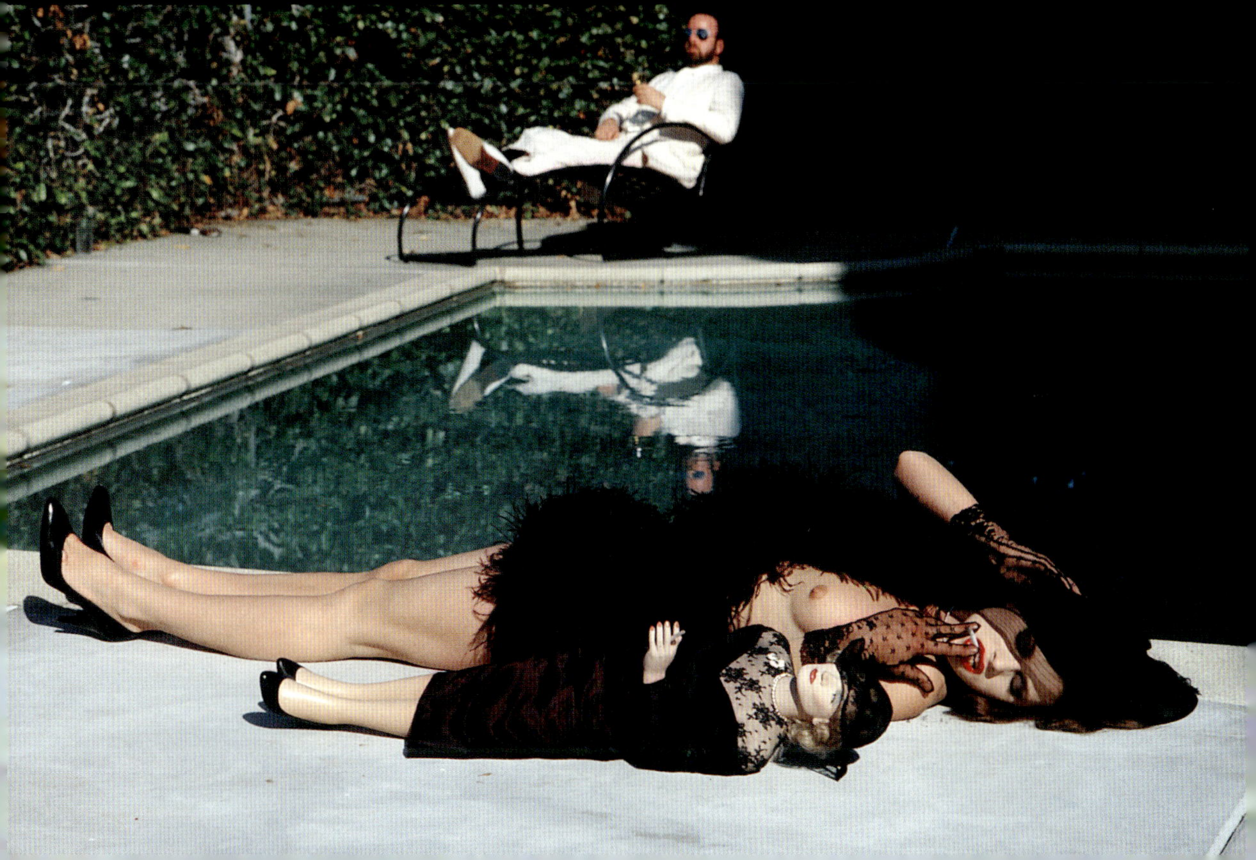

real dolls

March 2002, Unpublished

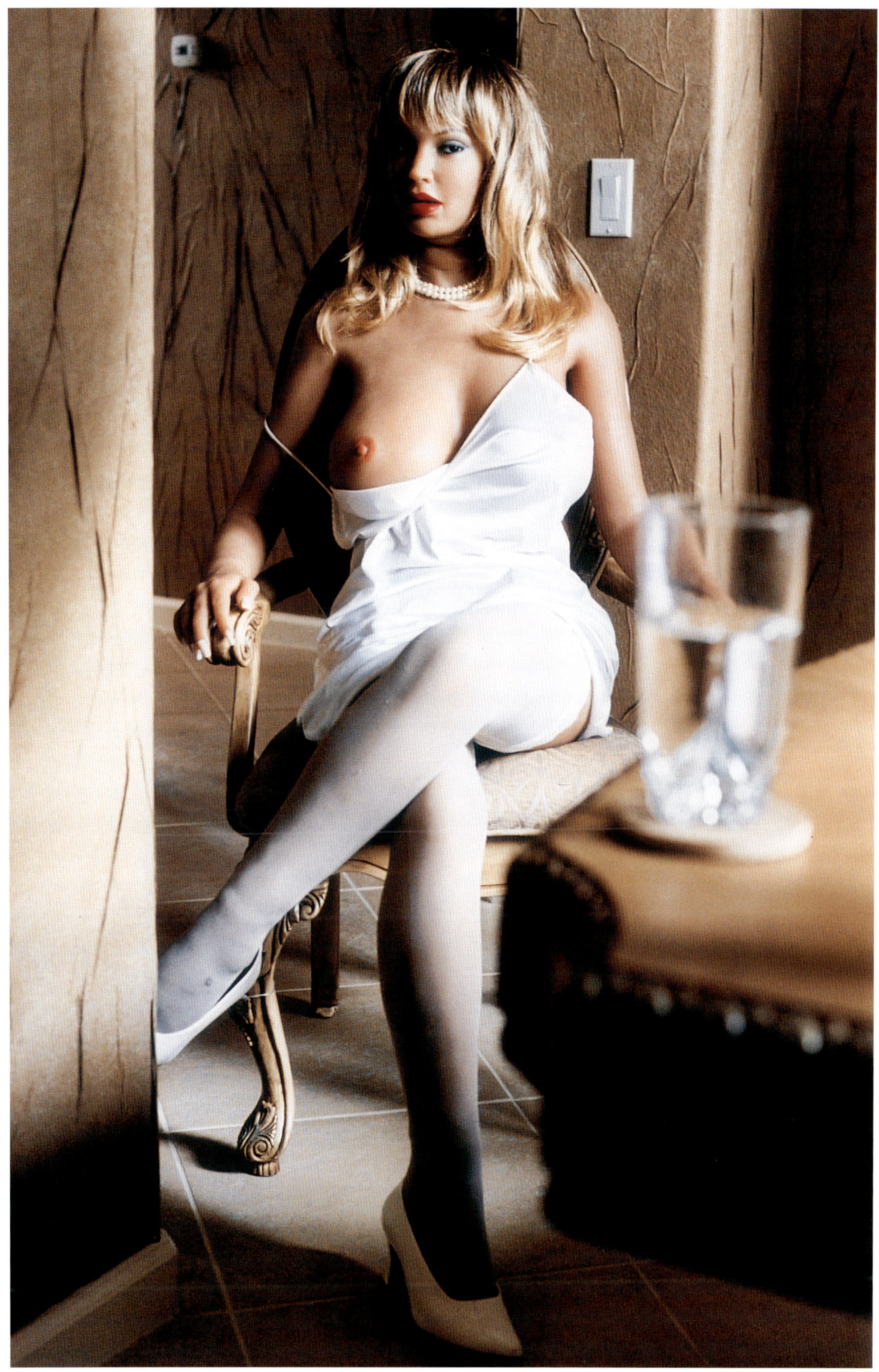

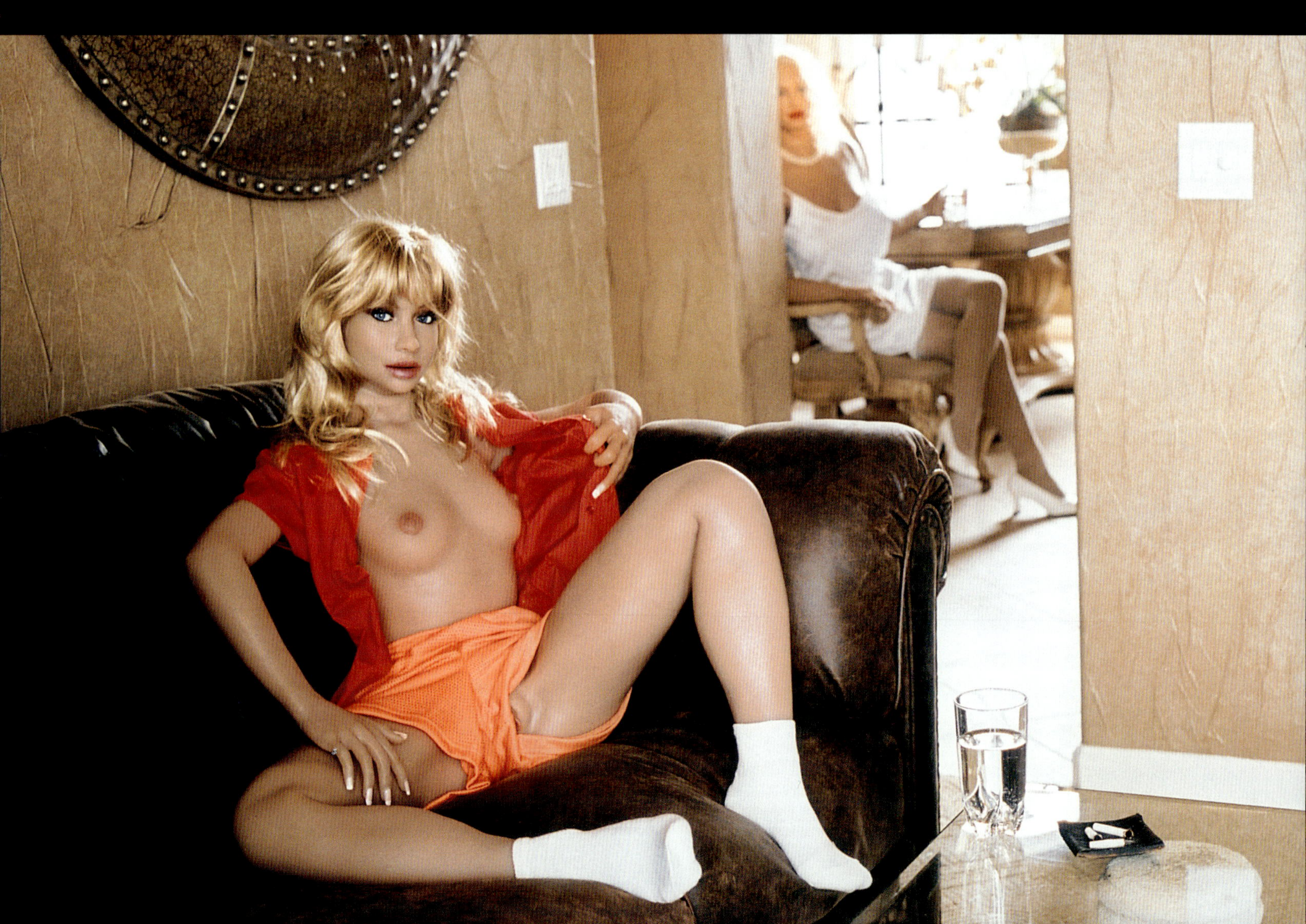

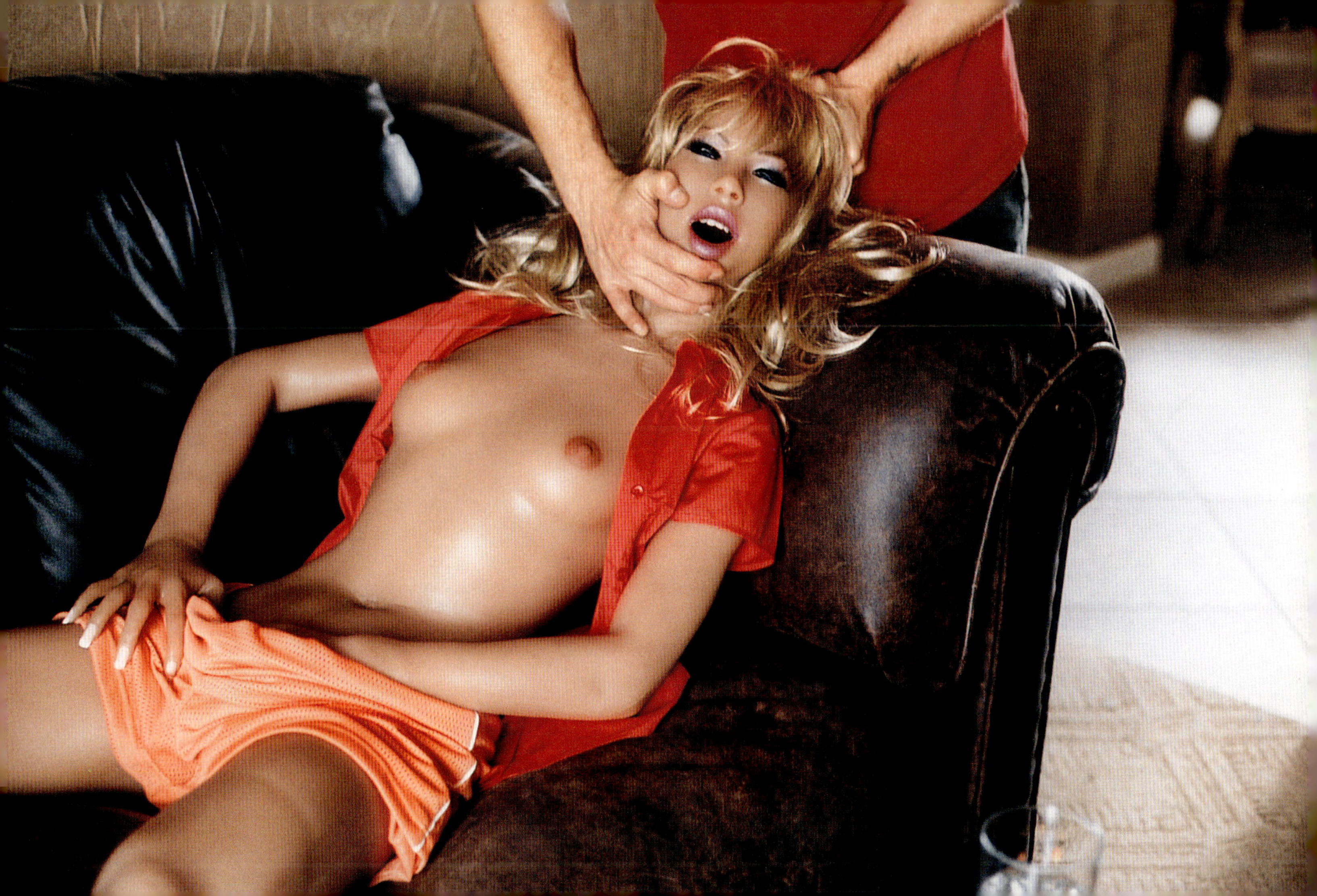

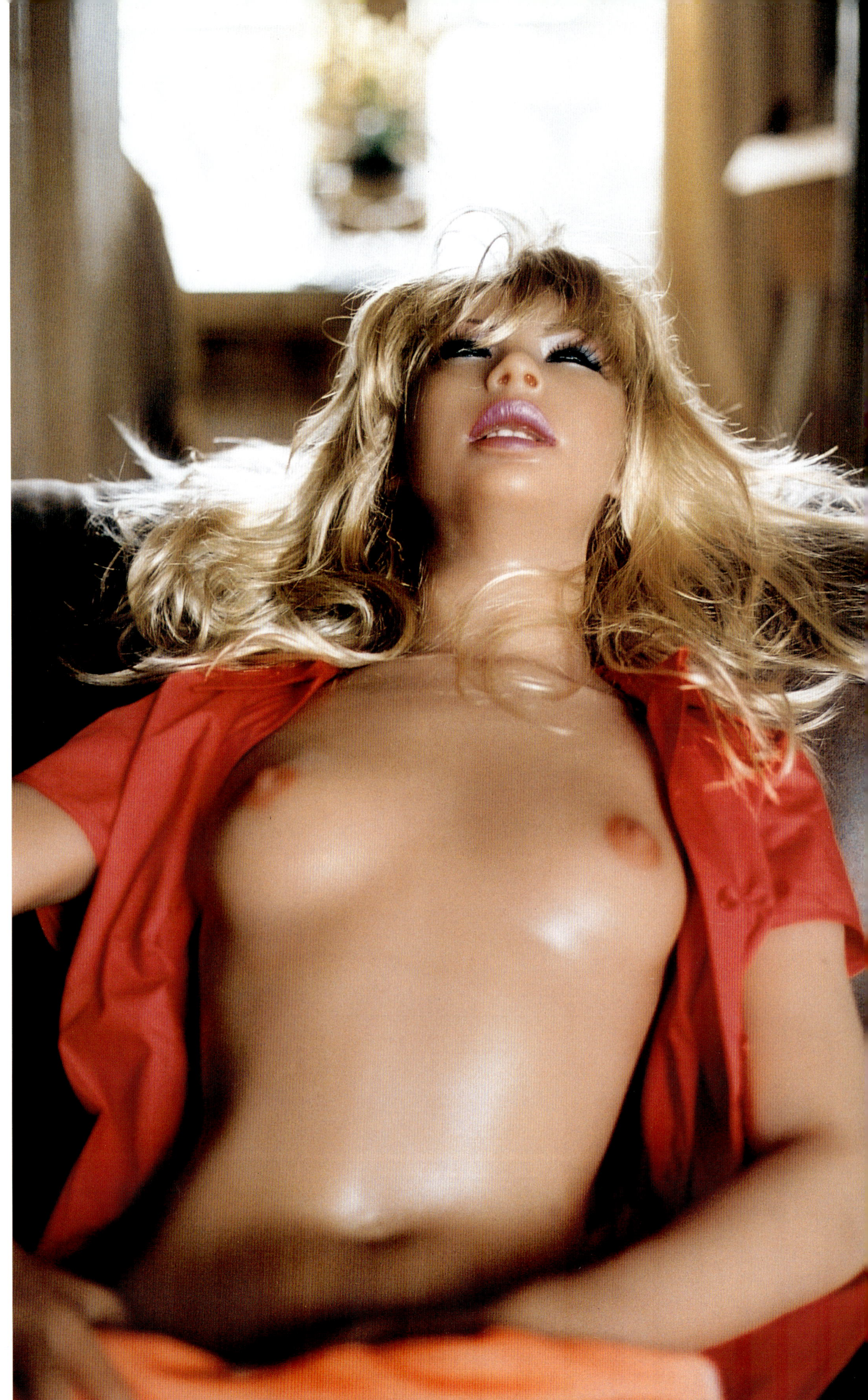

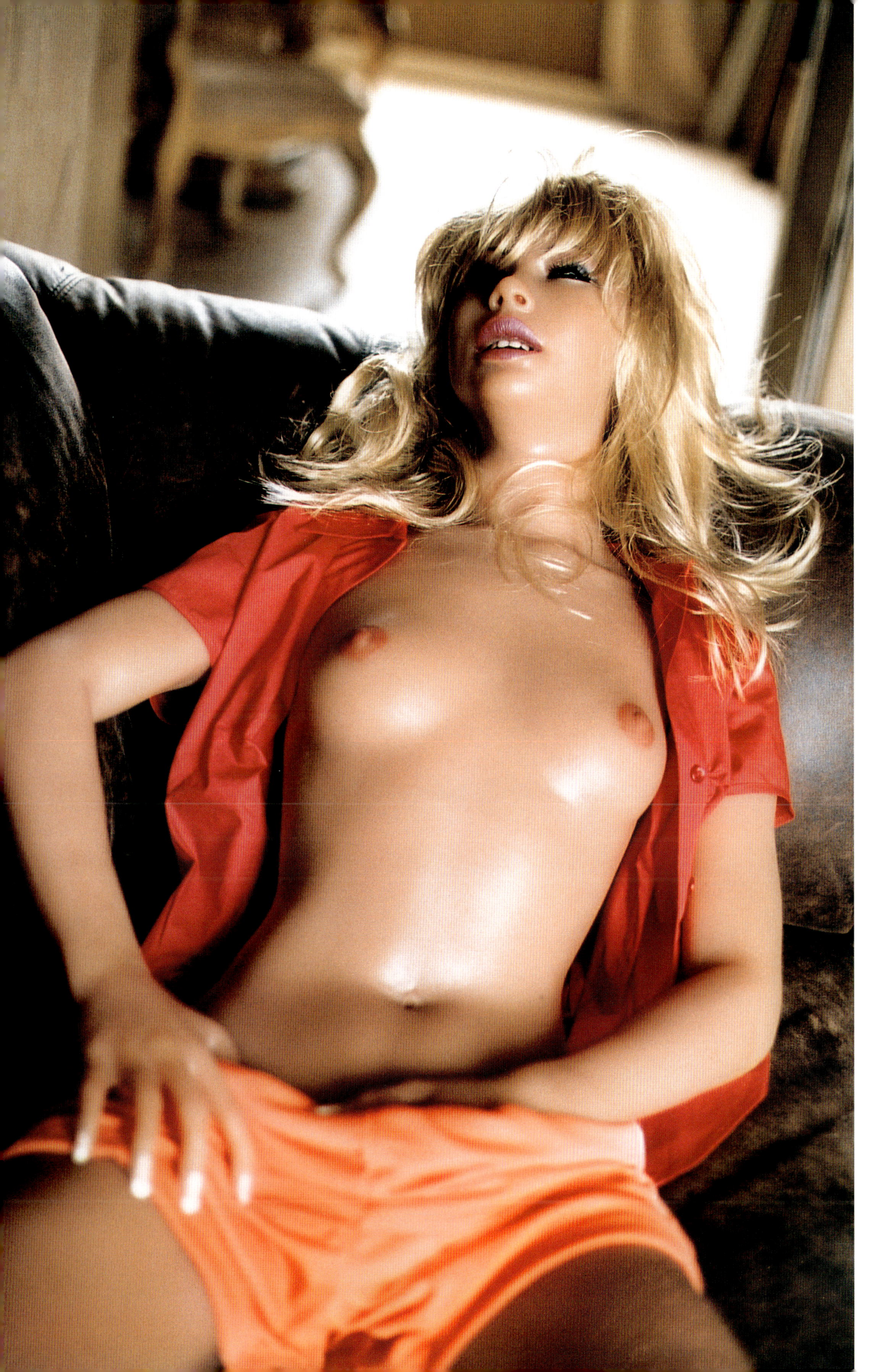

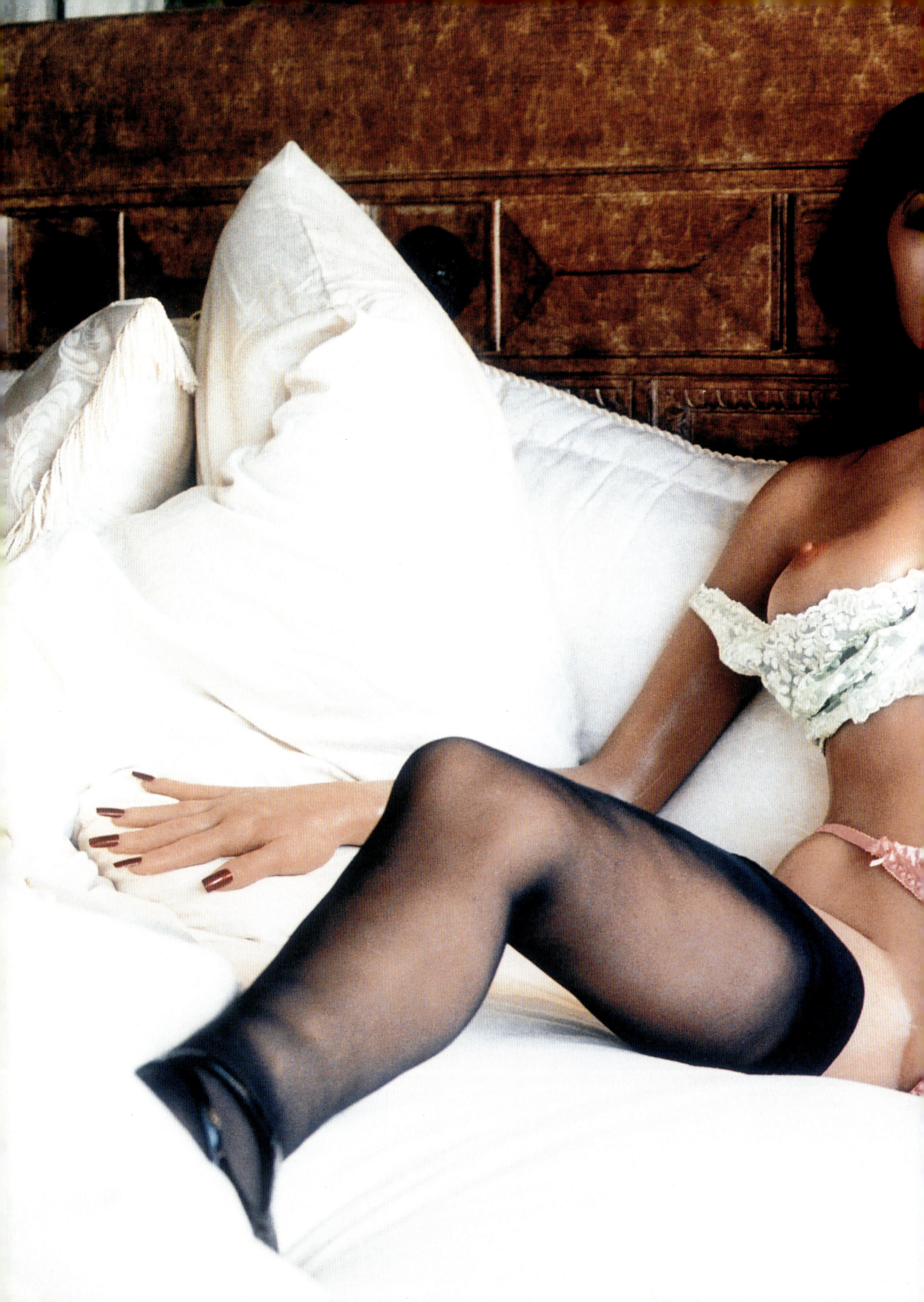

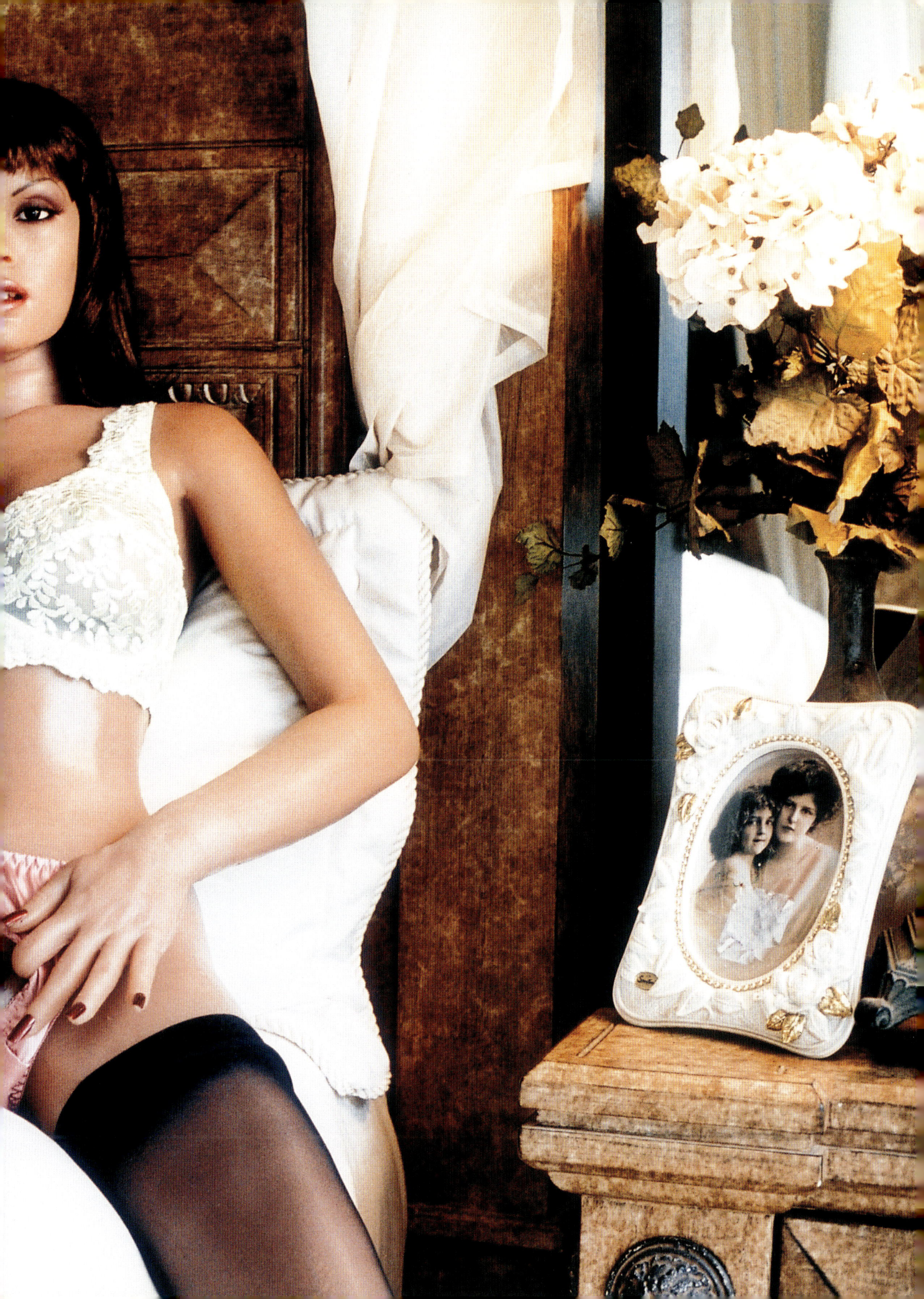

PRUSSIAN GUARD

FEATURING

Eva Tettamanti

August 1993, Unpublished

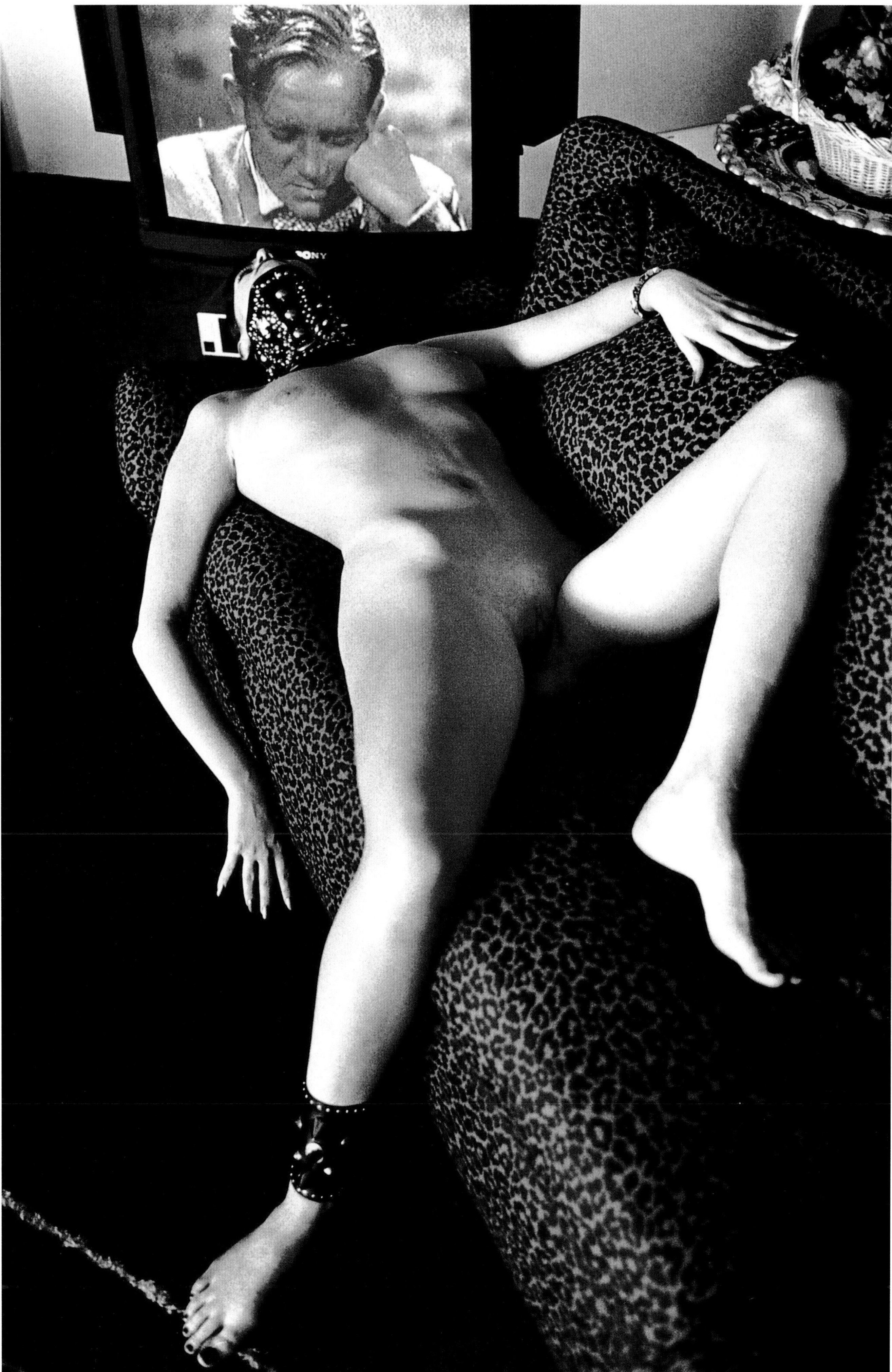

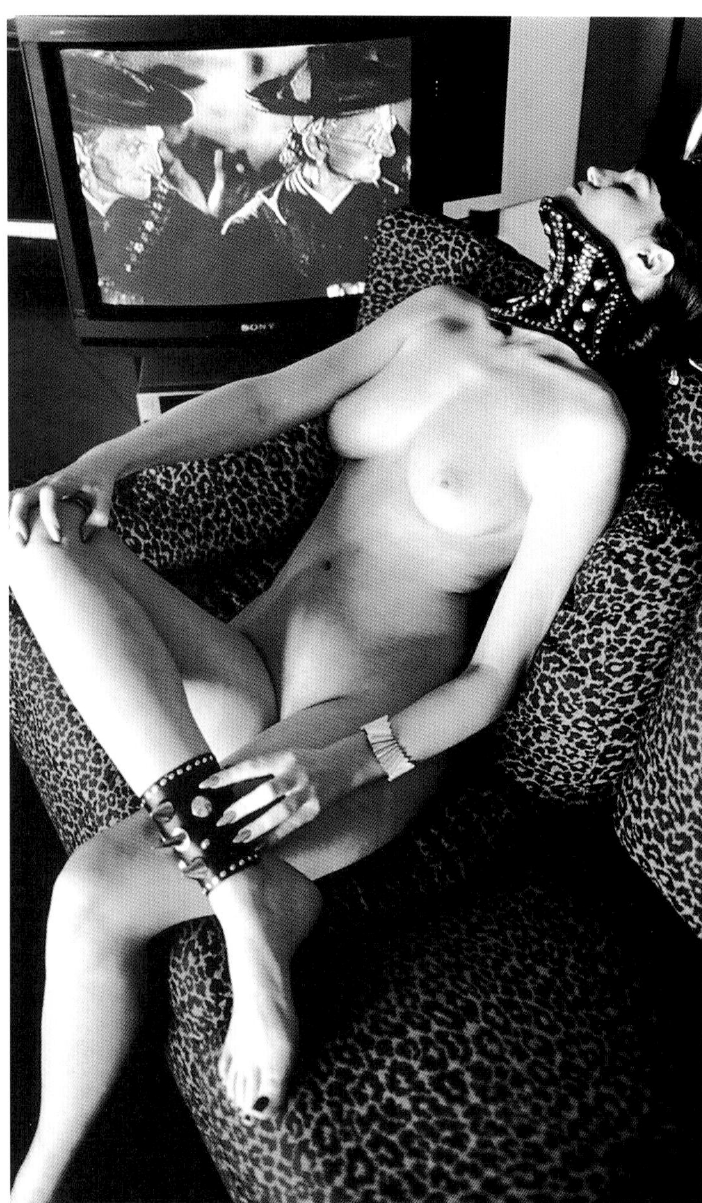
SONY

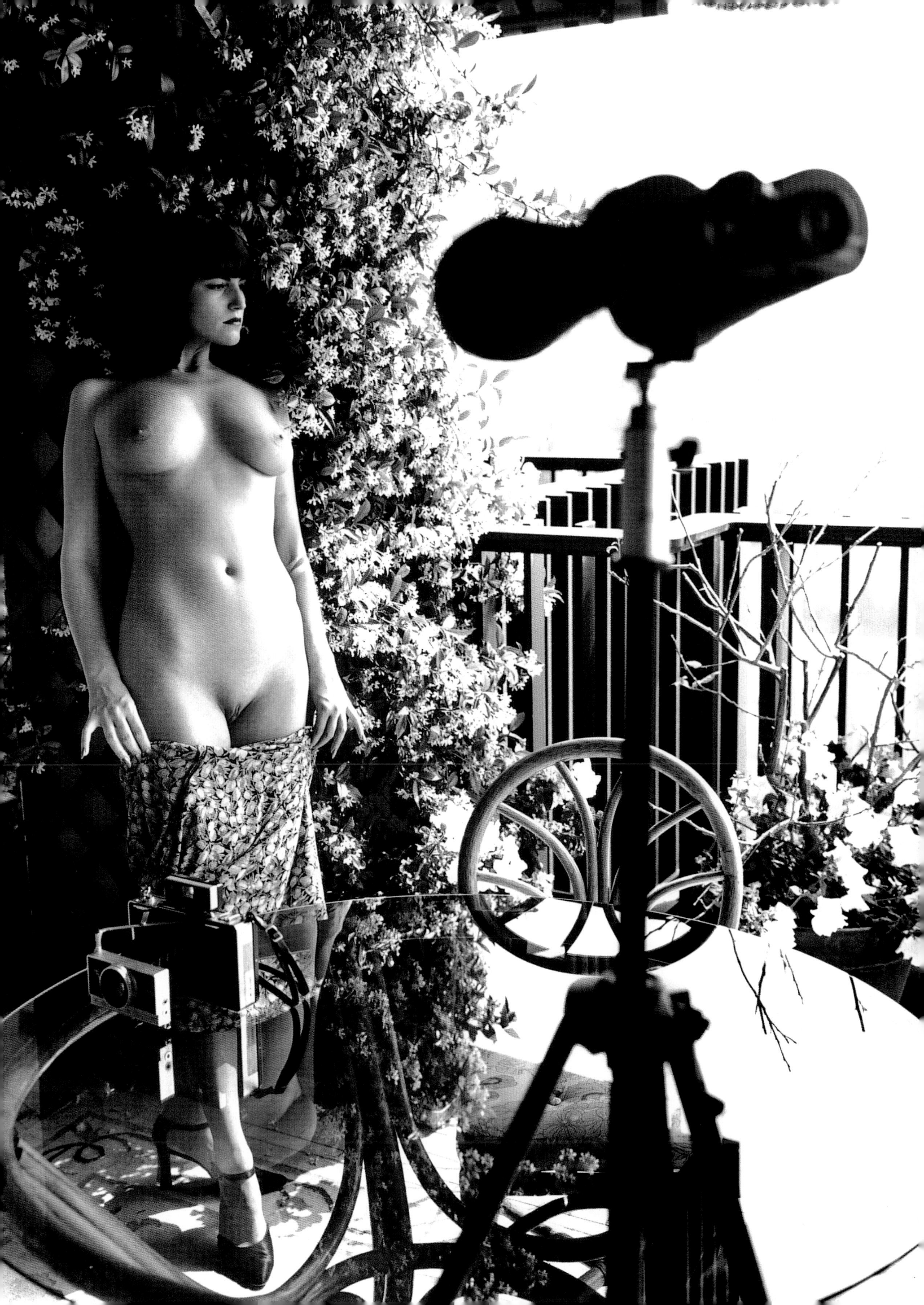

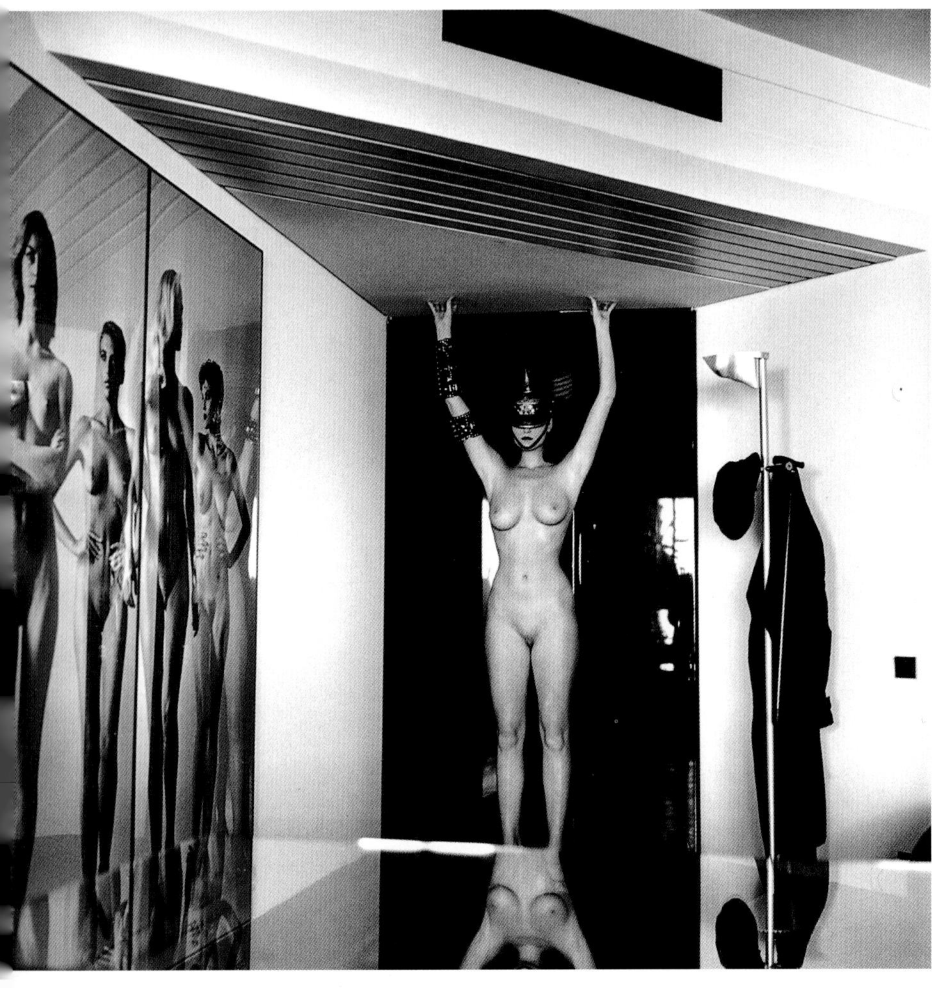

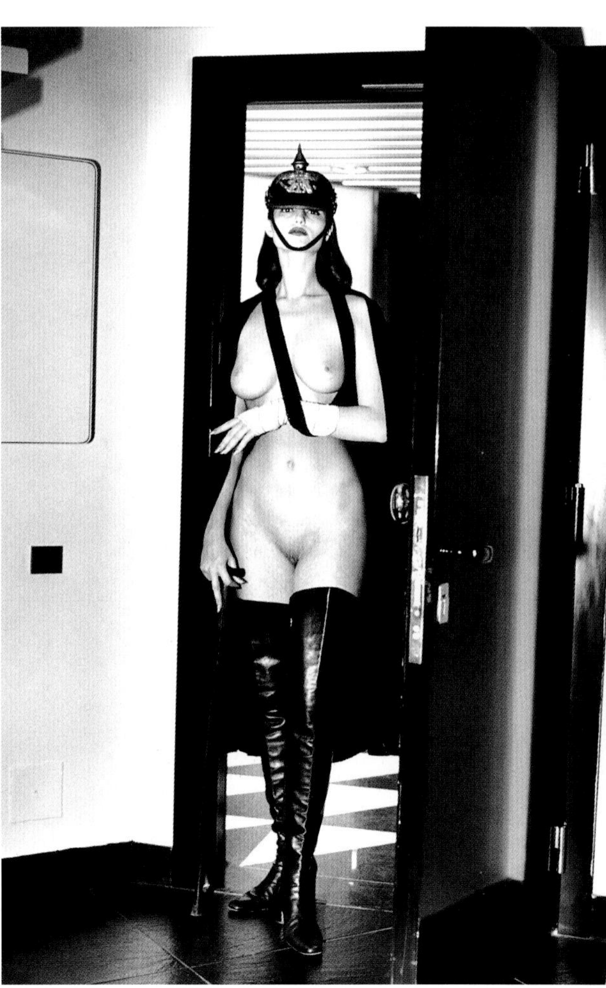

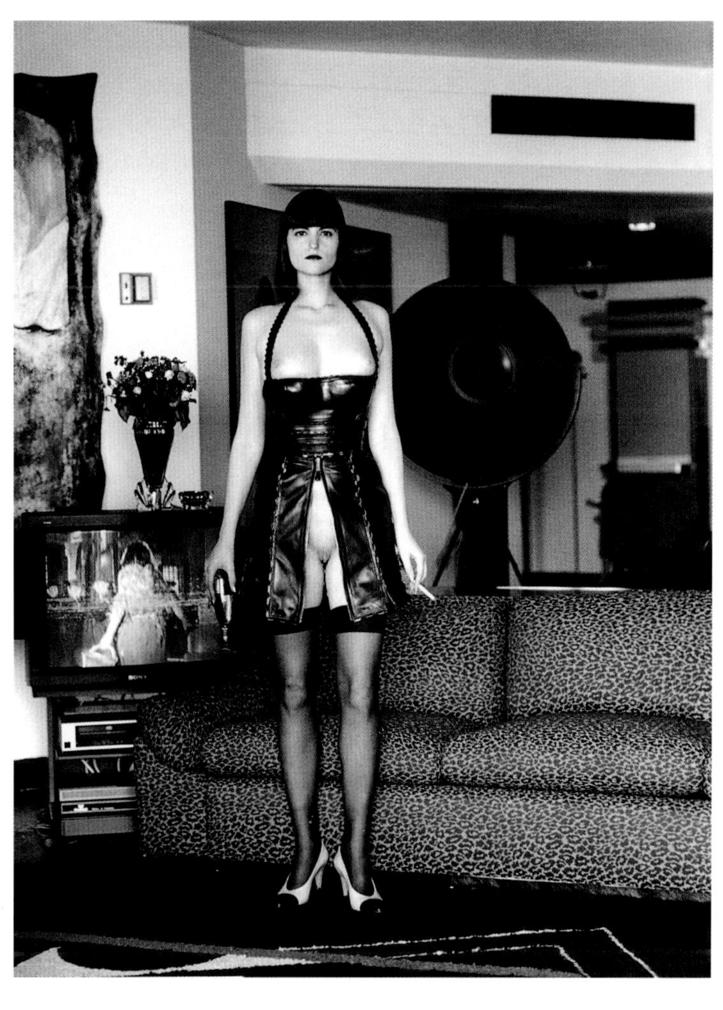

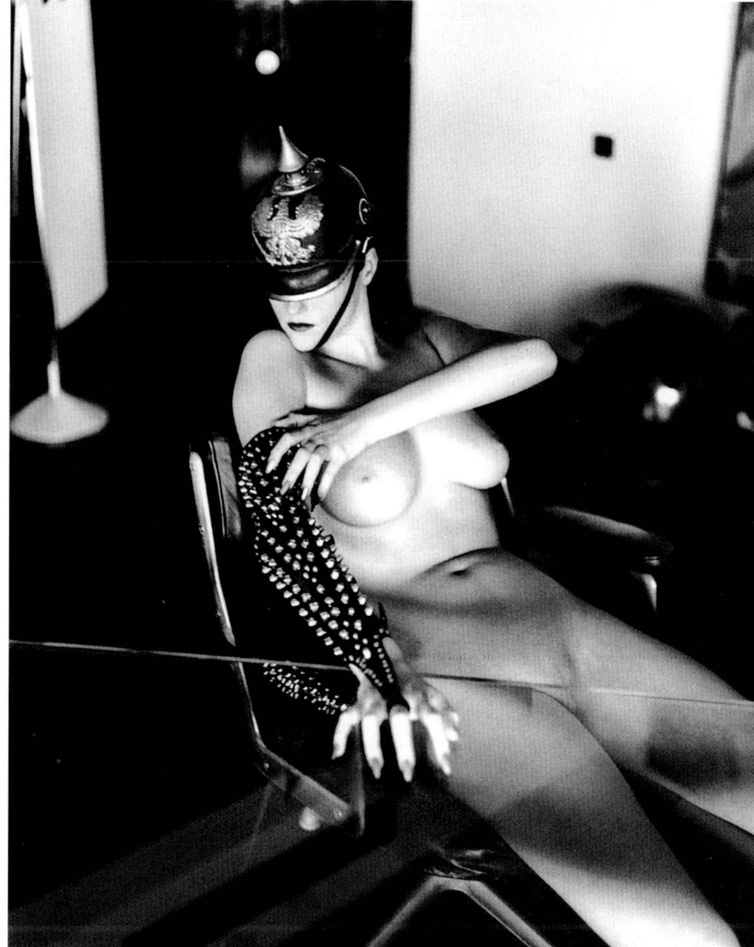

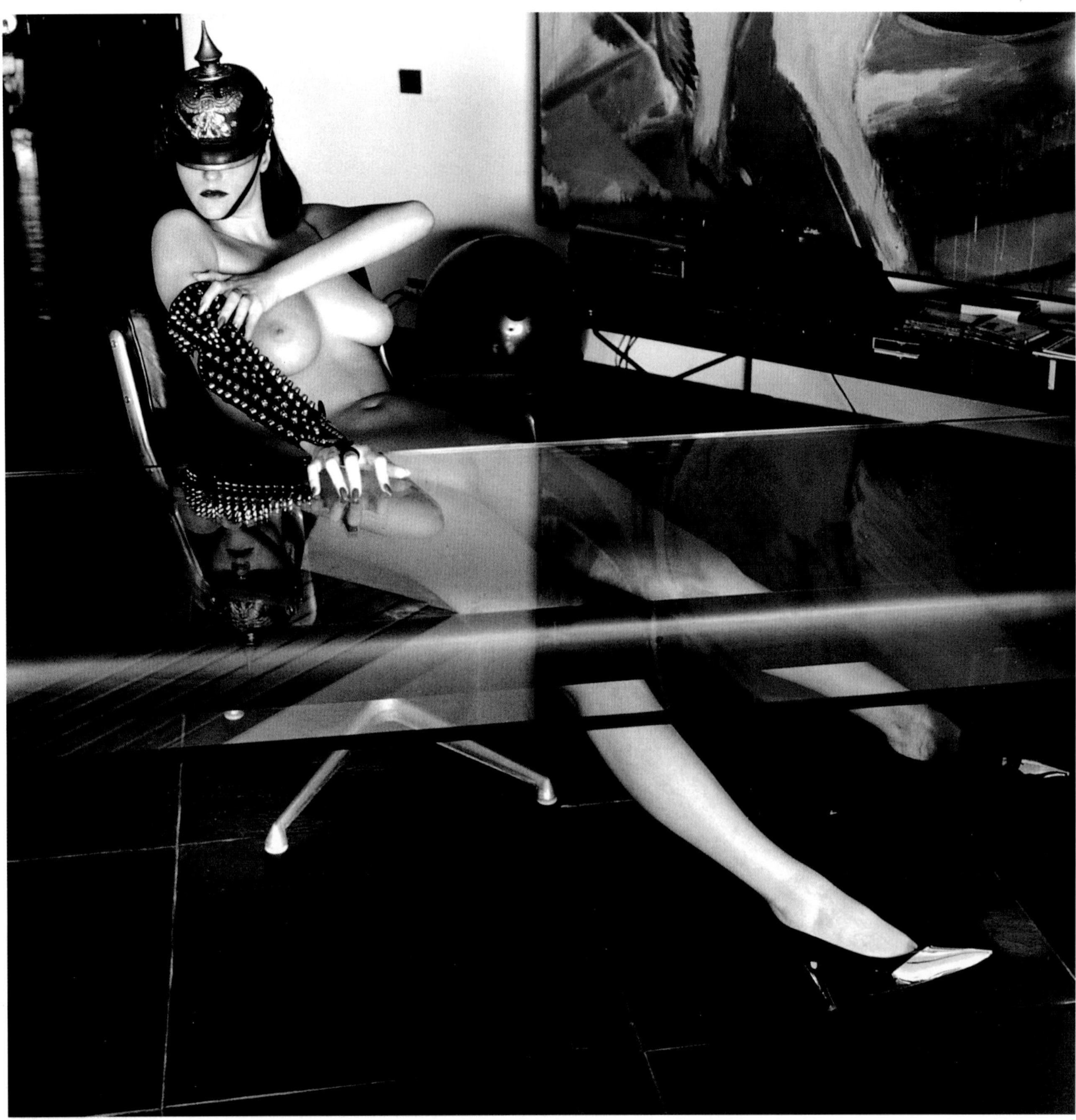

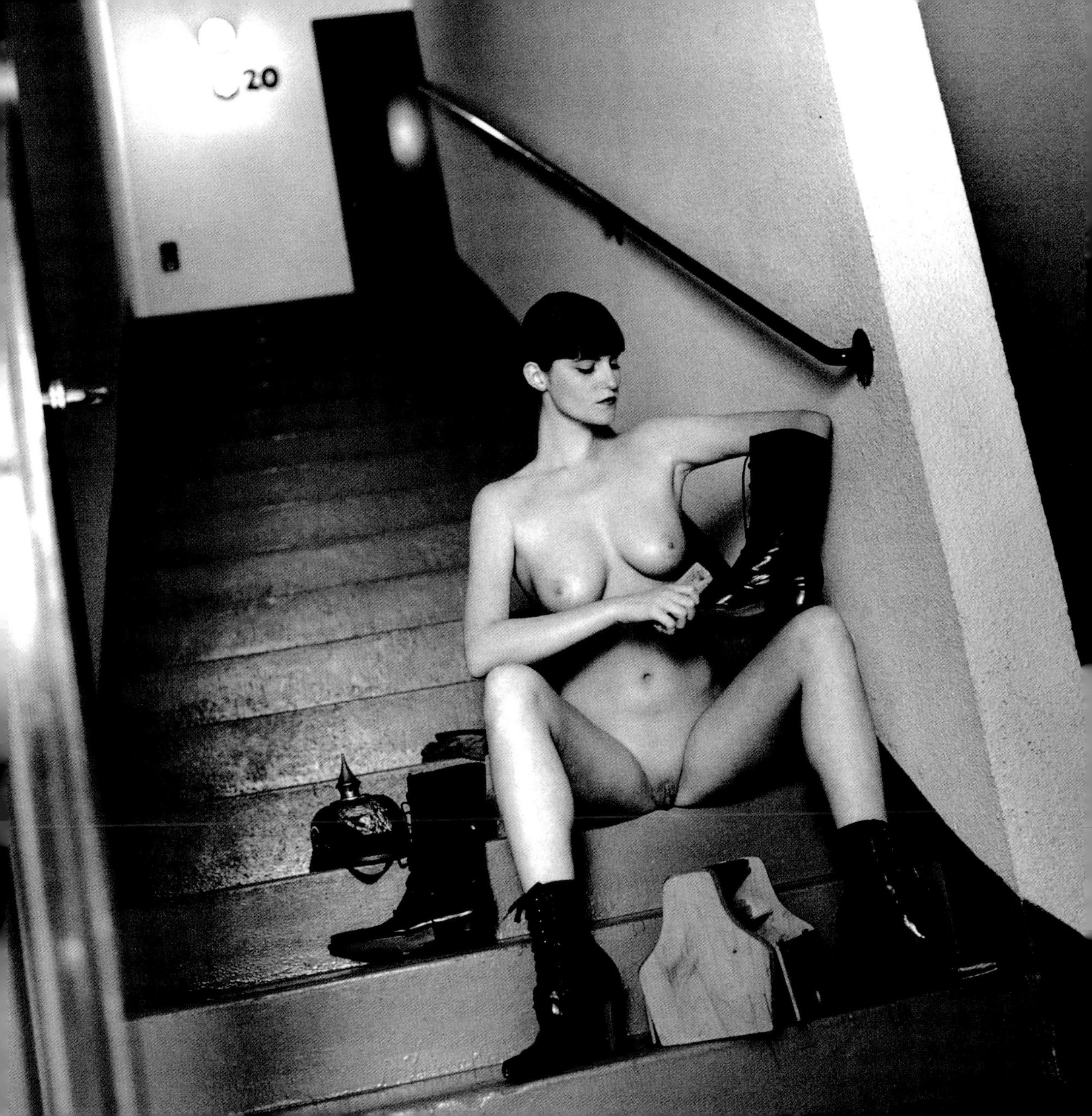
20

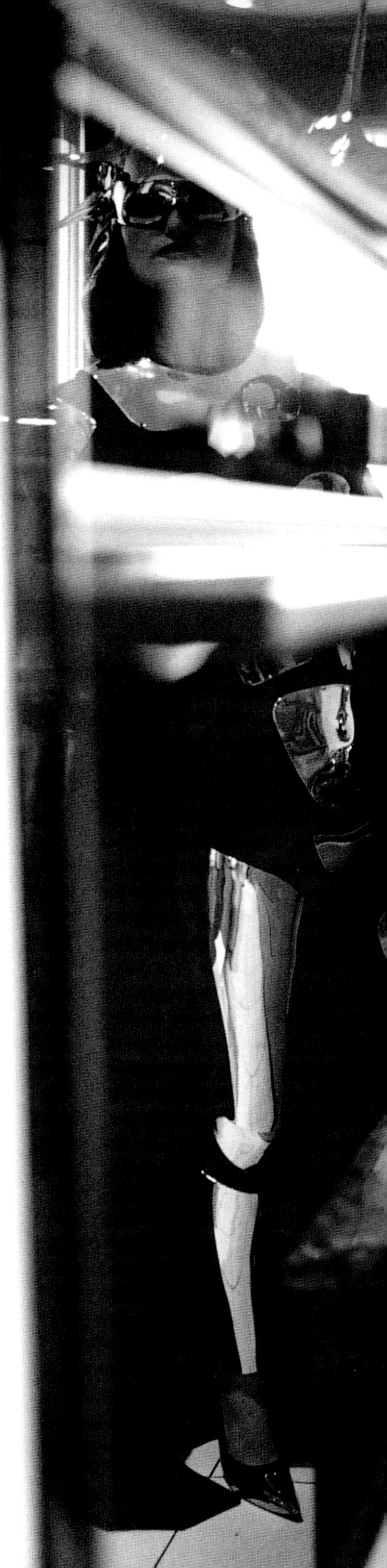

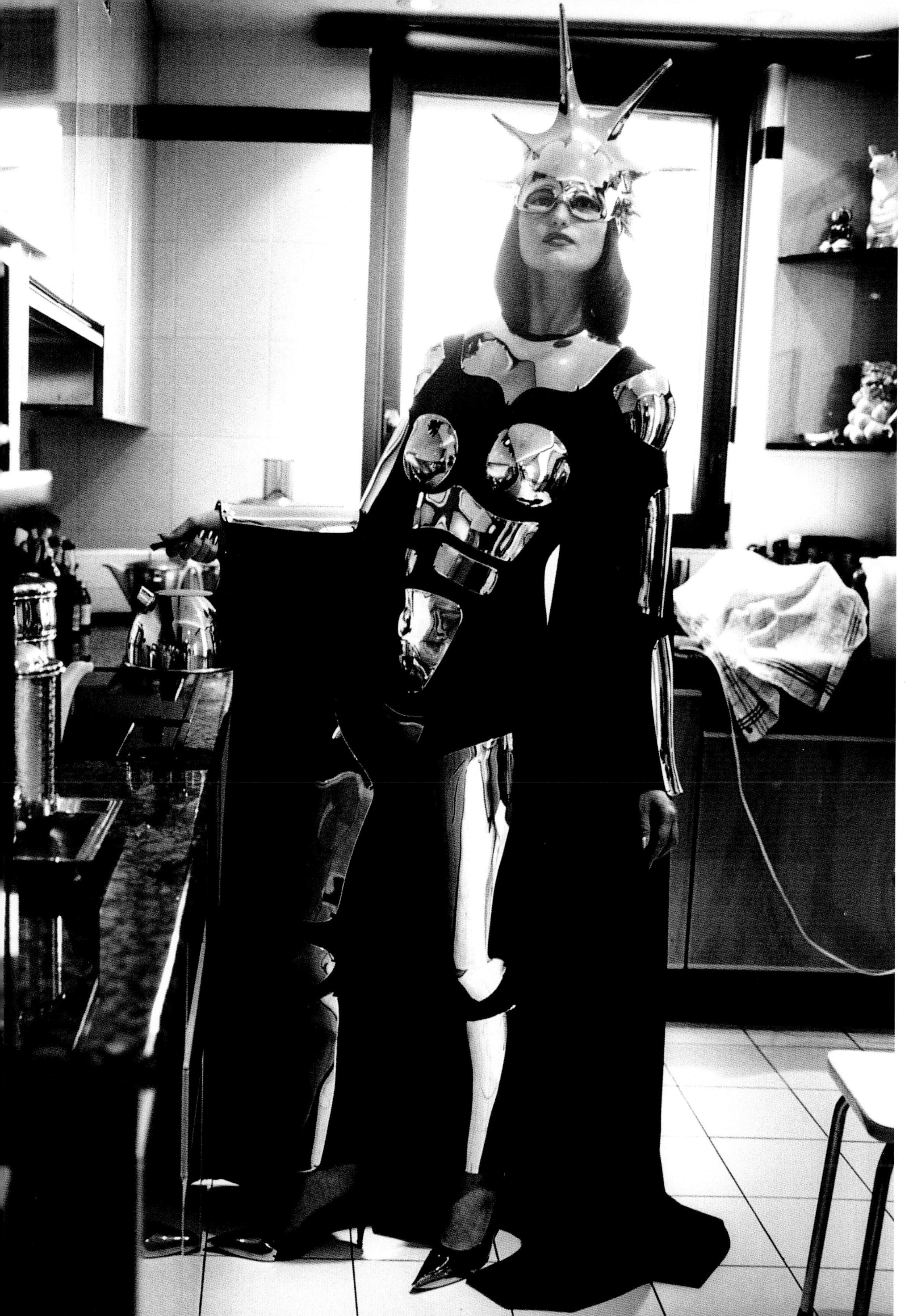

At your SERVICE

FEATURING

Eva Tettamanti

August 1993, Unpublished

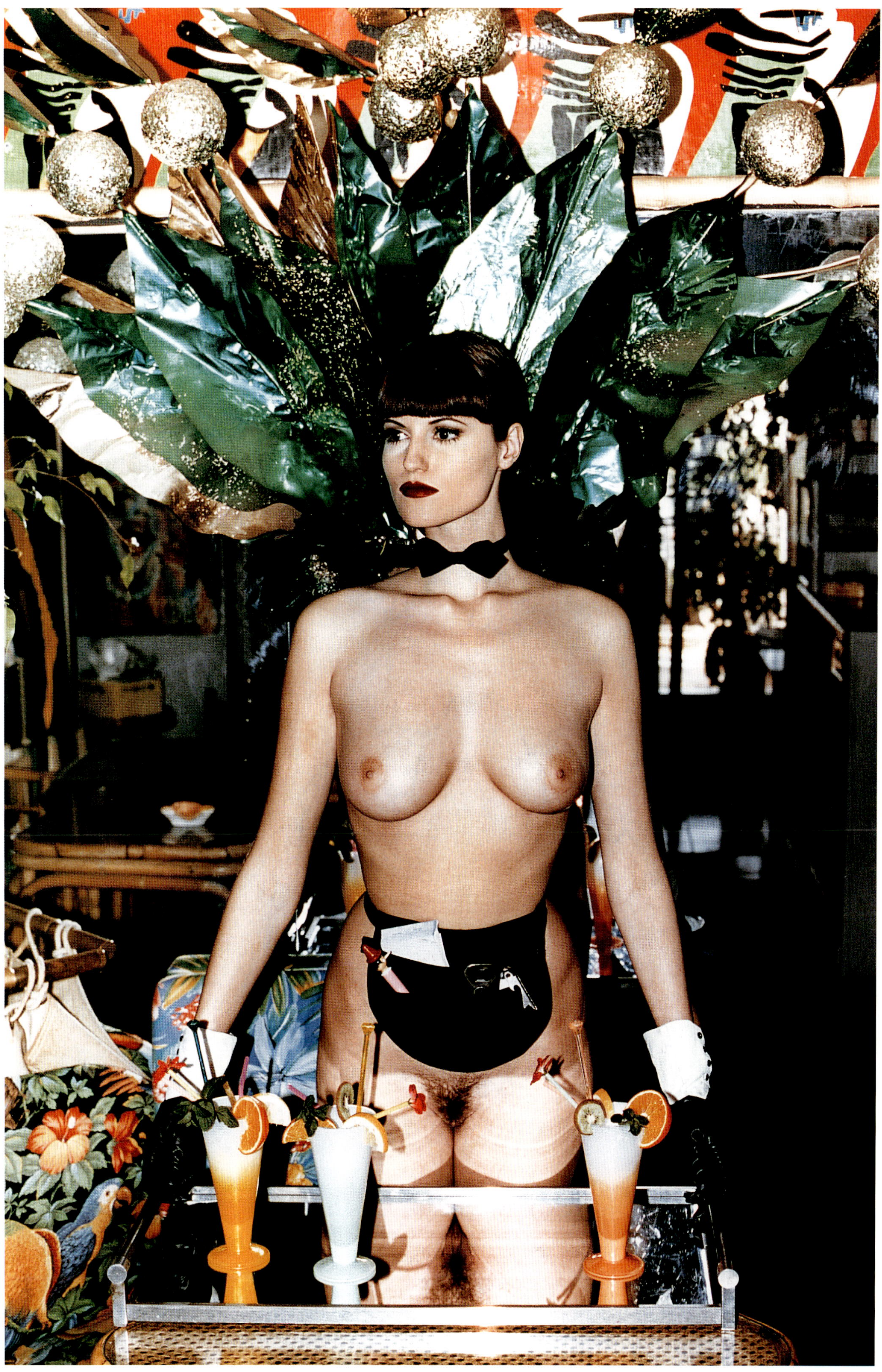

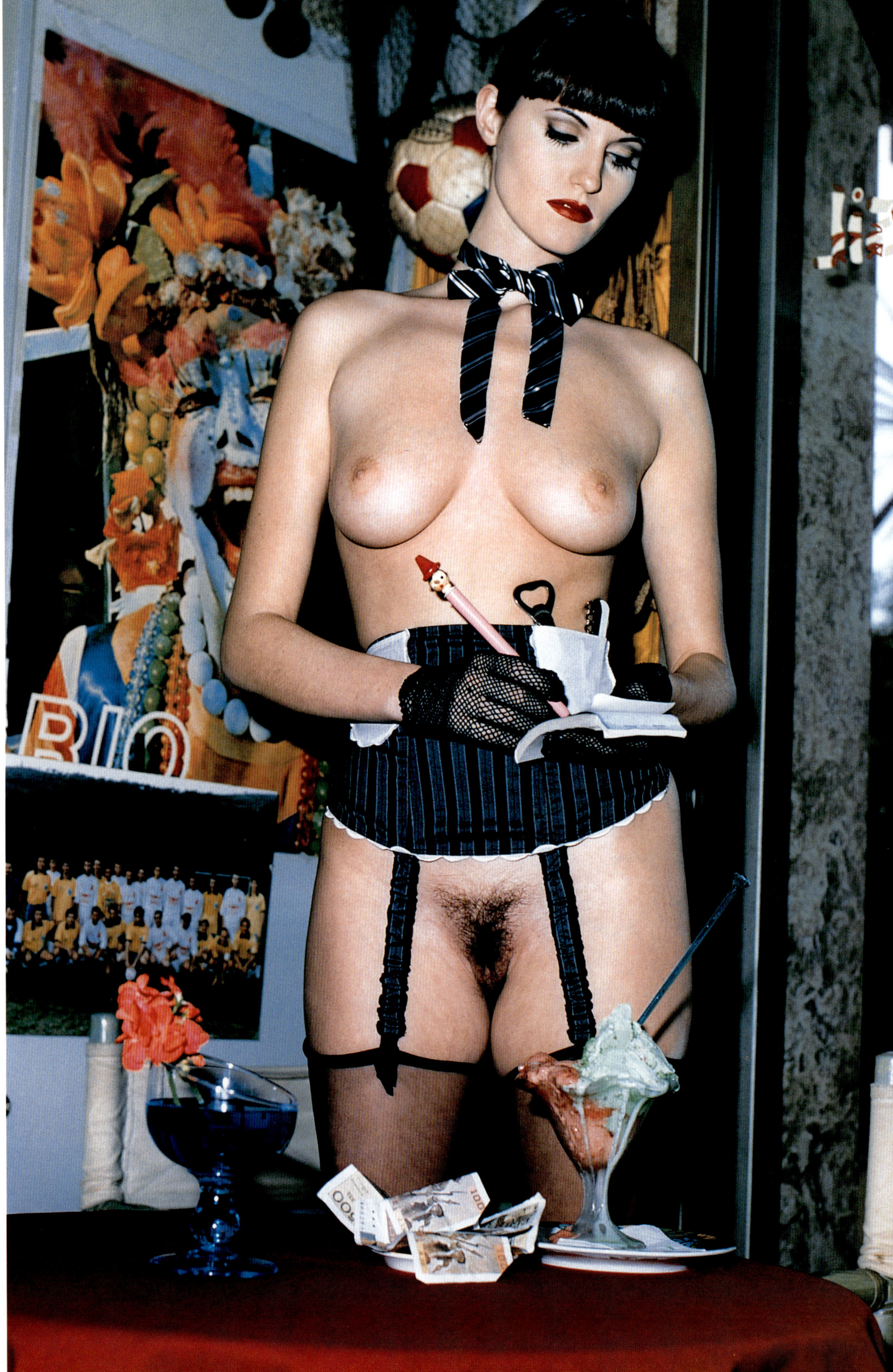
RIO

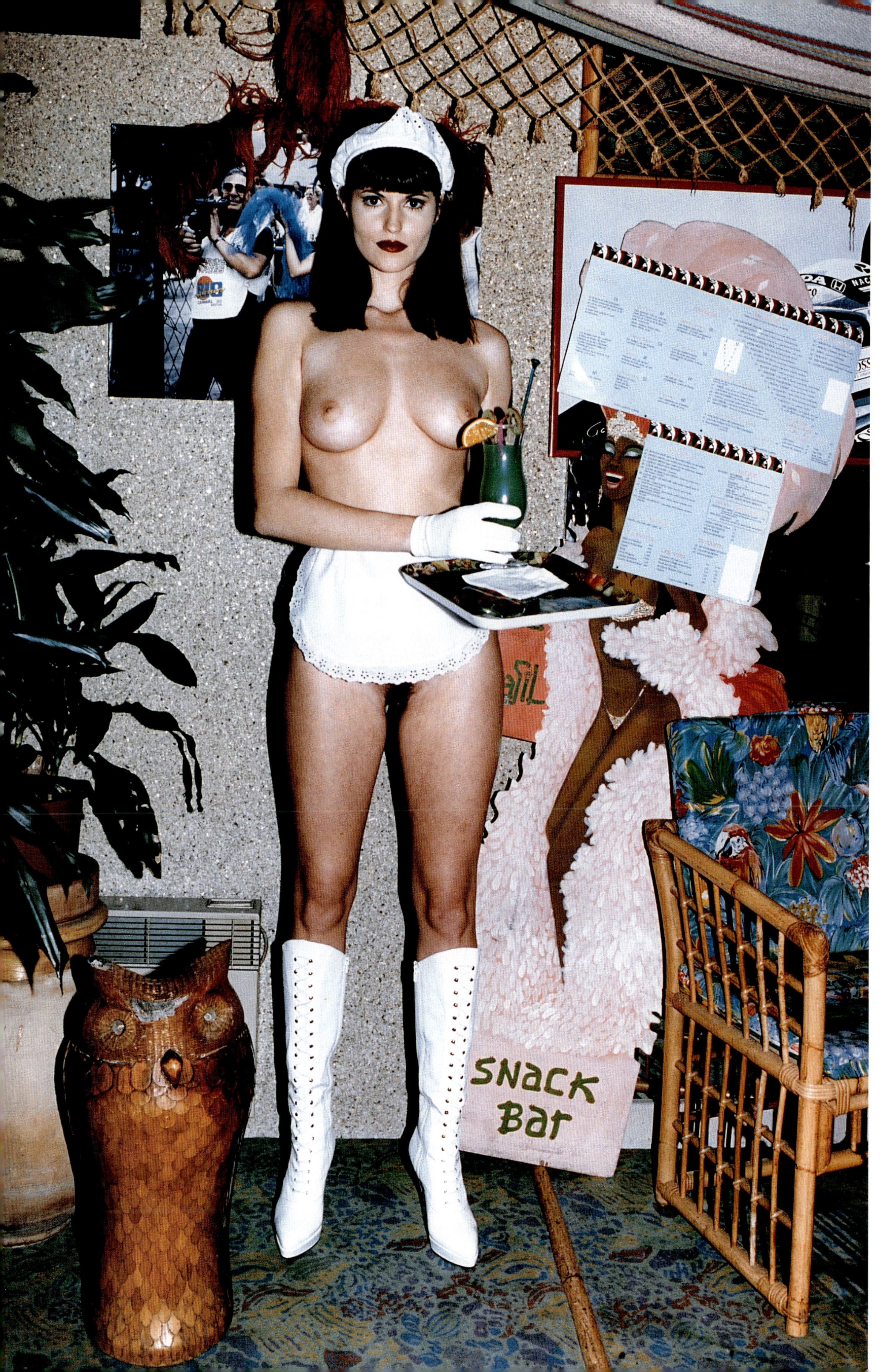
SNACK
Bar

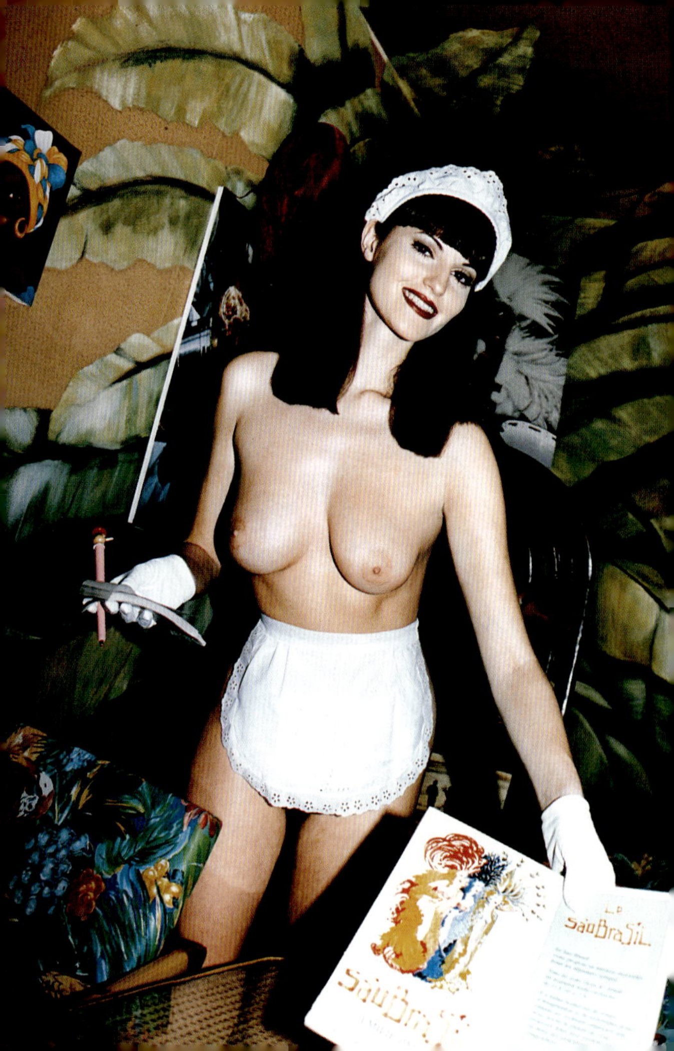
Le
São Brasil

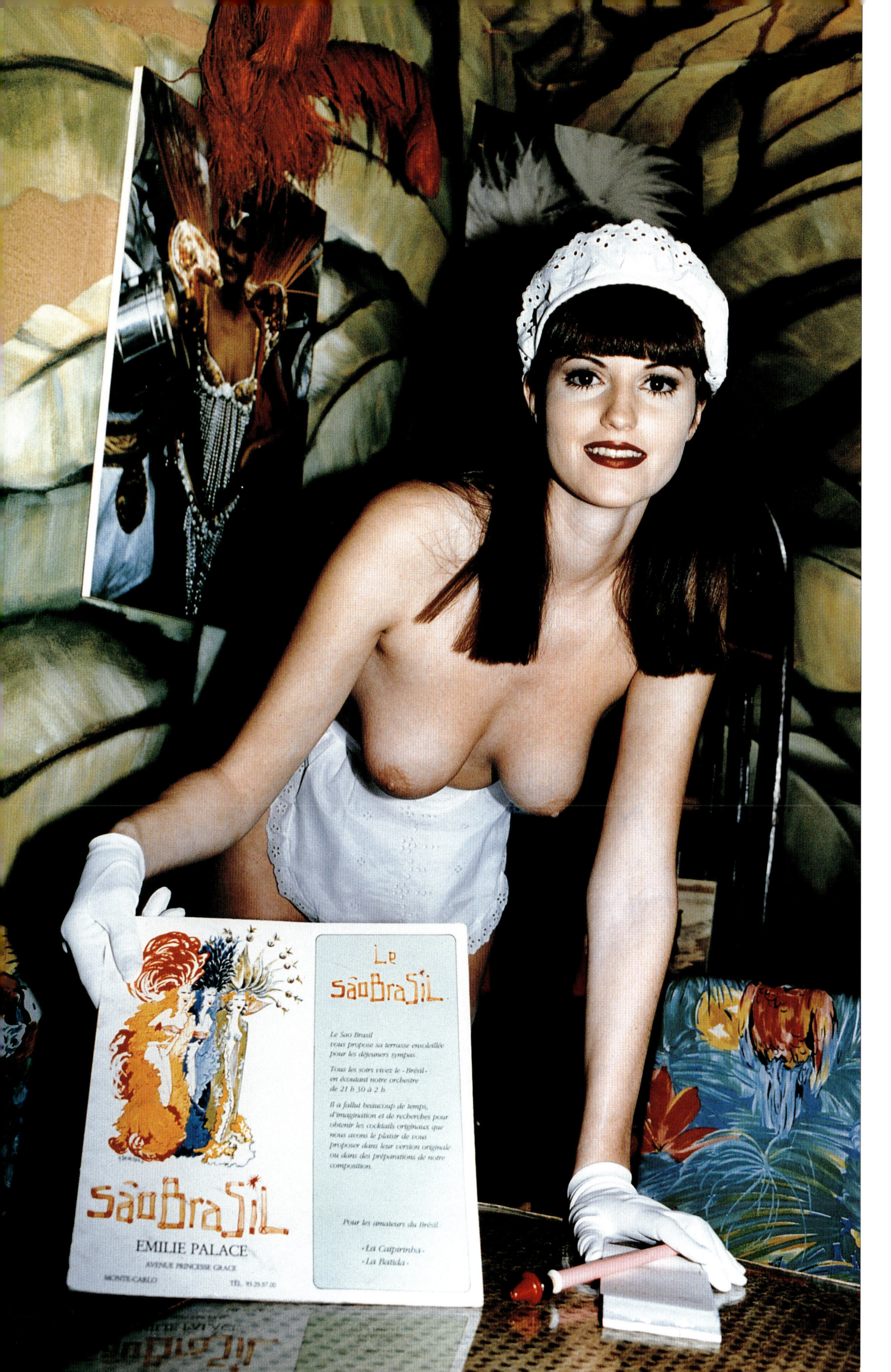
SãoBraSil
EMILIE PALACE
AVENUE PRINCESSE GRACE
MONTE-CARLO
TÉL. 93.25.57.00
Le SãoBraSil
Le Sao Brasil
vous propose sa terrasse ensoleillée
pour les déjeuners sympas.
Tous les soirs vivez le - Brésil -
en écoutant notre orchestre
de 21 h 30 à 2 h.
Il a fallut beaucoup de temps,
d'imagination et de recherches pour
obtenir les cocktails originaux que
nous avons le plaisir de vous
proposer dans leur version originale
ou dans des préparations de notre
composition.
Pour les amateurs du Brésil
- La Caipirinha -
- La Batida -

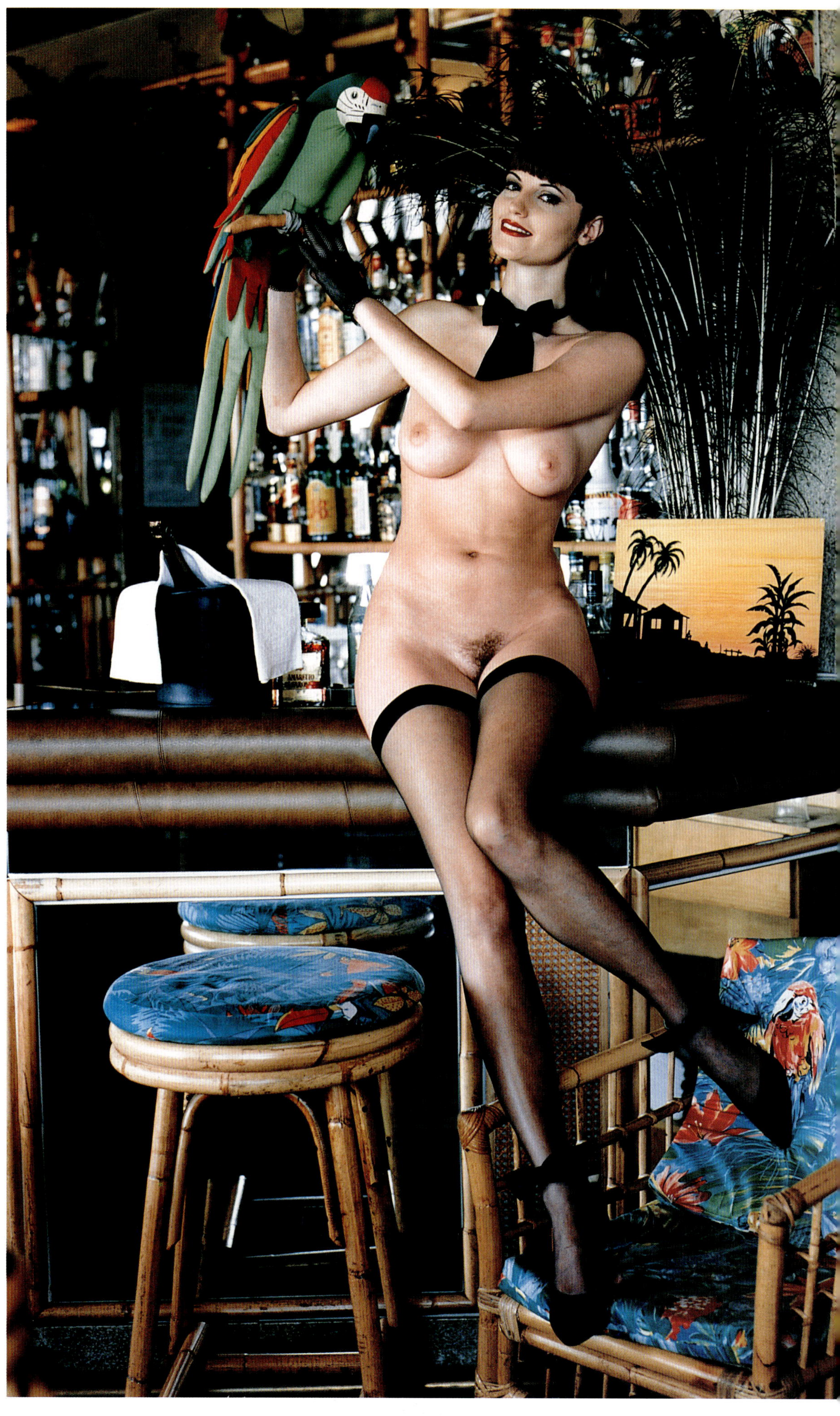

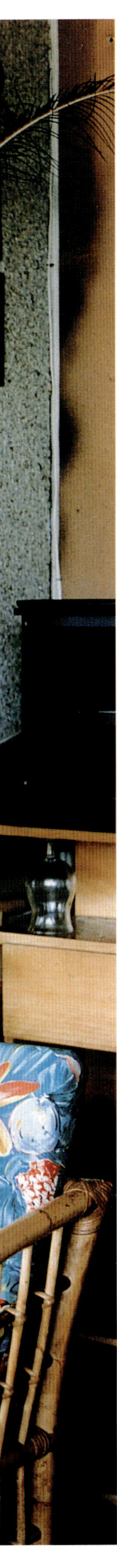

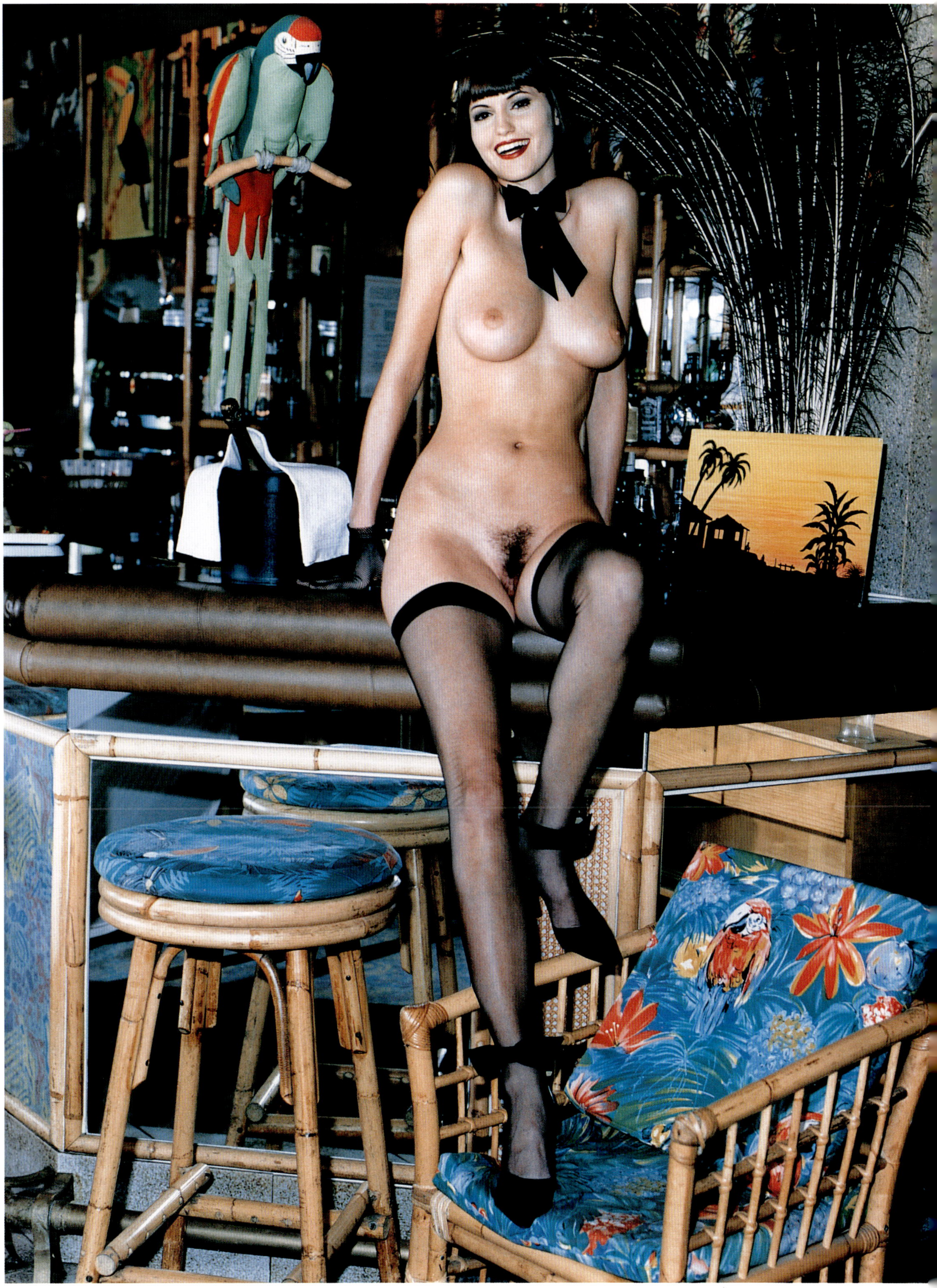

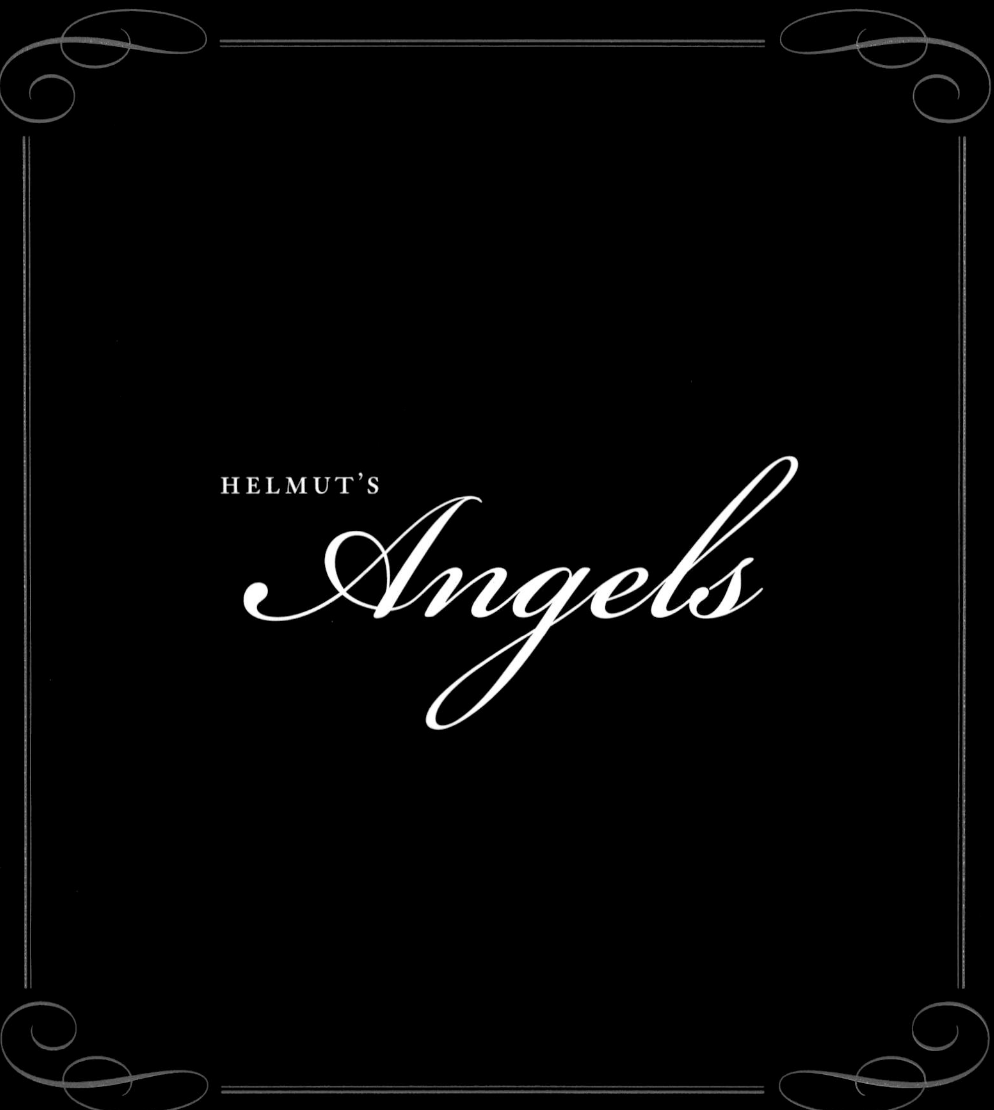

FEATURING

Lené Hefner, Naydean Sophiea Fisher, Helle Michaelsen, Kimberley Conrad

May 1988

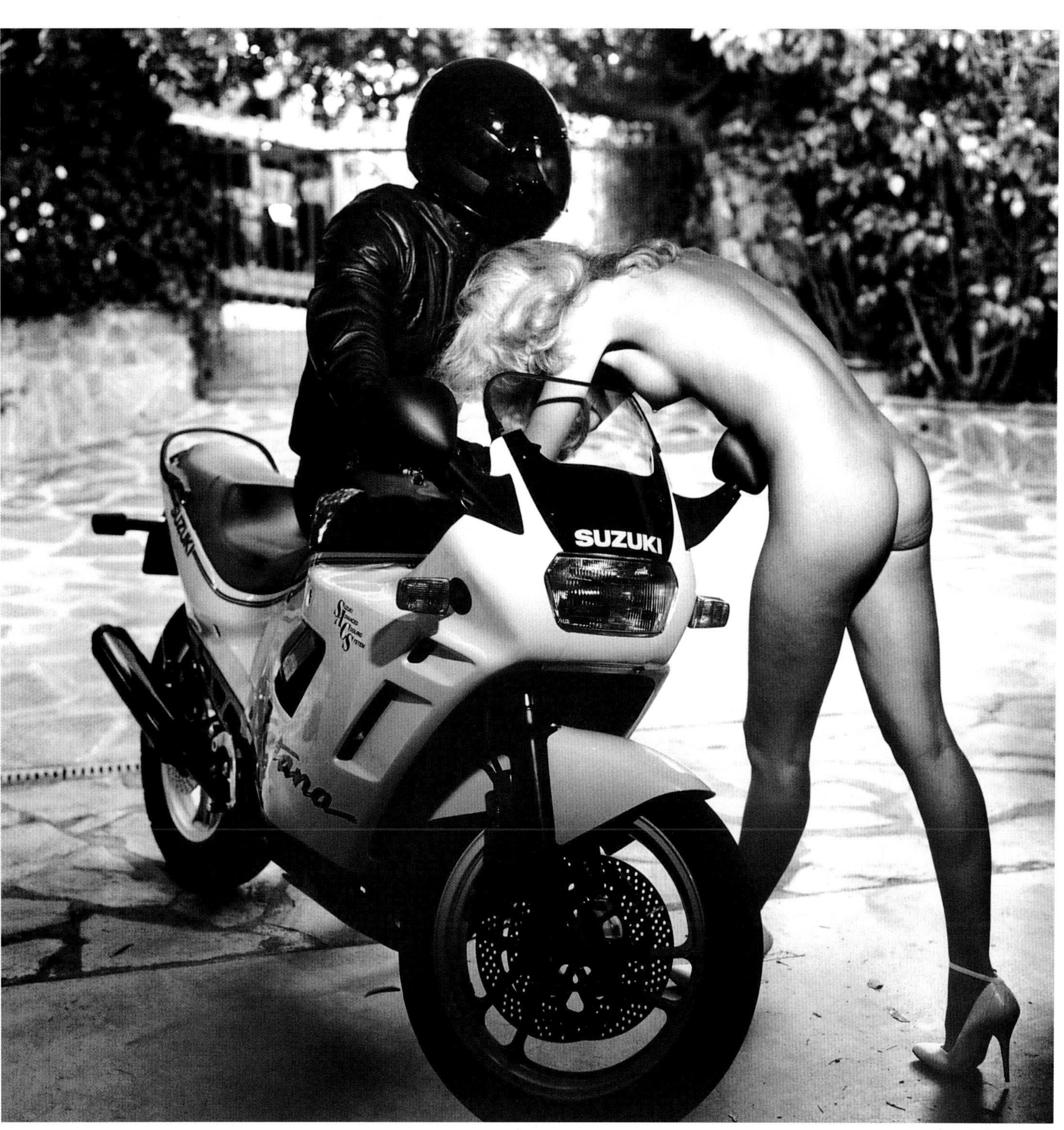
SUZUKI

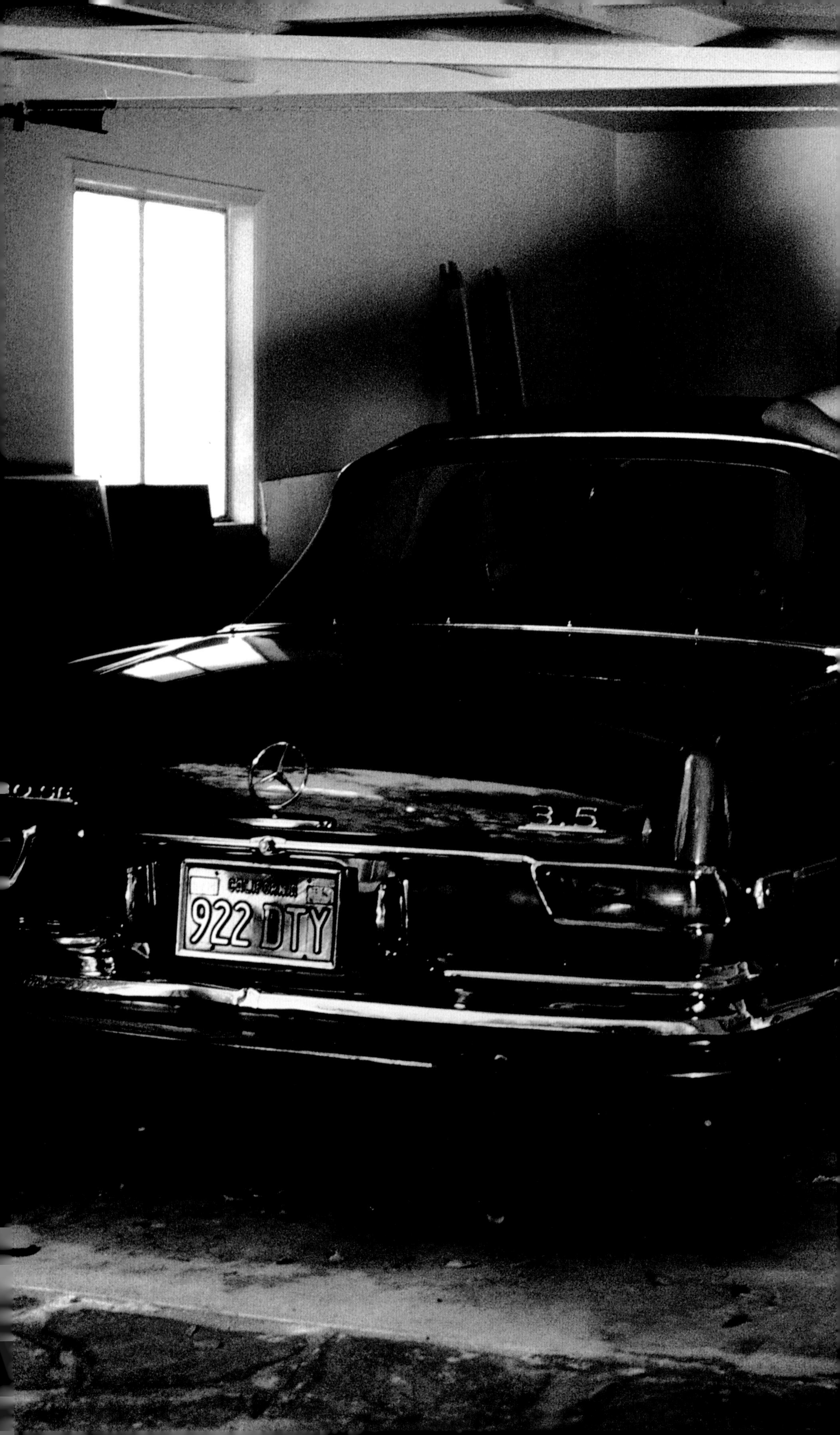

922 DTY
3.5

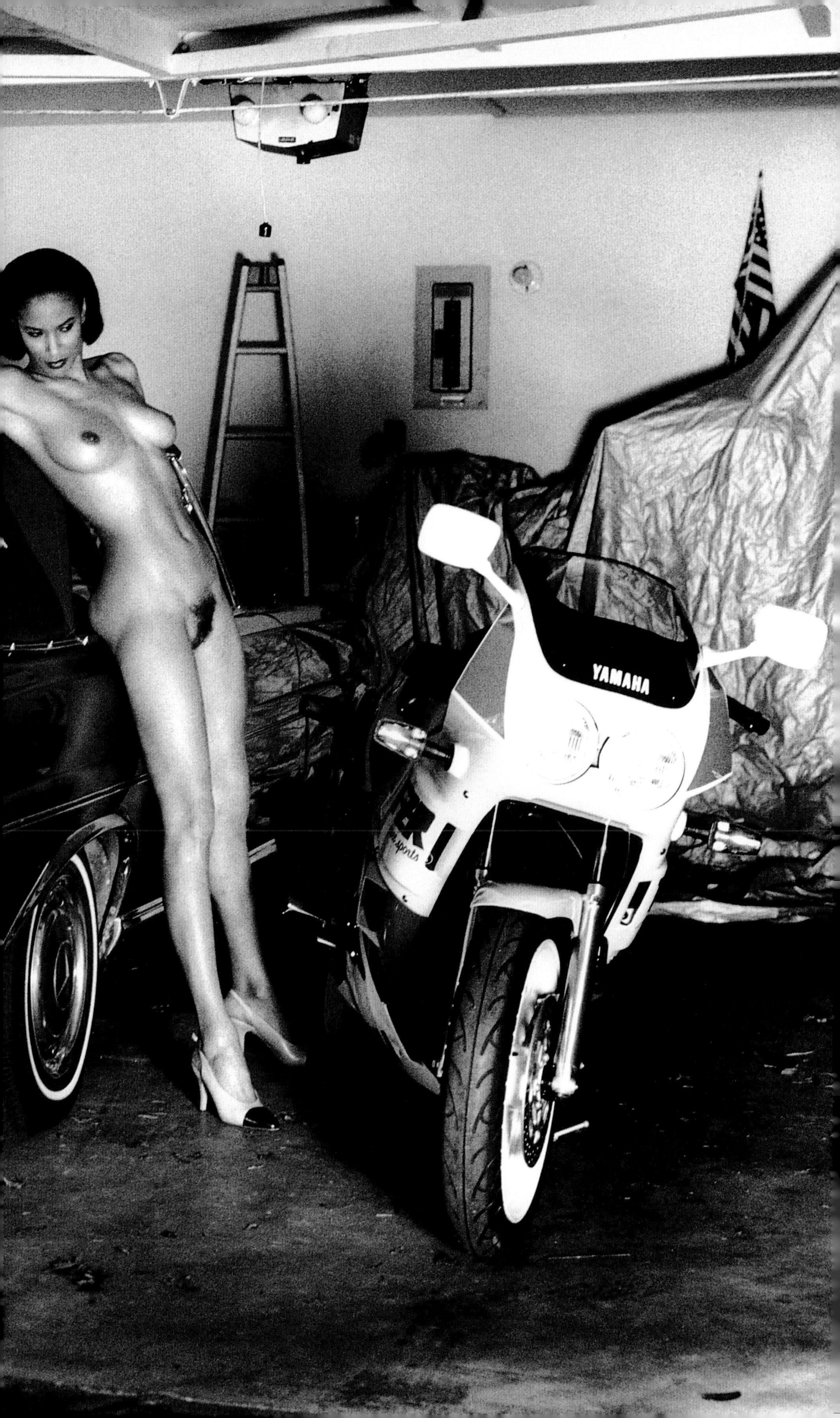
YAMAHA

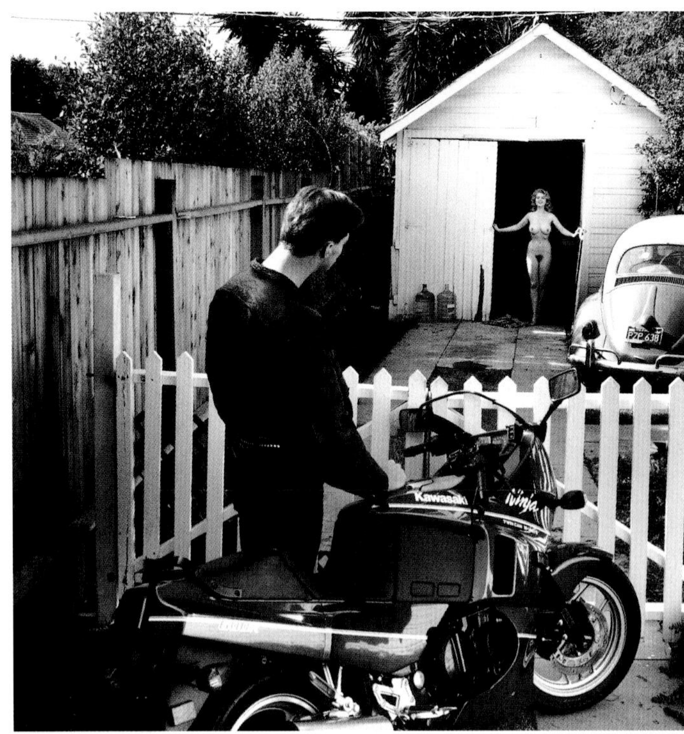
Kawasaki
Ninja

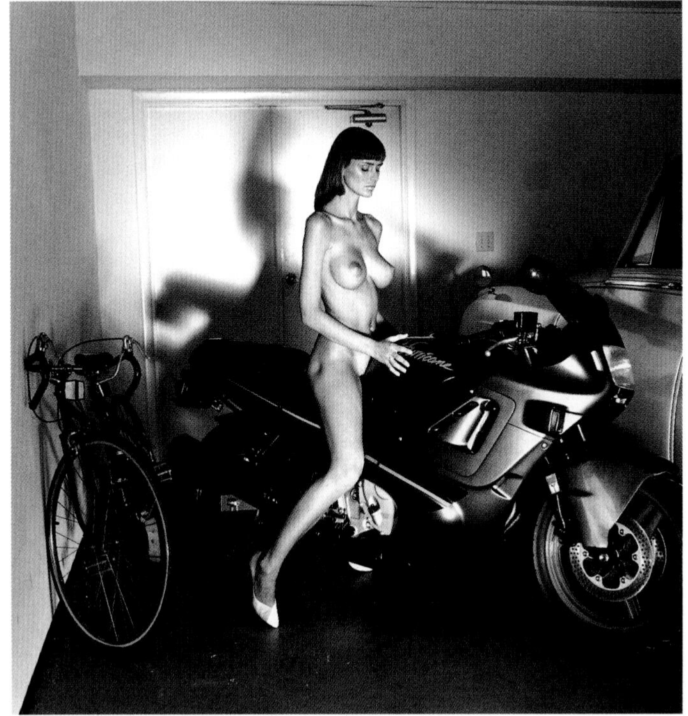

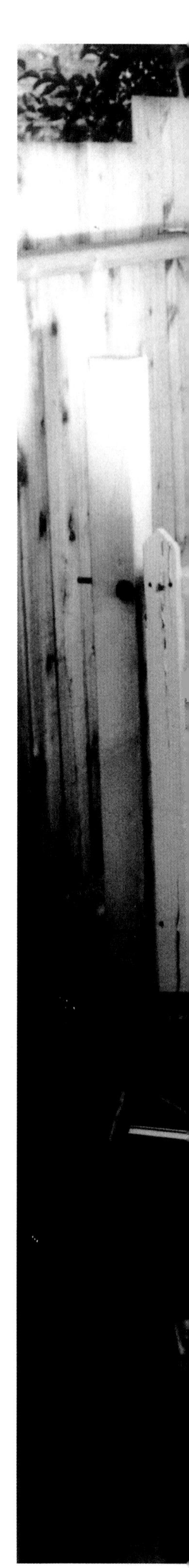

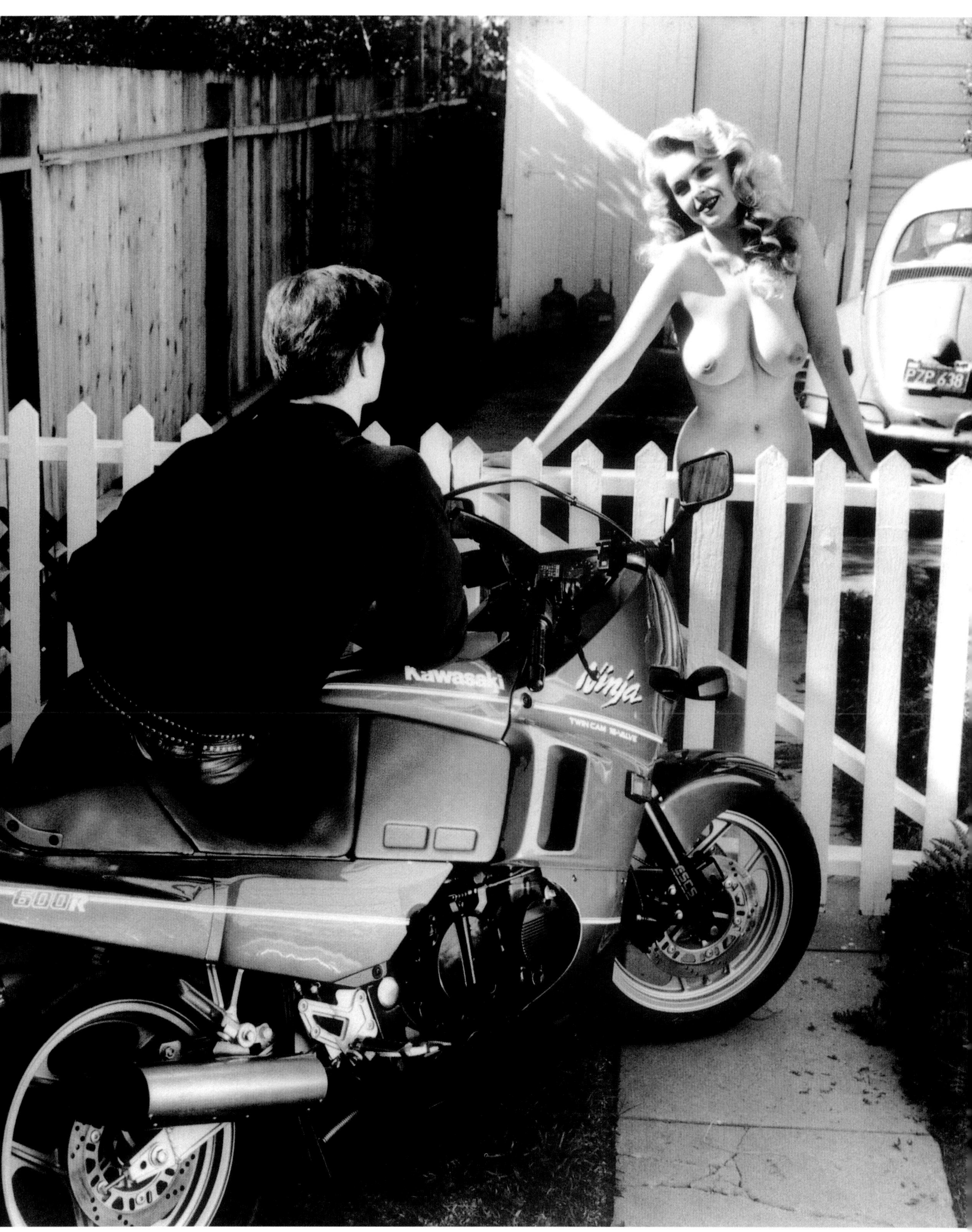
Kawasaki
Ninja
600R
PZP 638

BIG LITTLE LADY LADY

FEATURING

Brigitte Ariel and Roanne Rogers

August 1977, Unpublished

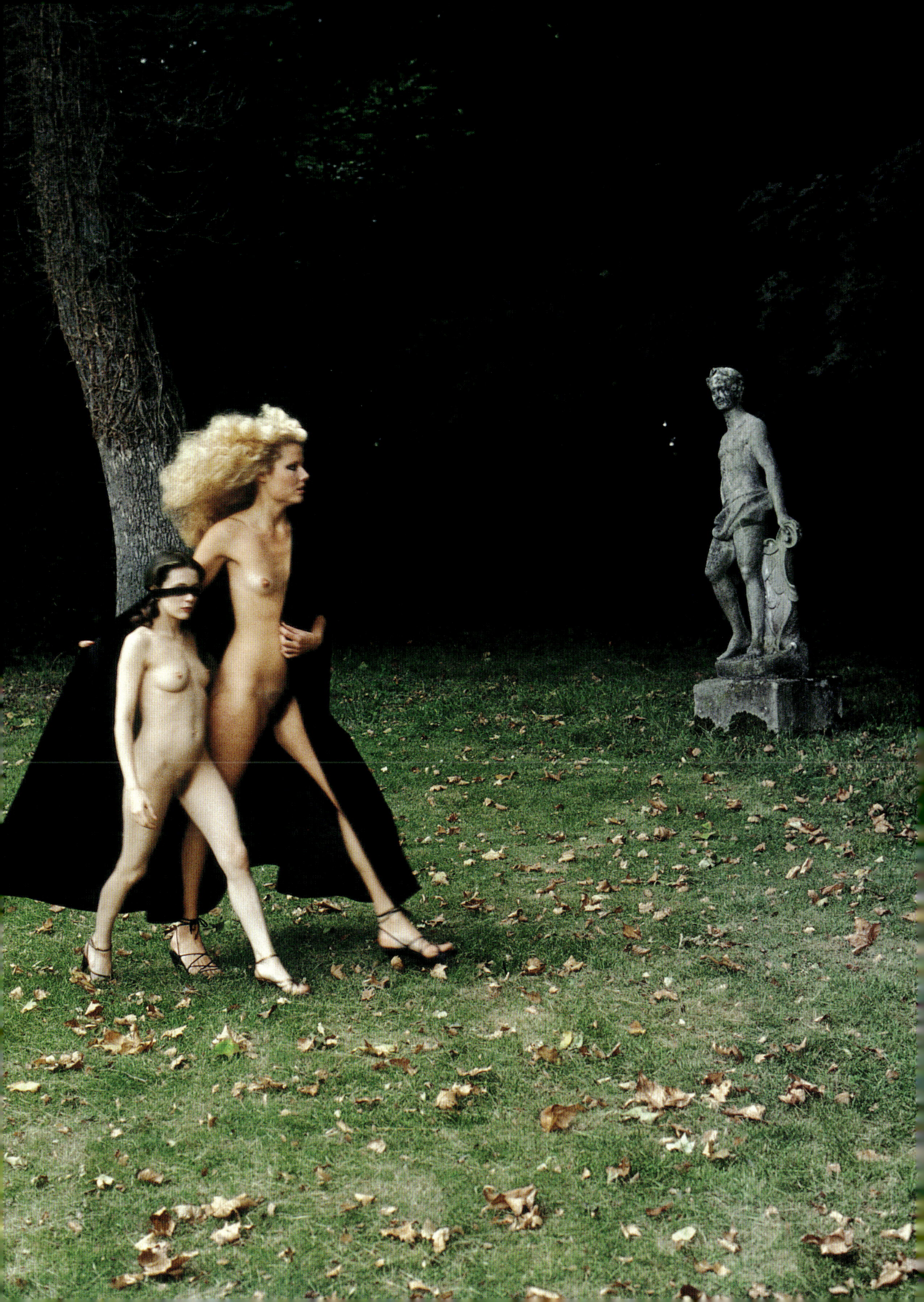

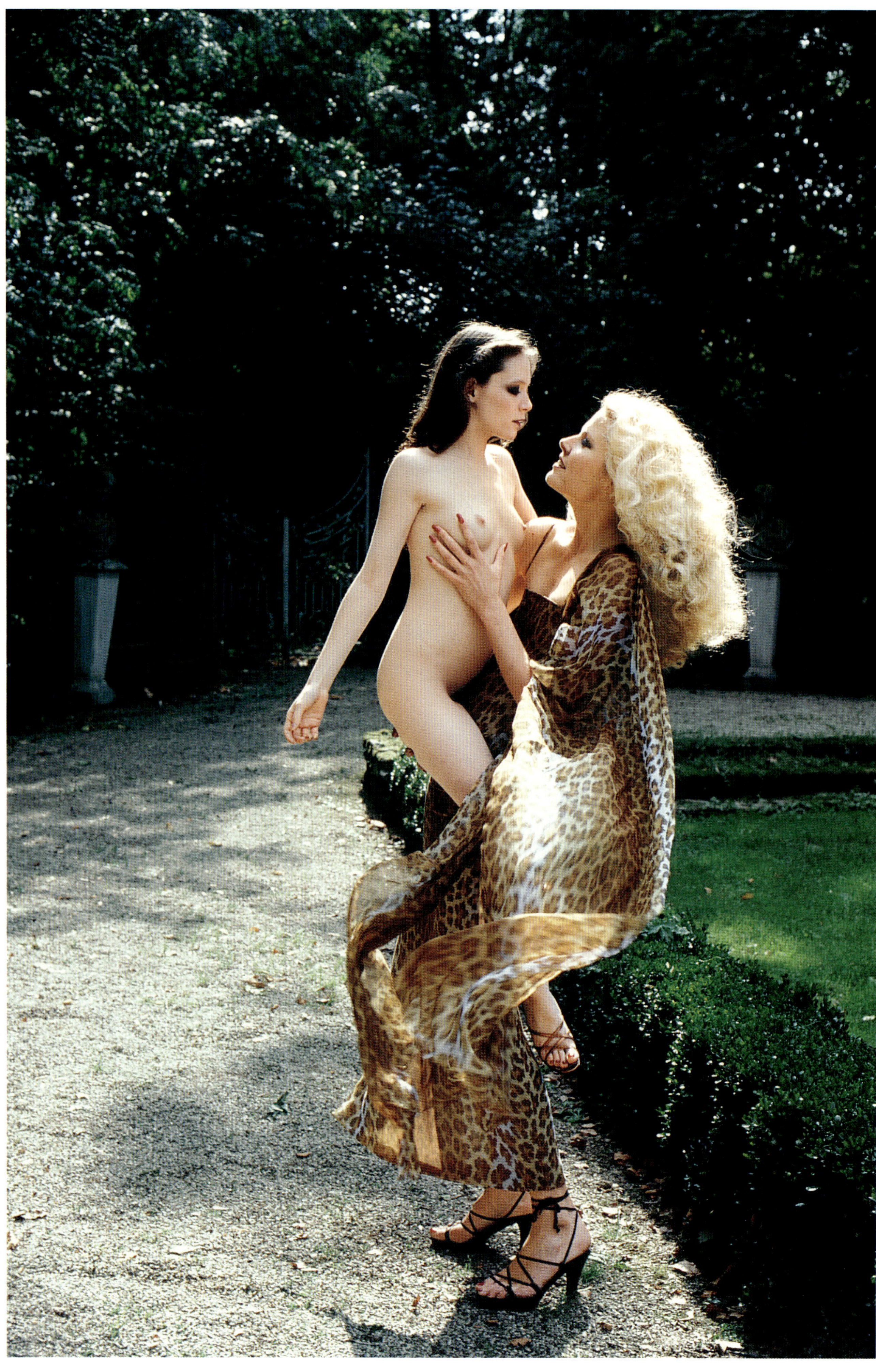

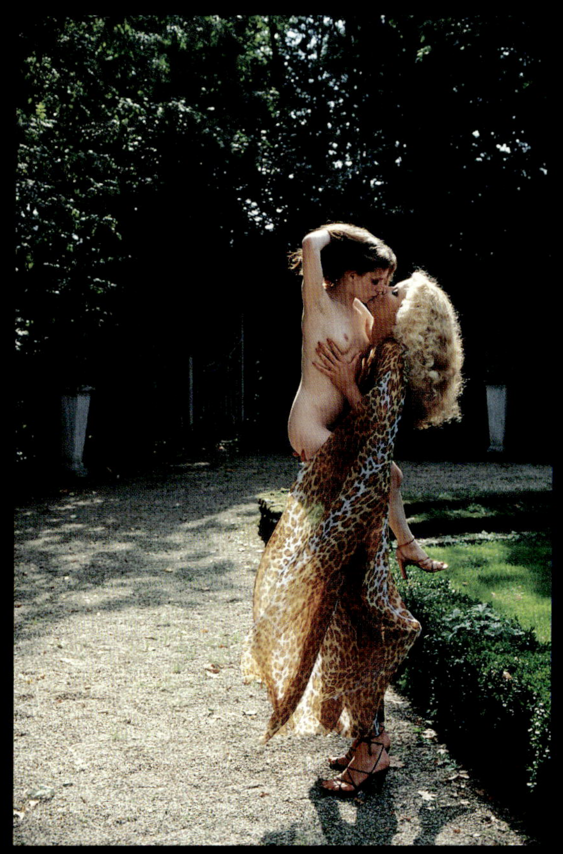

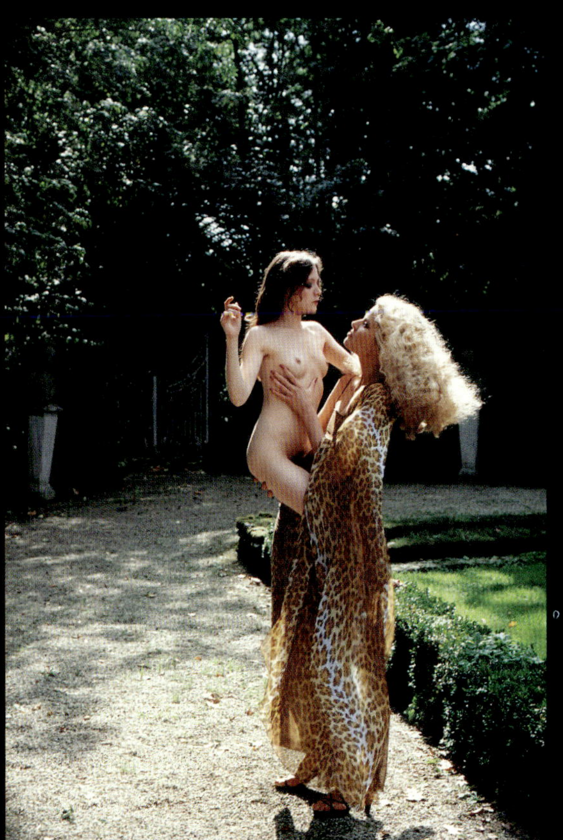

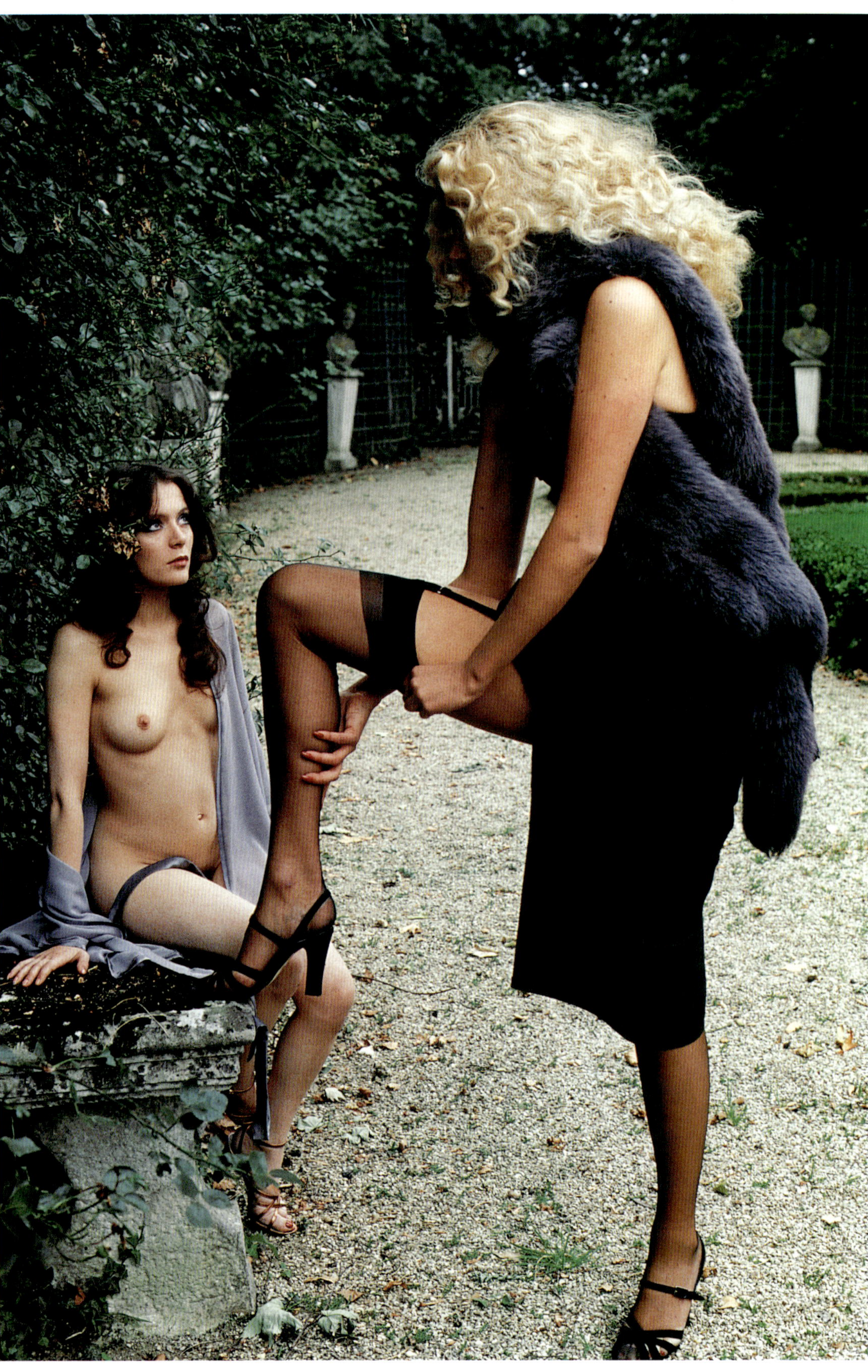

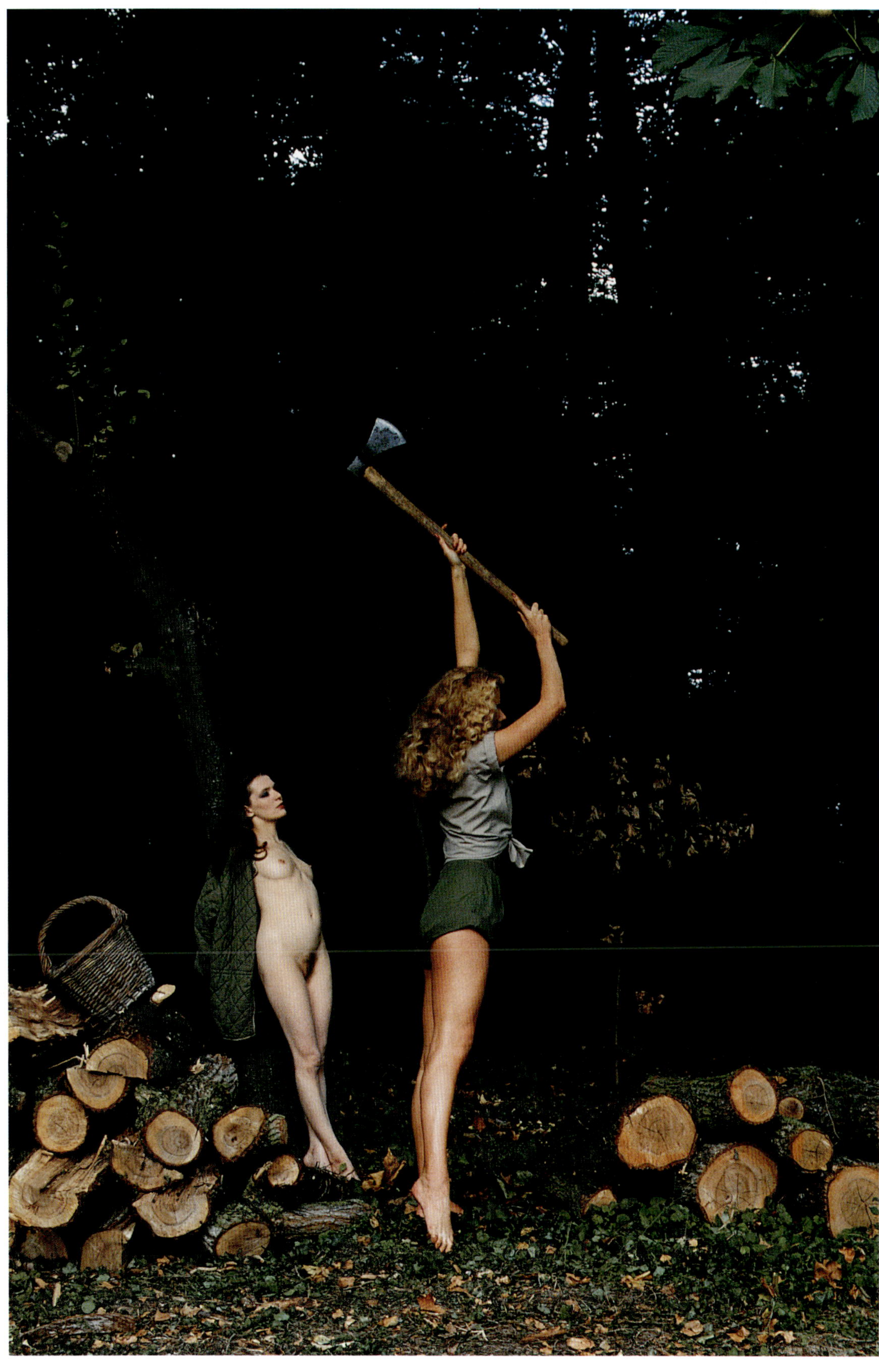

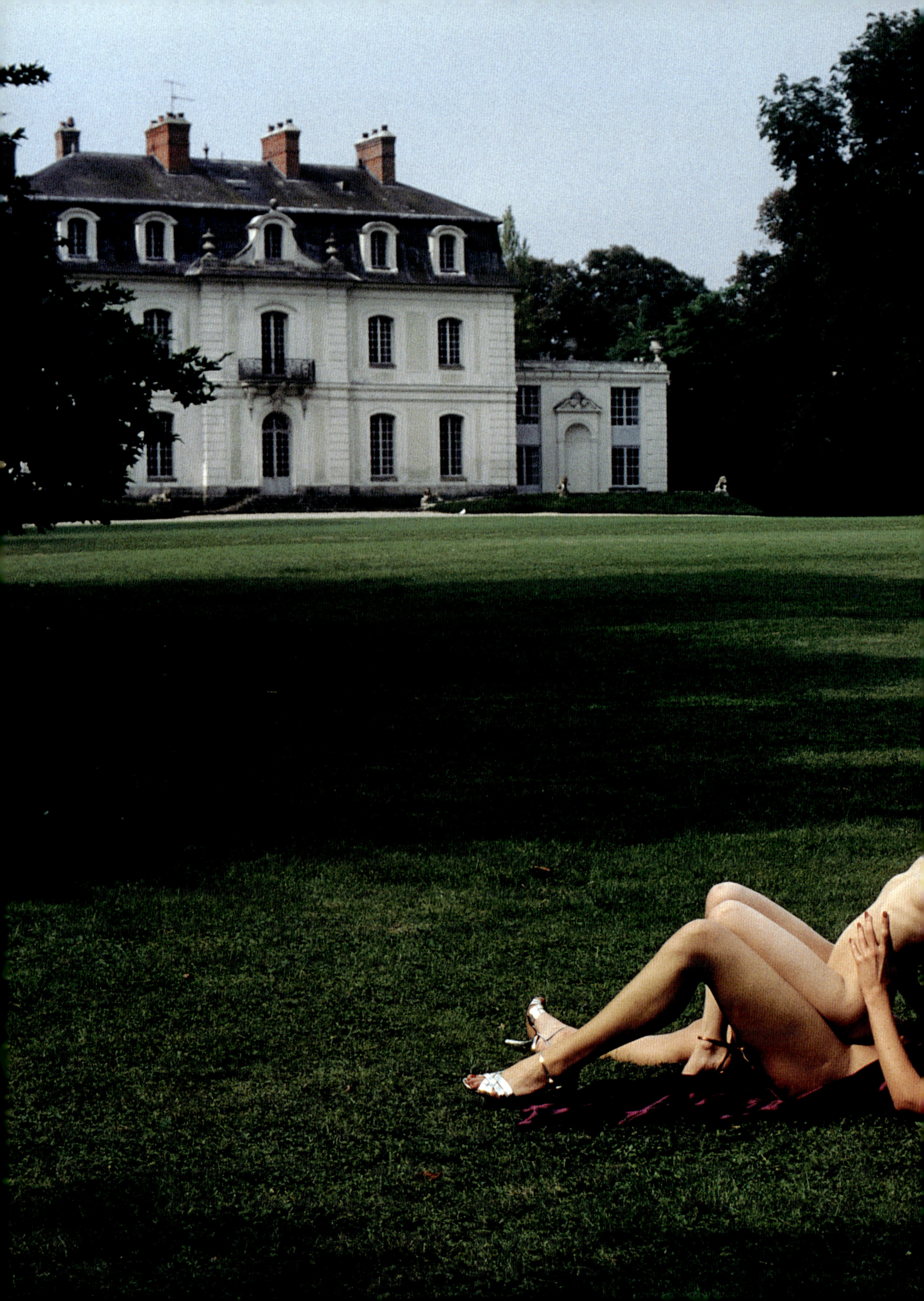

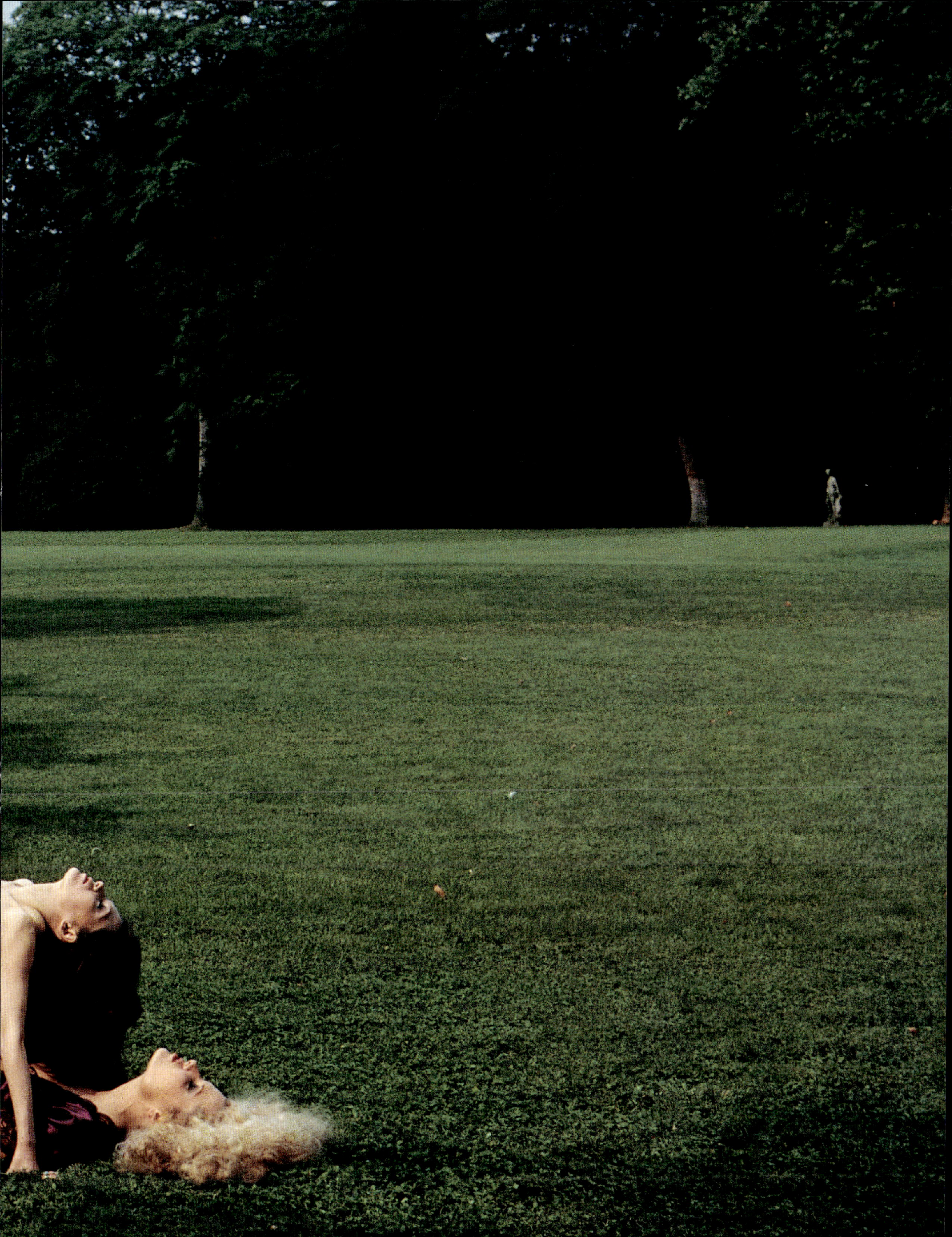

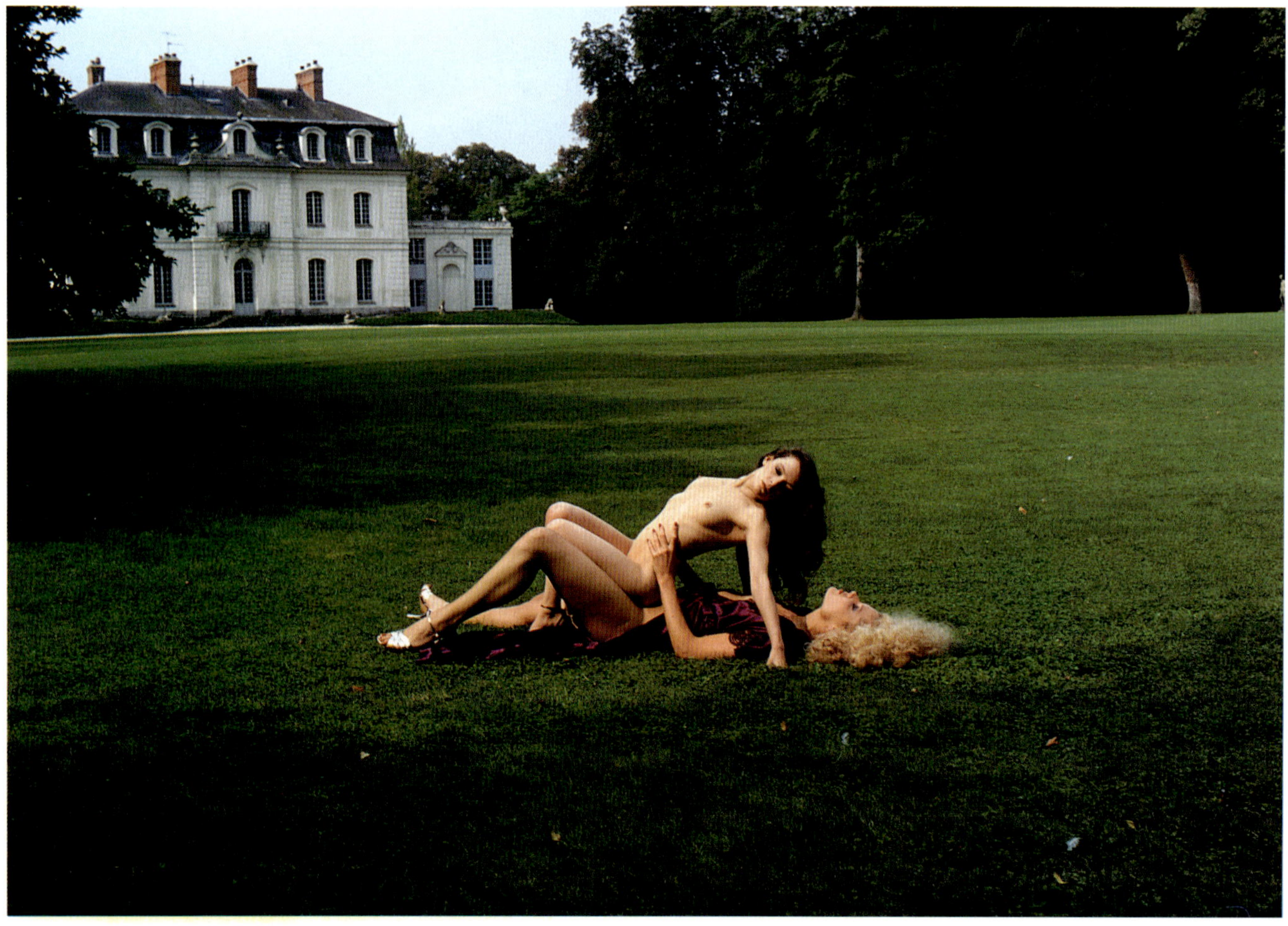

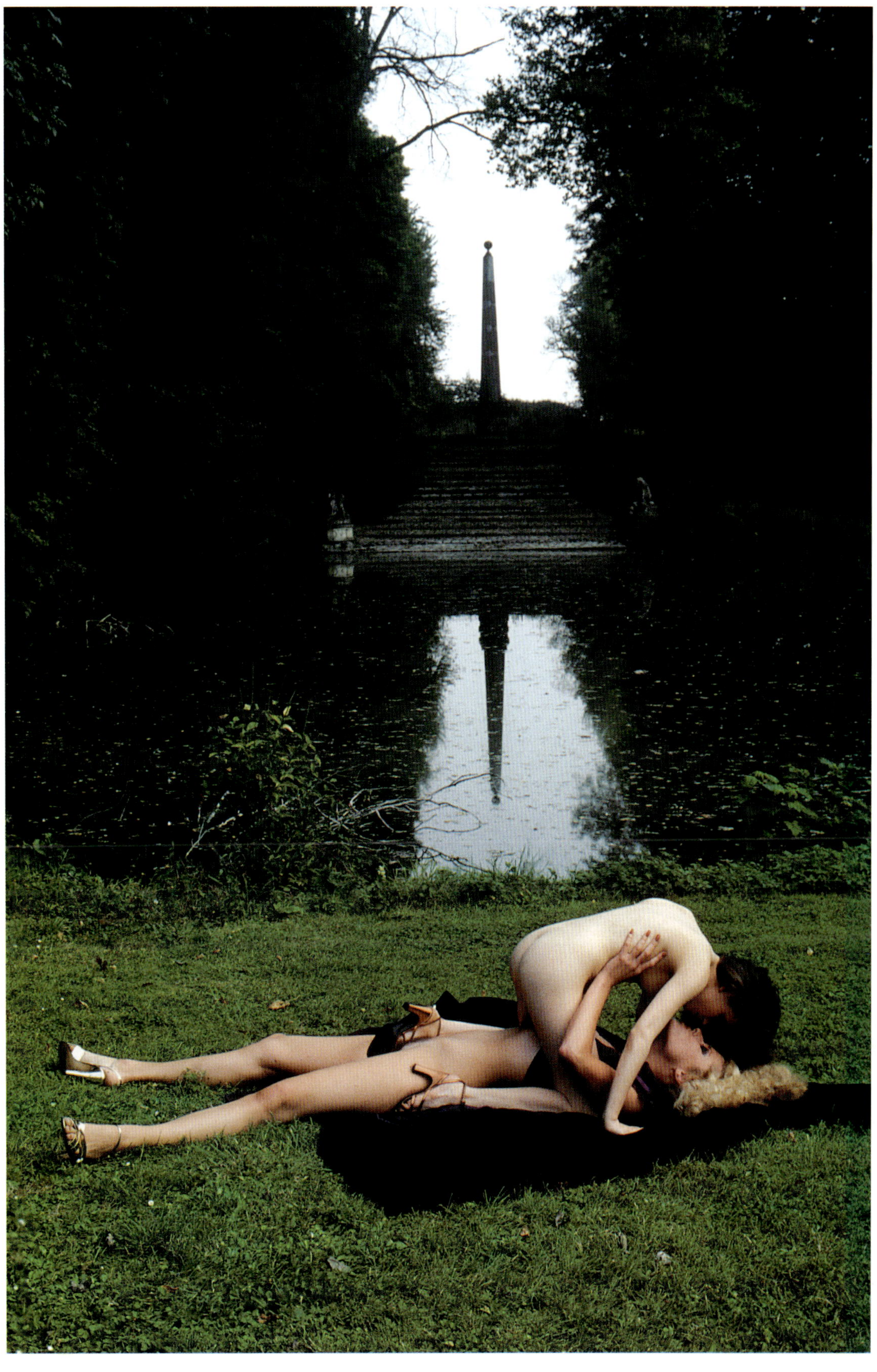

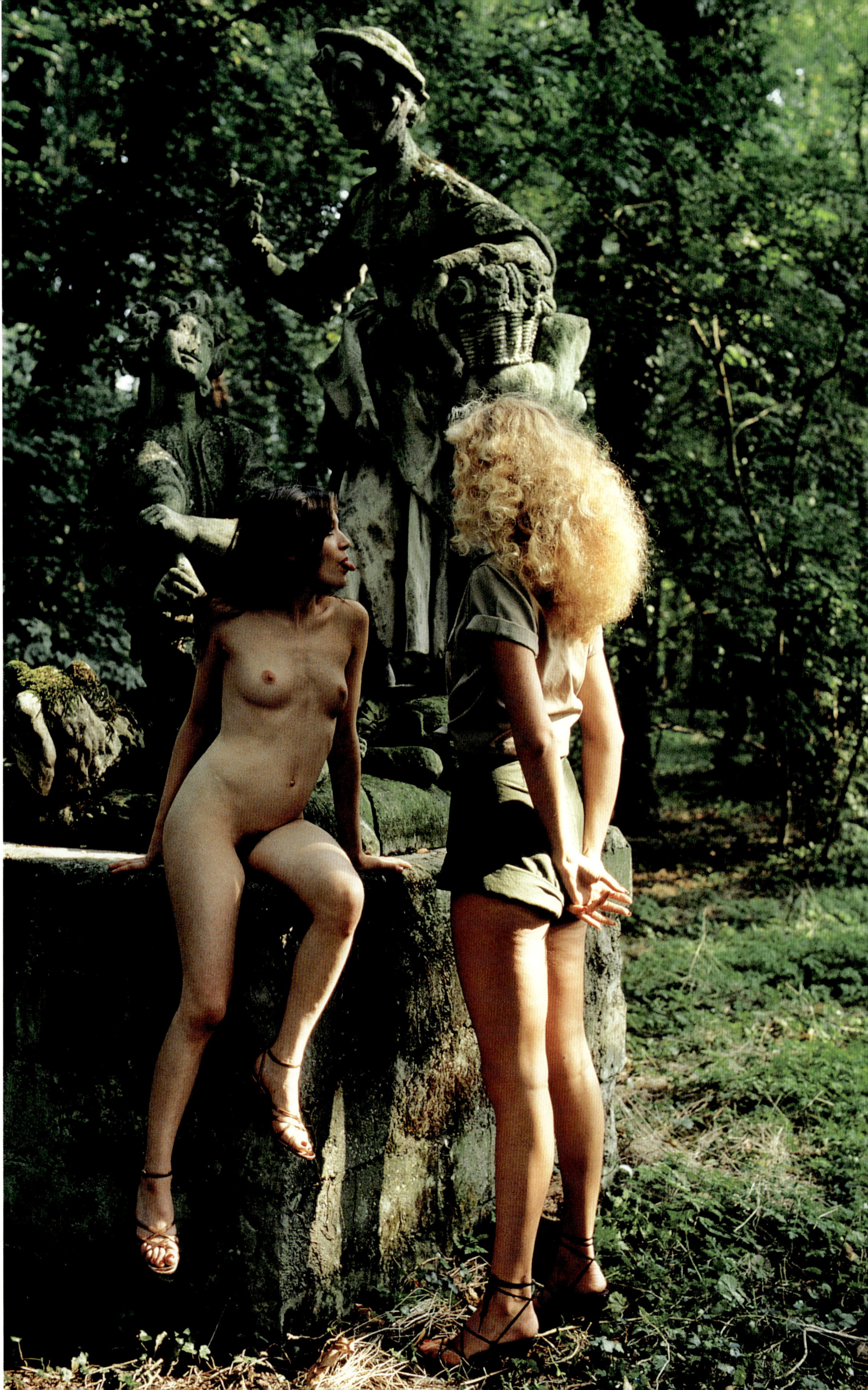

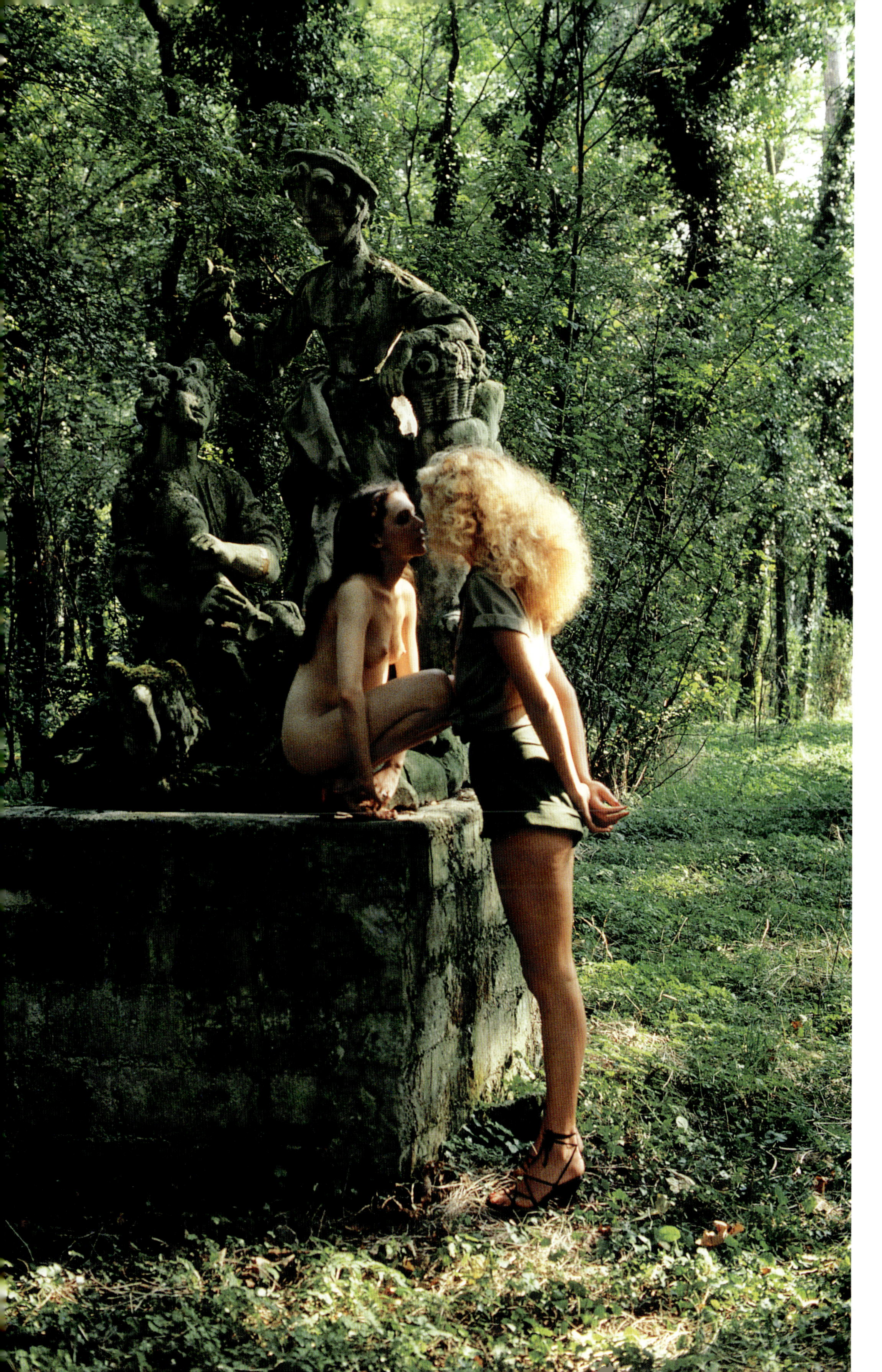

the NEWTON *girls*

FEATURING

Kimber West, Carrie Stevens, Barbara Moore, Julie Cialini, Traci Adell, and Victoria Fuller

July 1998

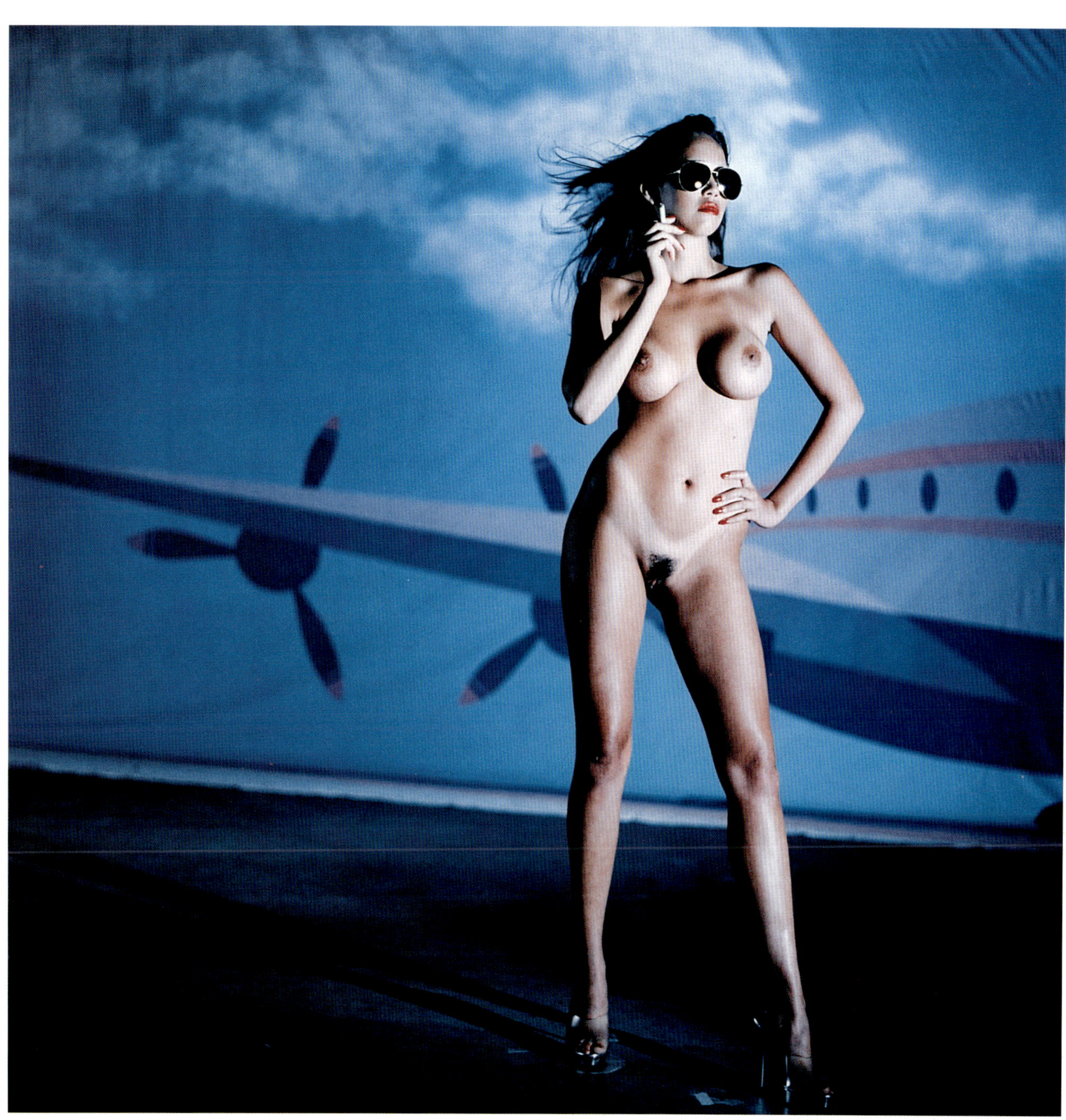

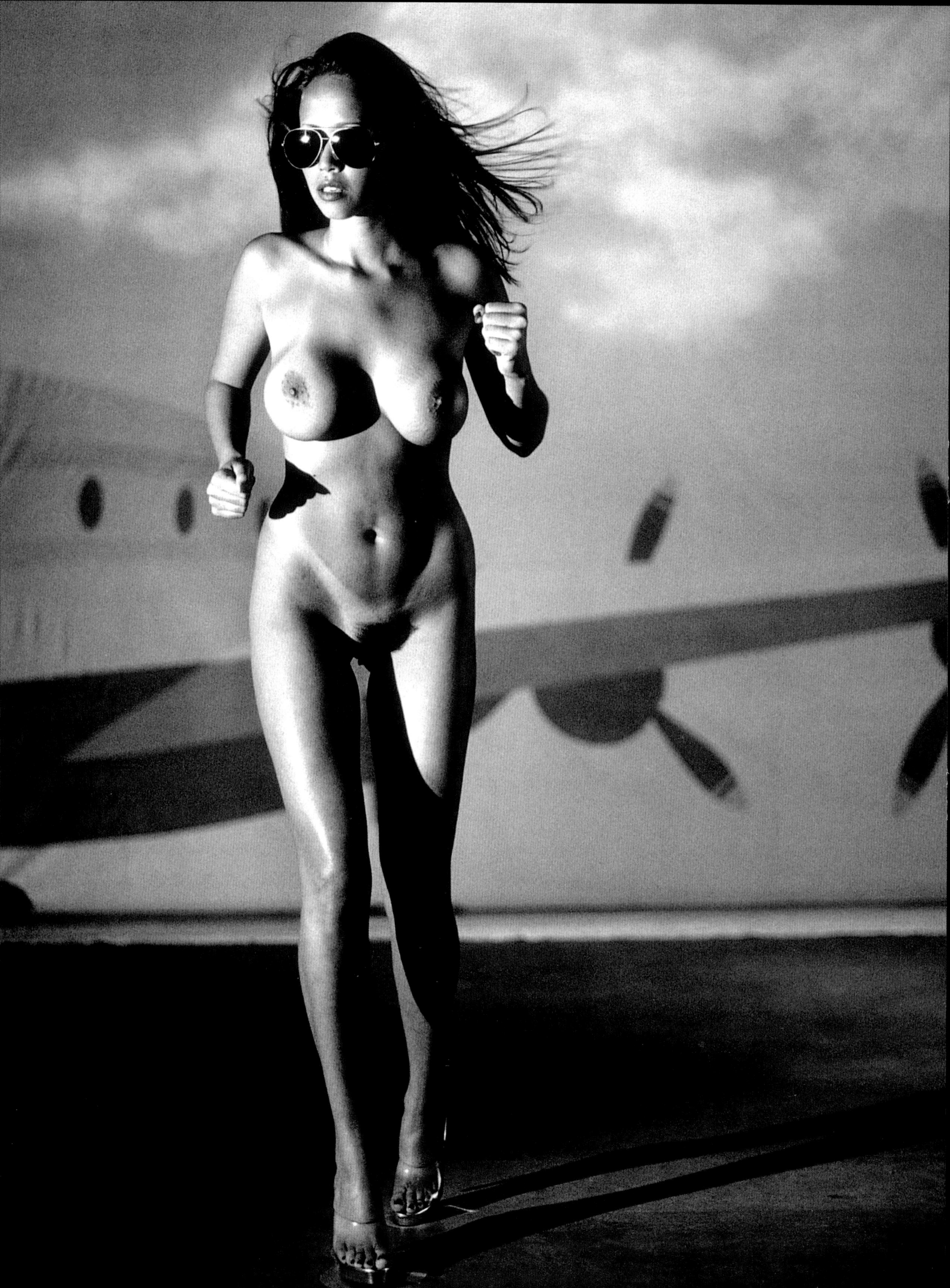

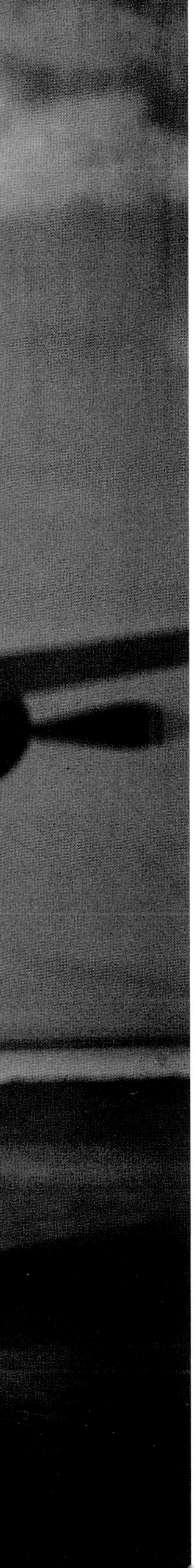

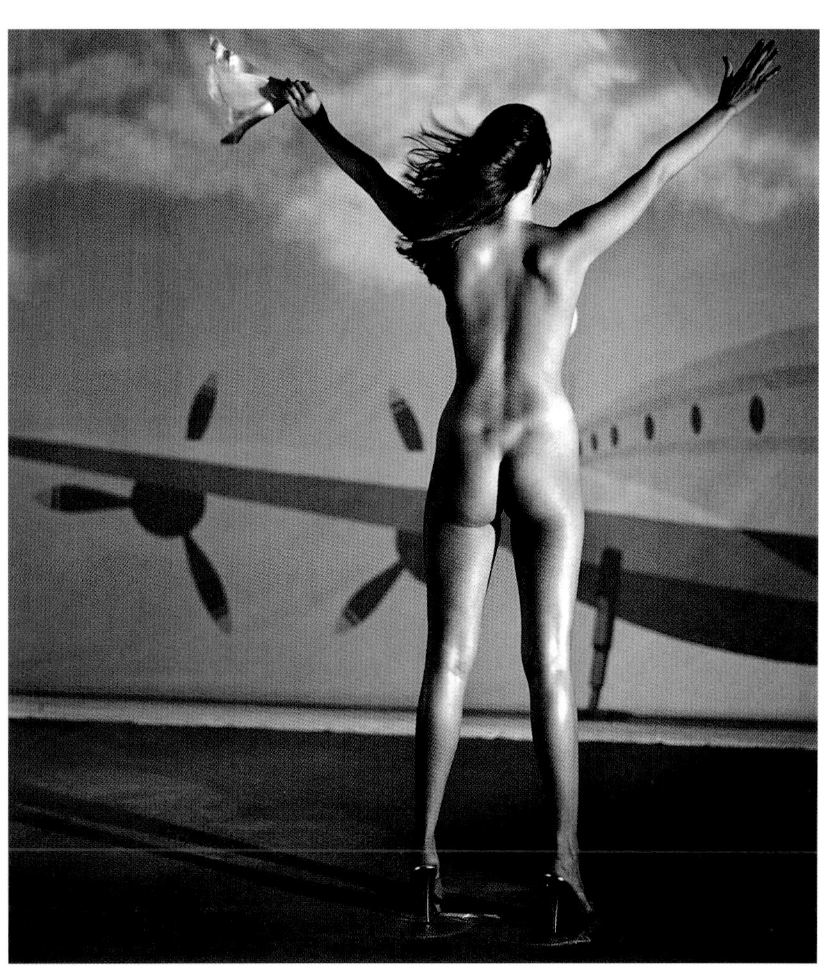

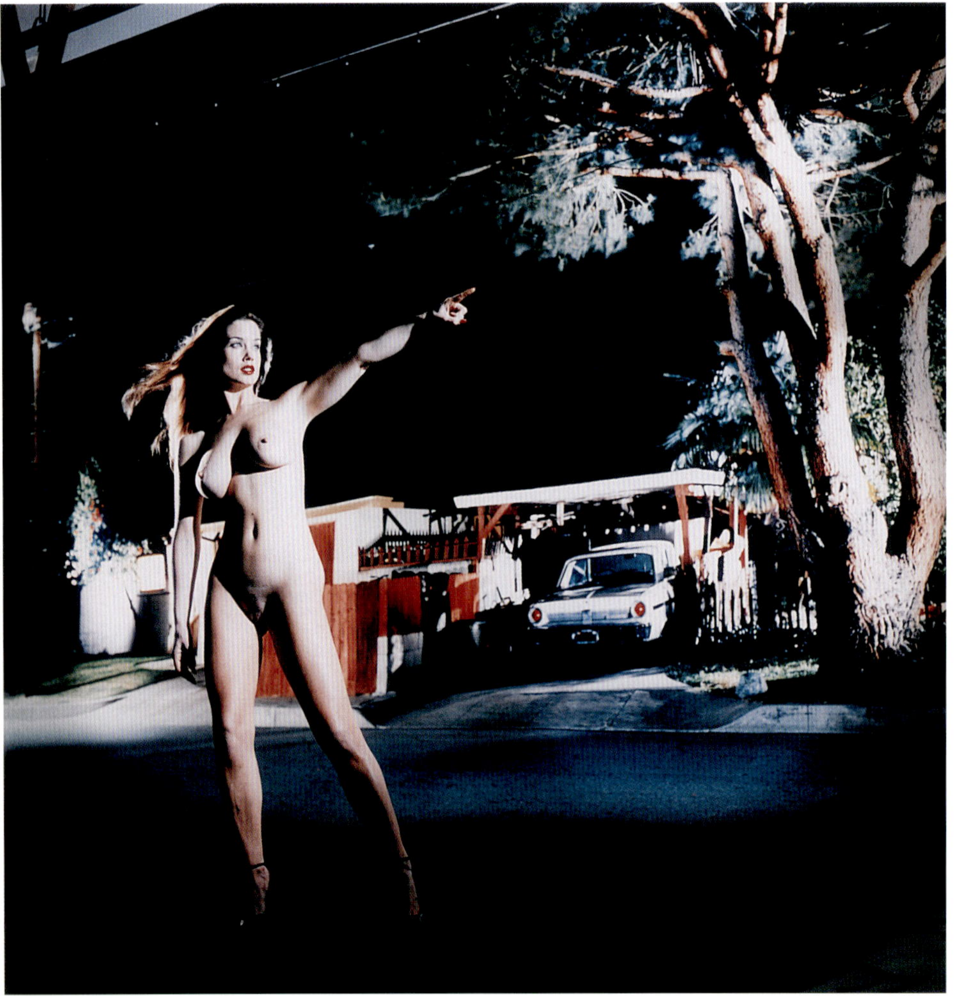

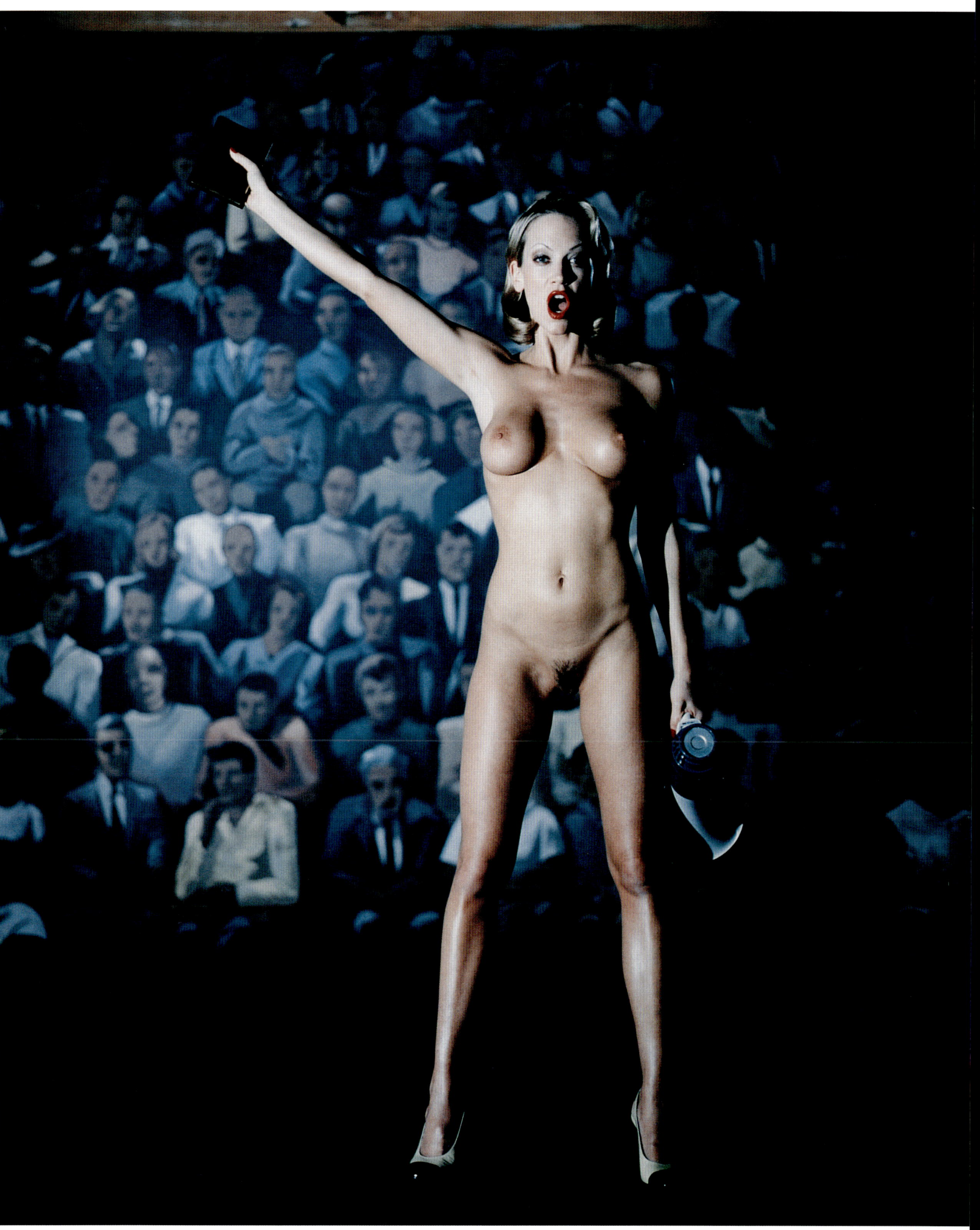

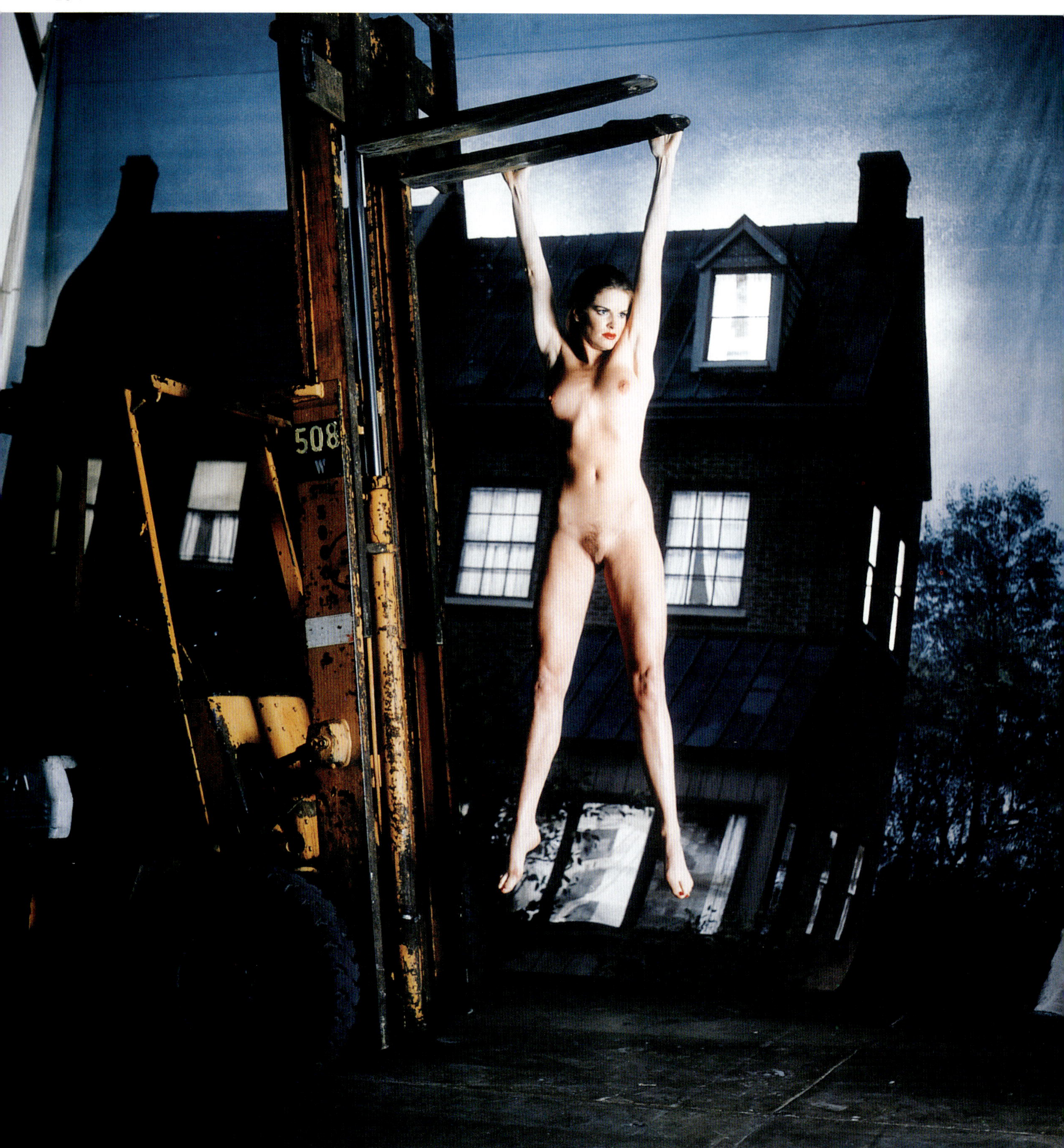
508

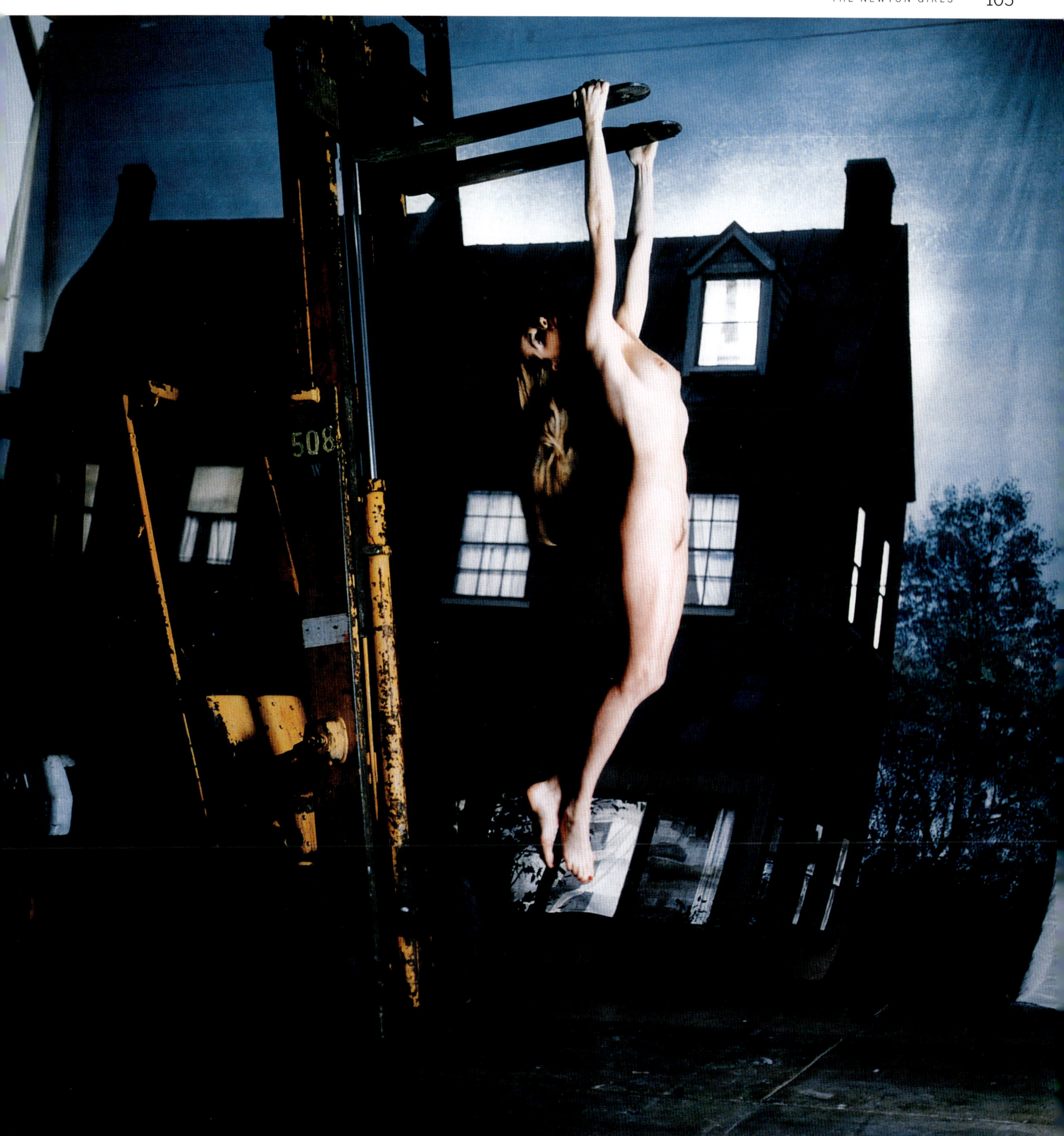
508

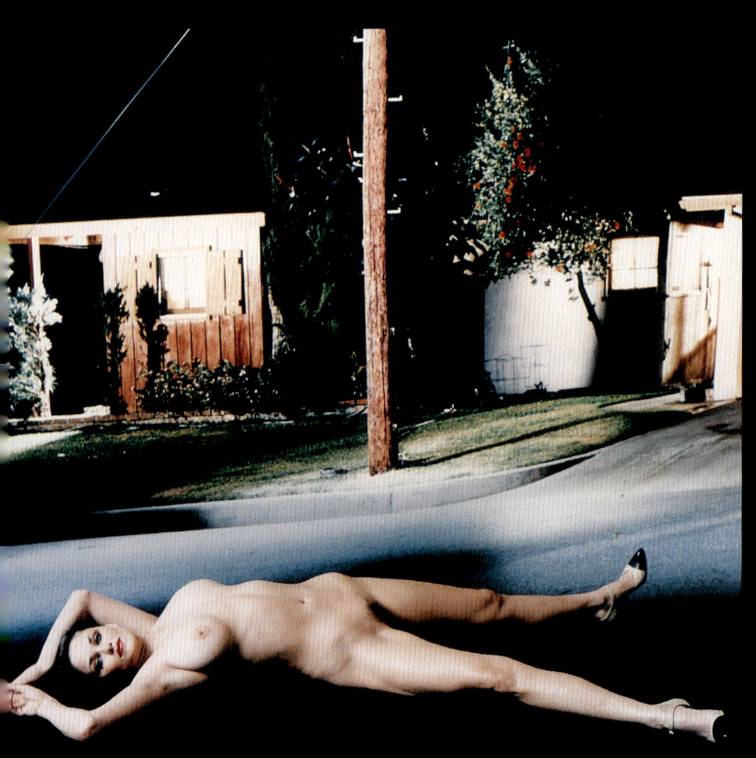

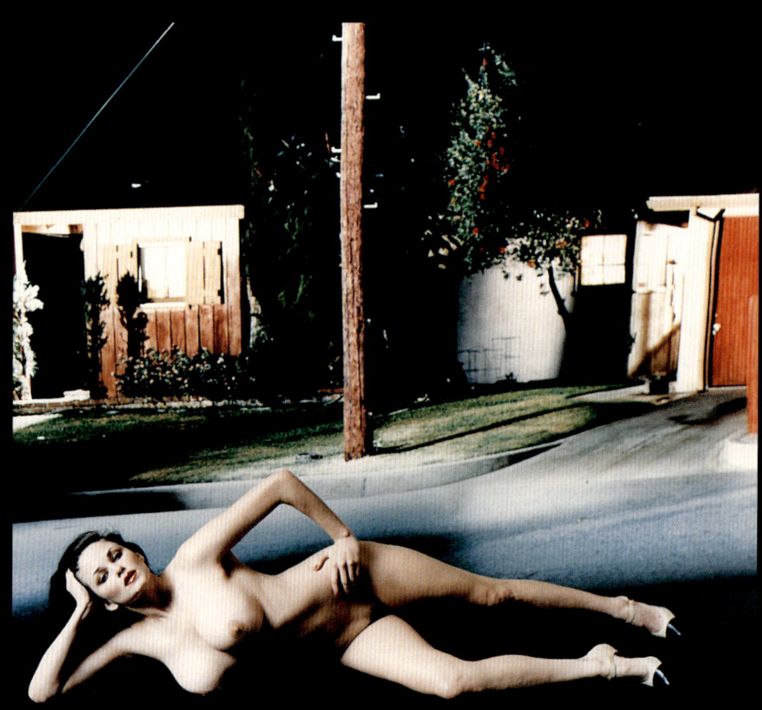

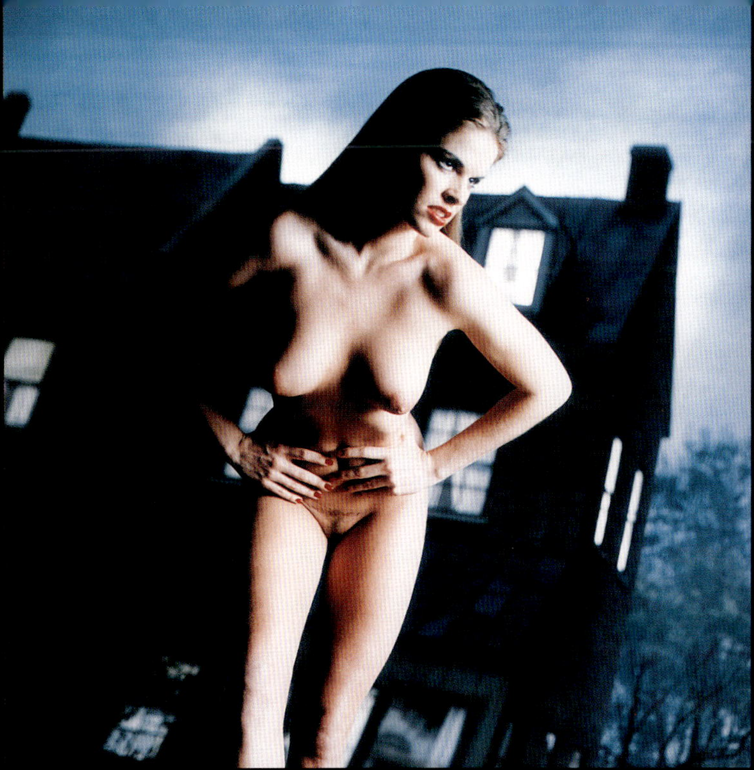

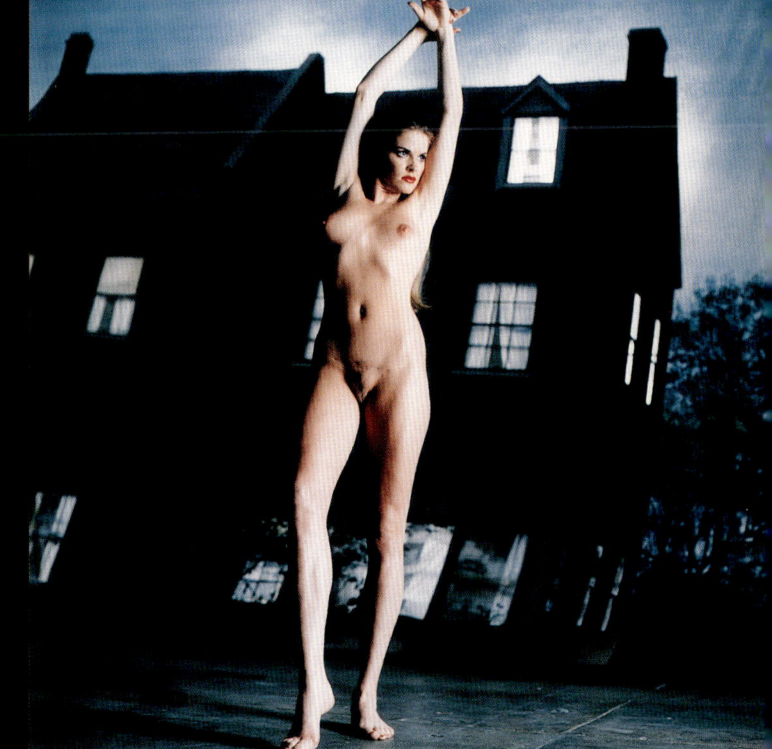

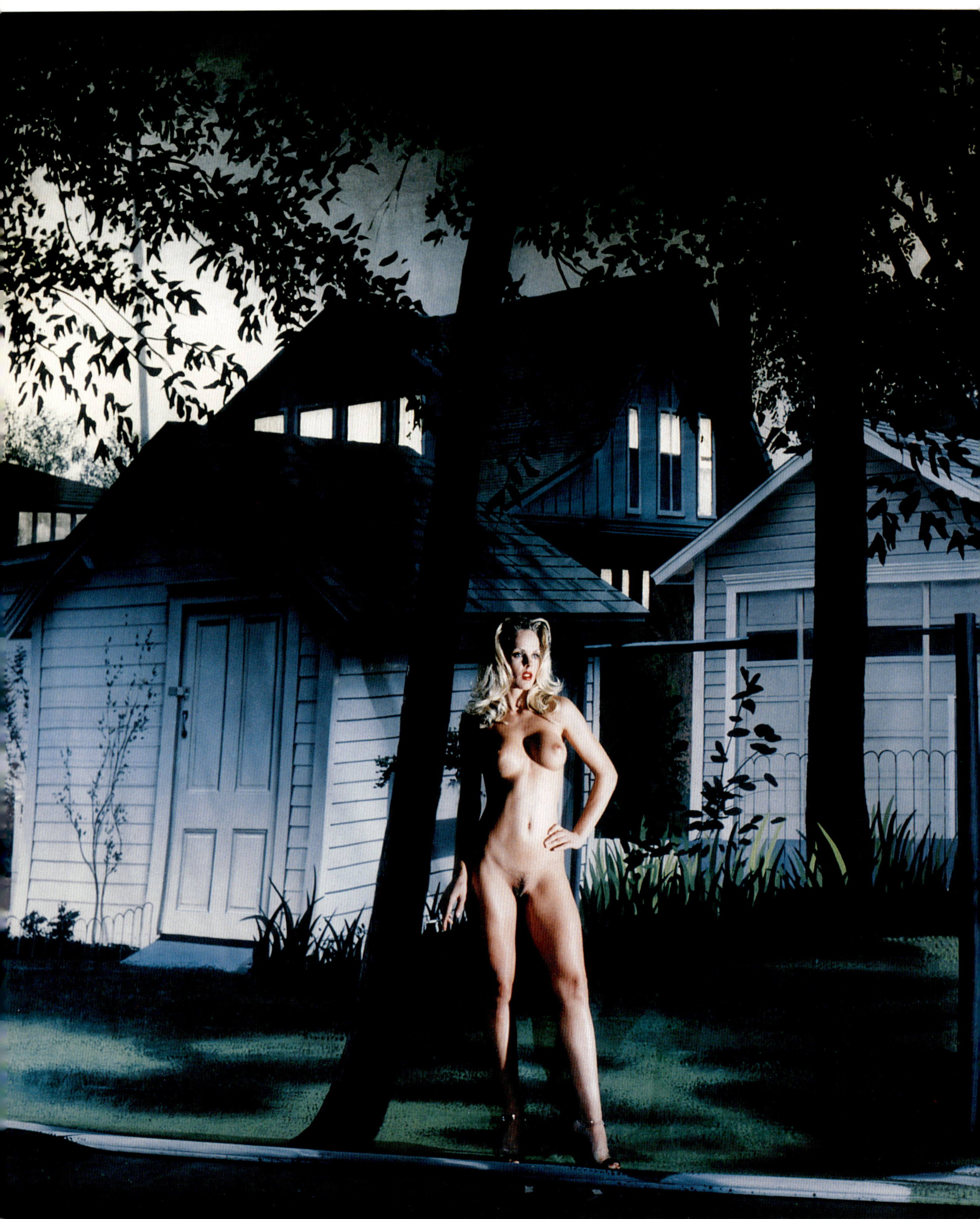

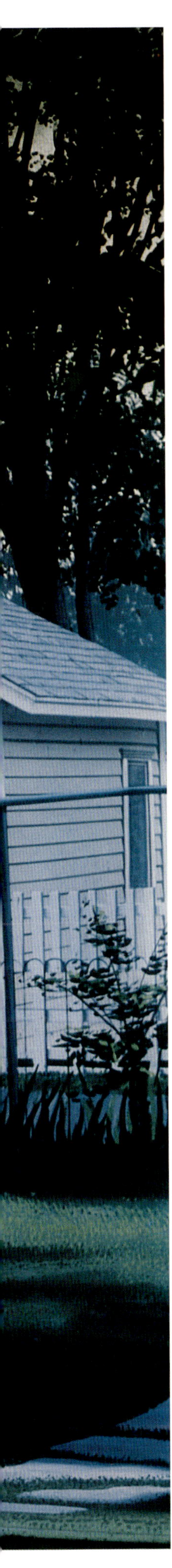

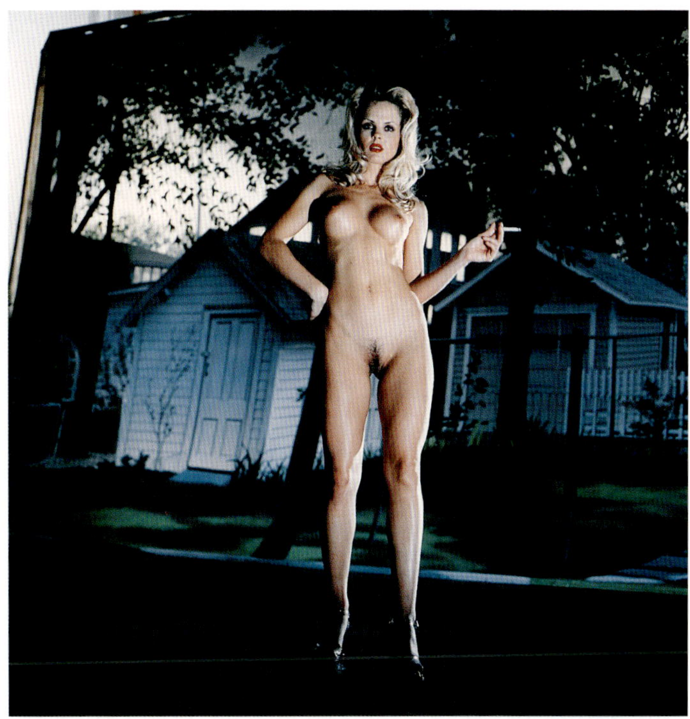

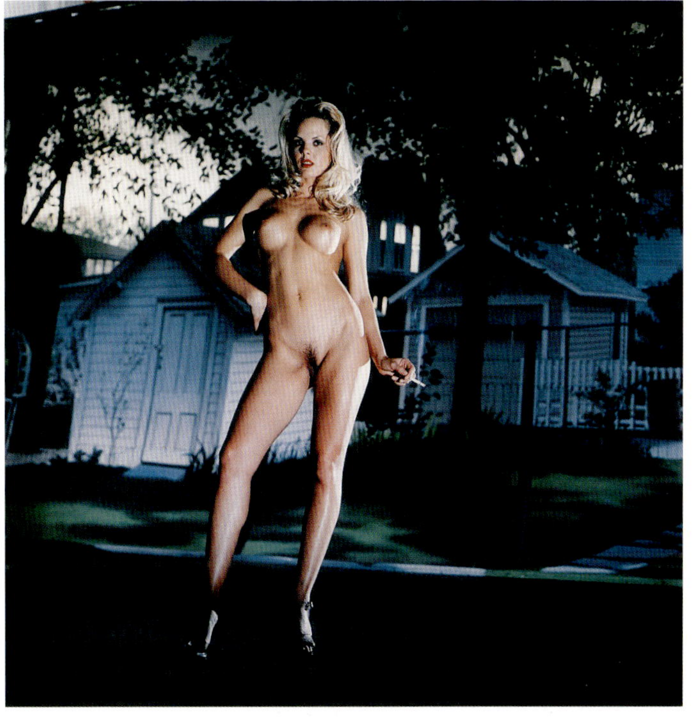

BED *And* BOARD

FEATURING

Uschi Obermaier

April 1975

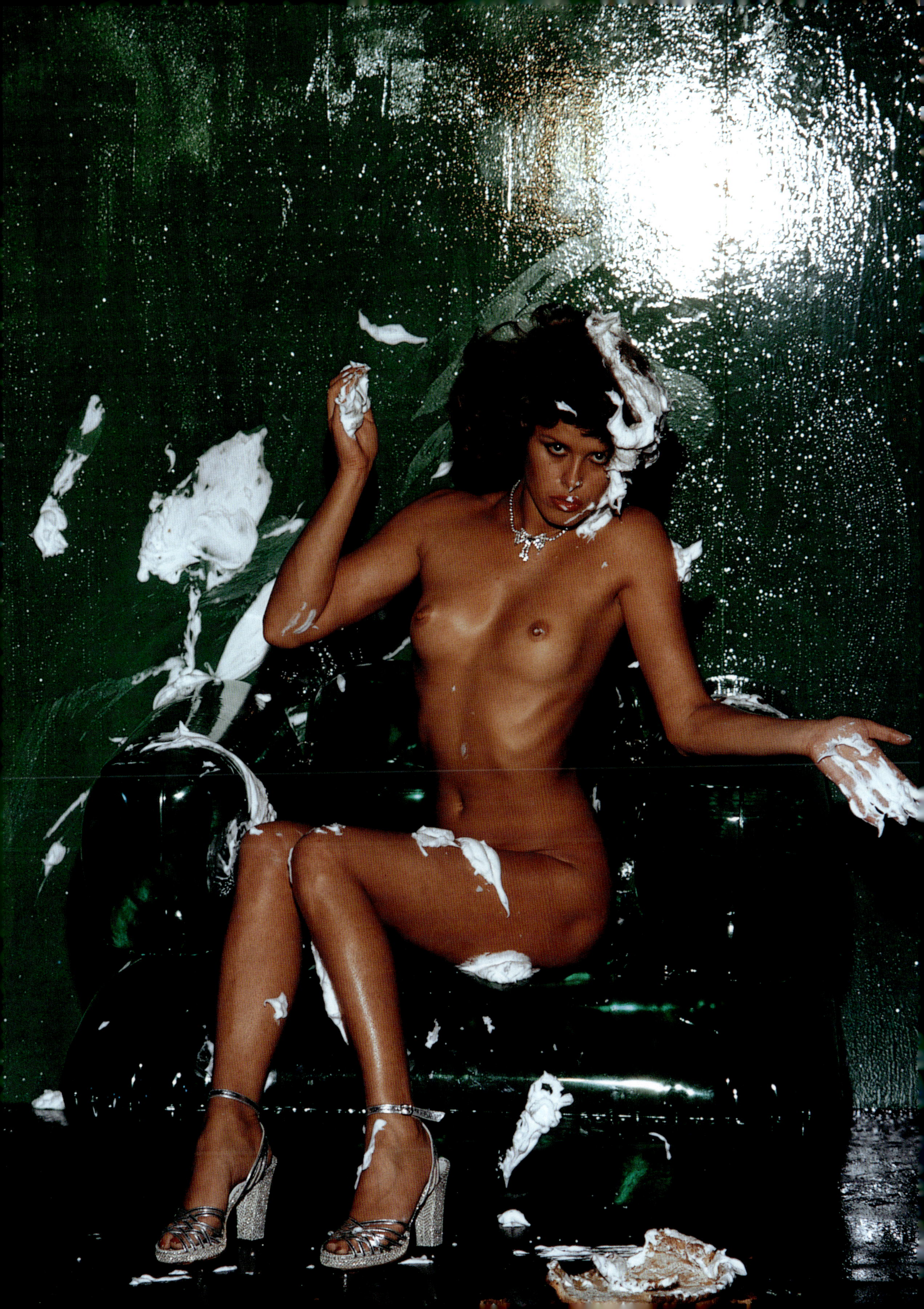

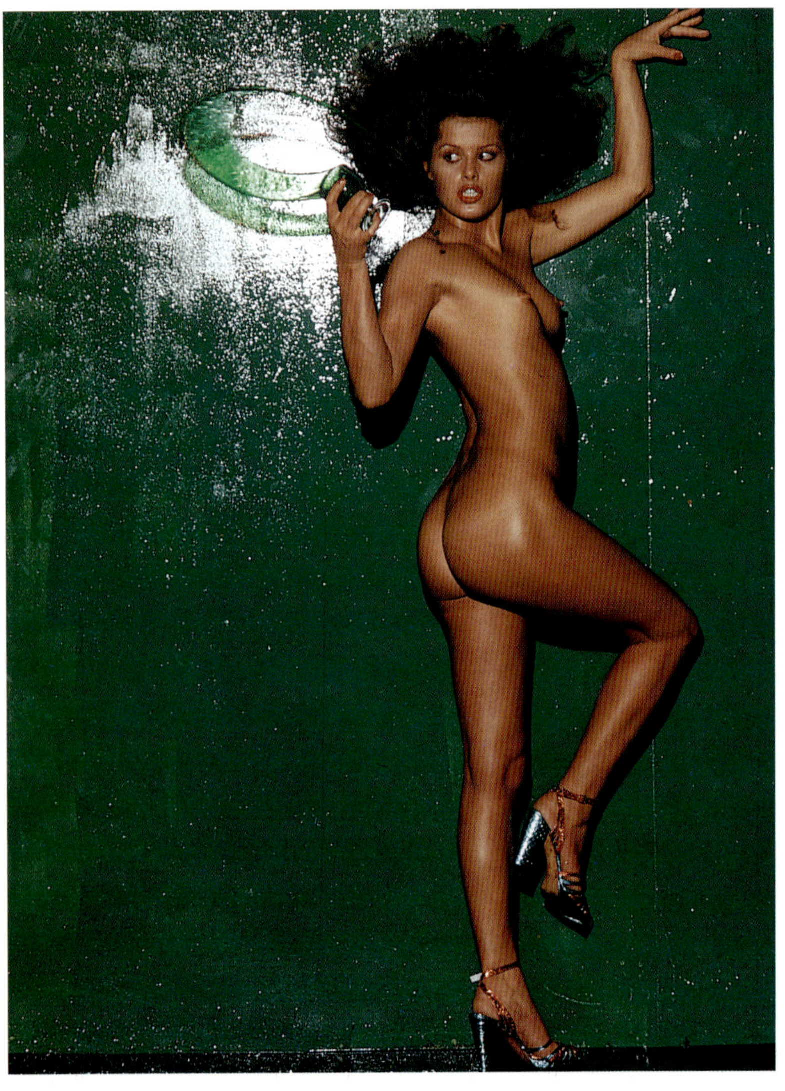

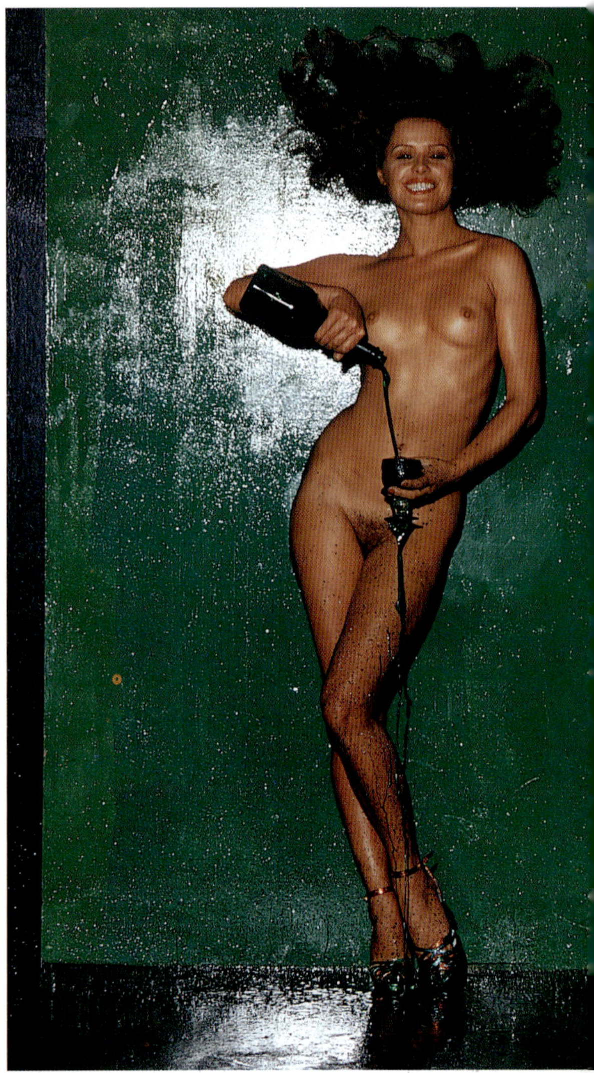

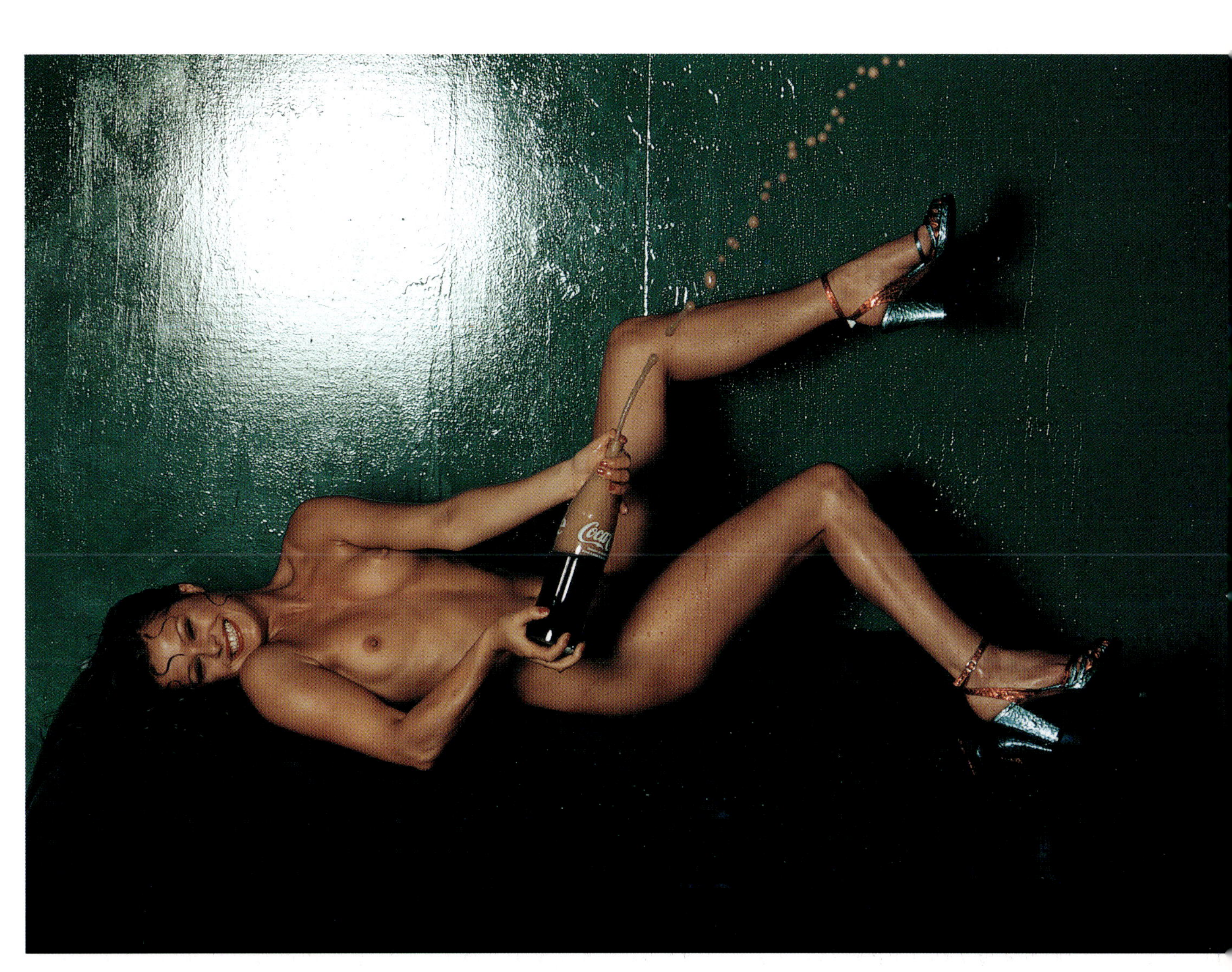

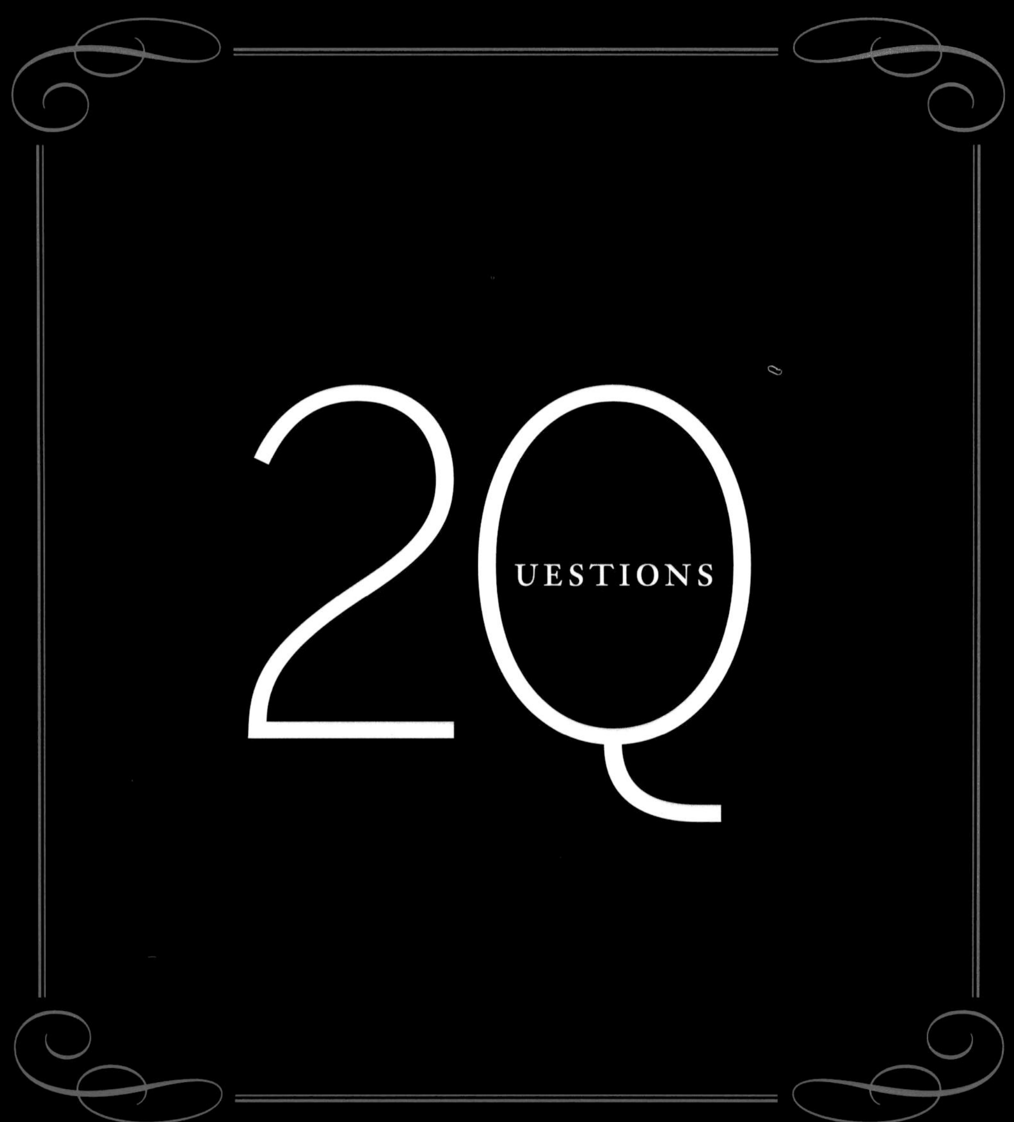

FEATURING

Debra Winger

June 1983

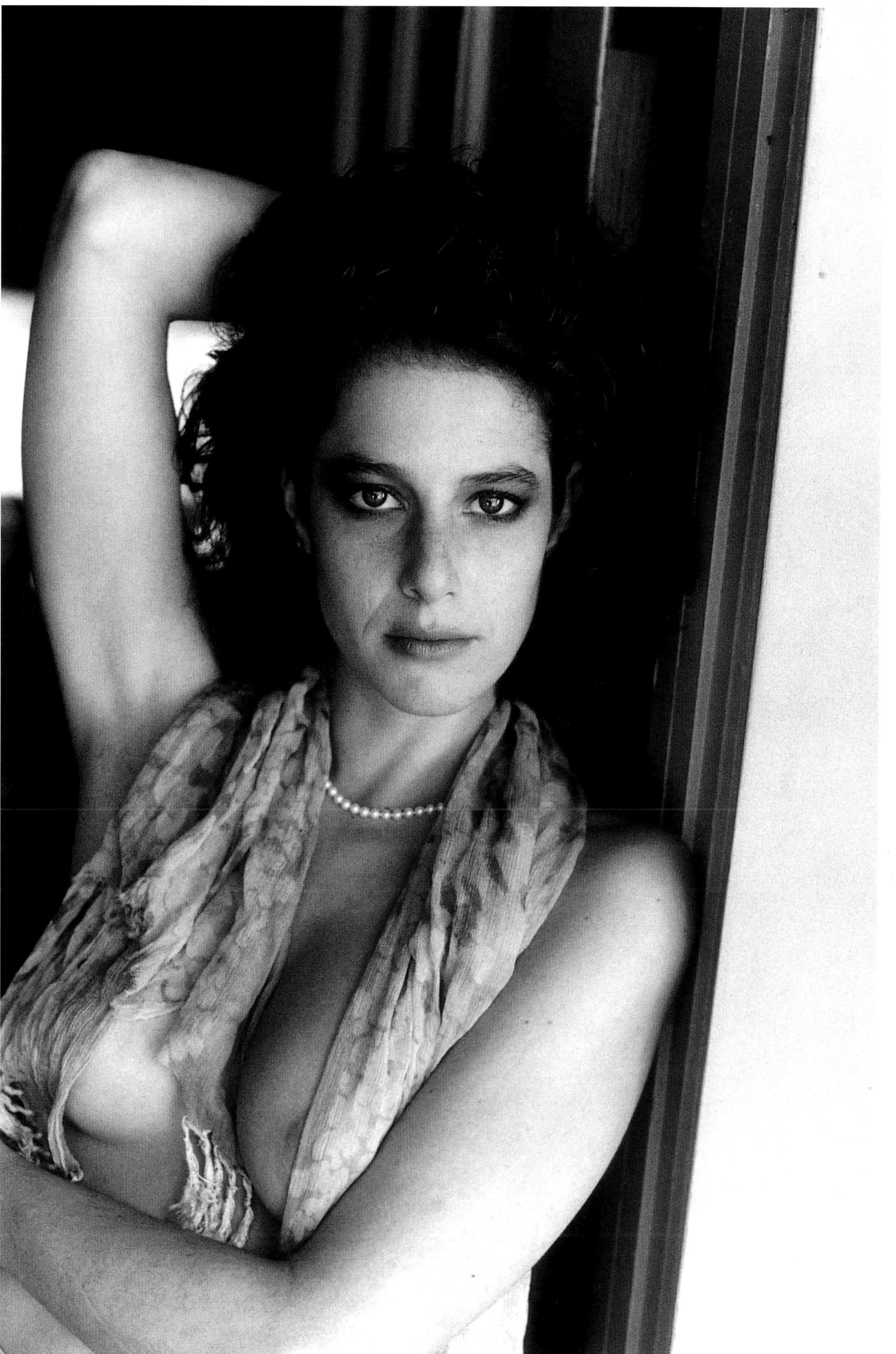

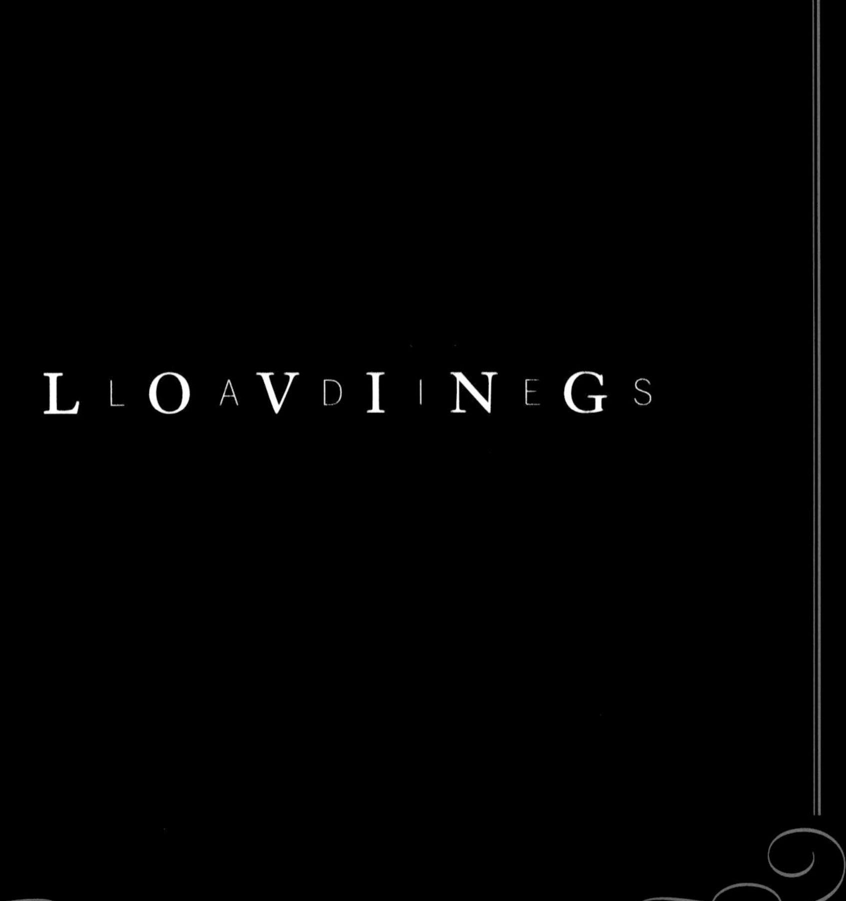

FEATURING

Sylvie Benard and Prunellia Favaron

February 1977. Unpublished

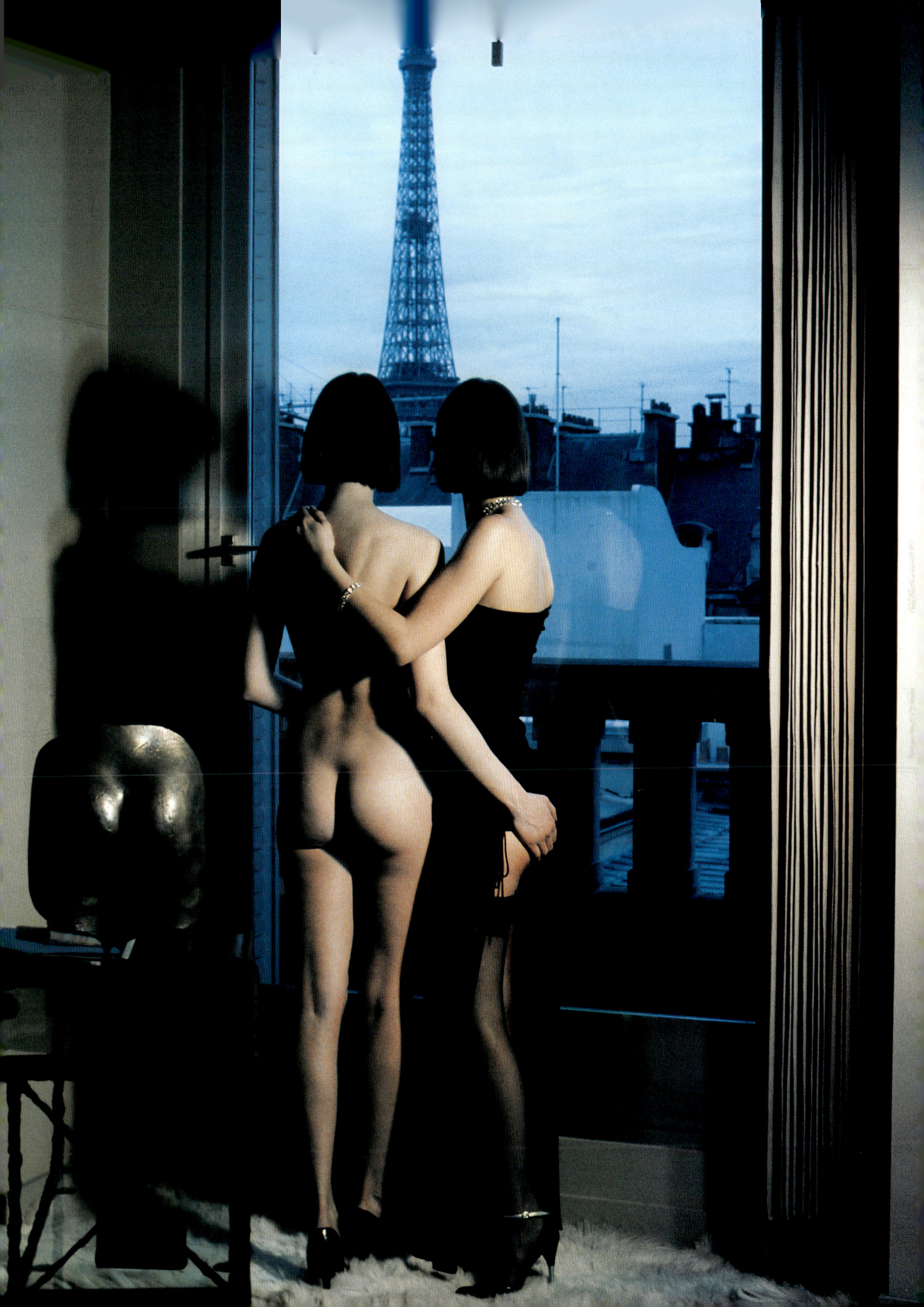

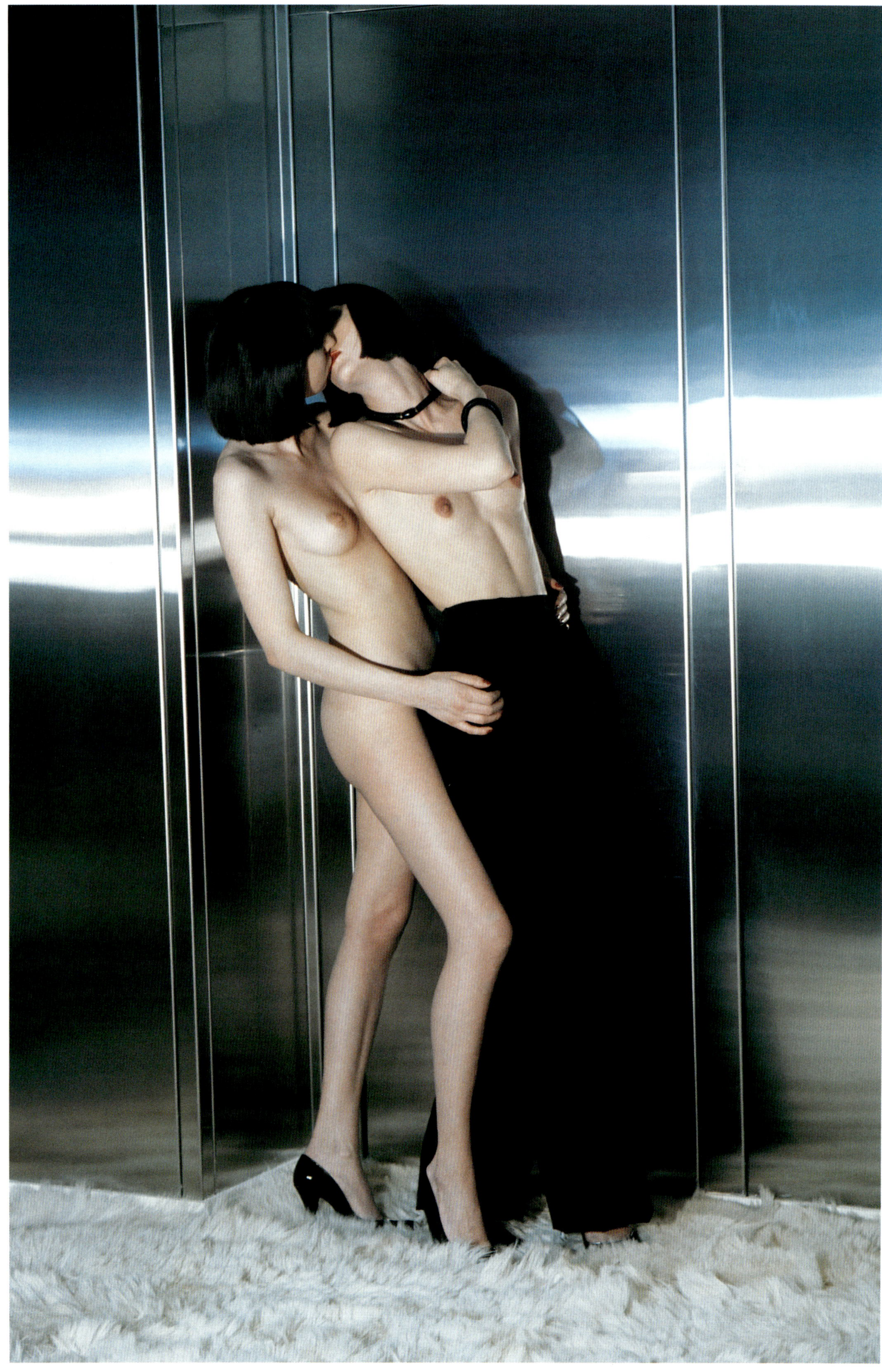

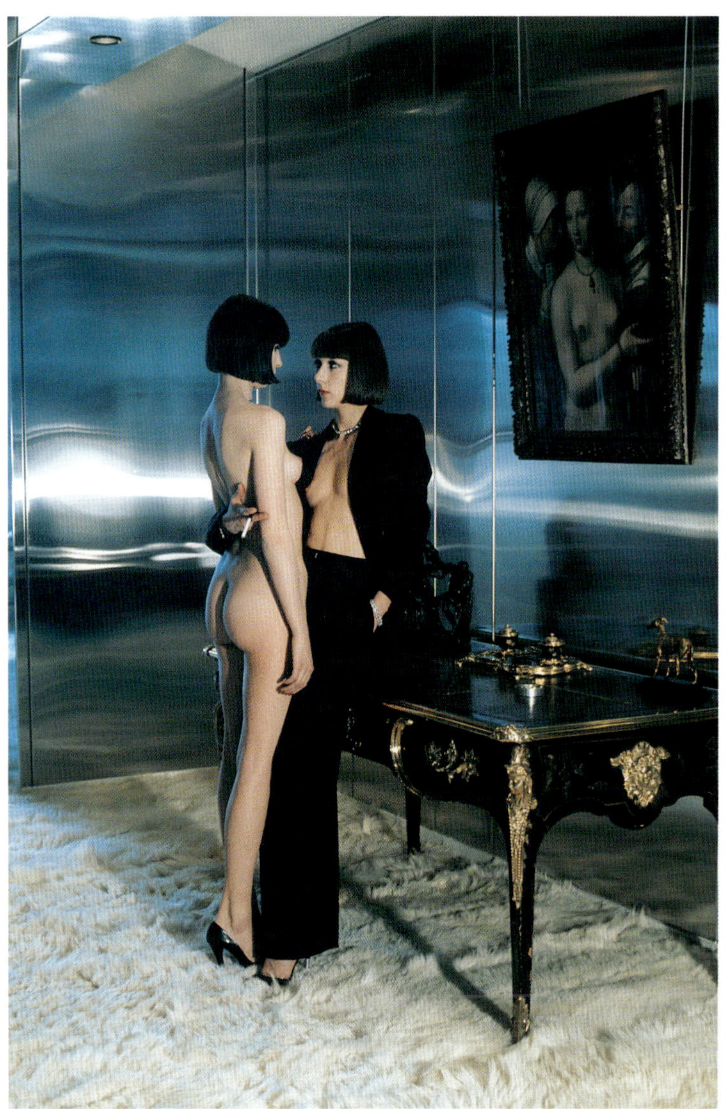

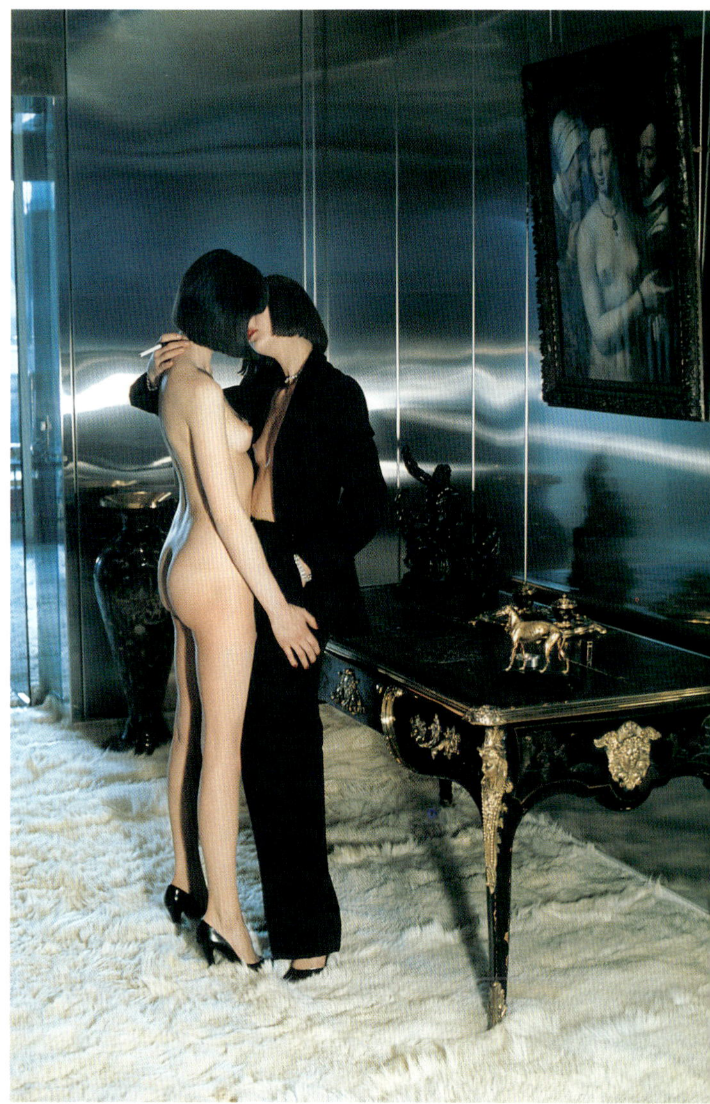

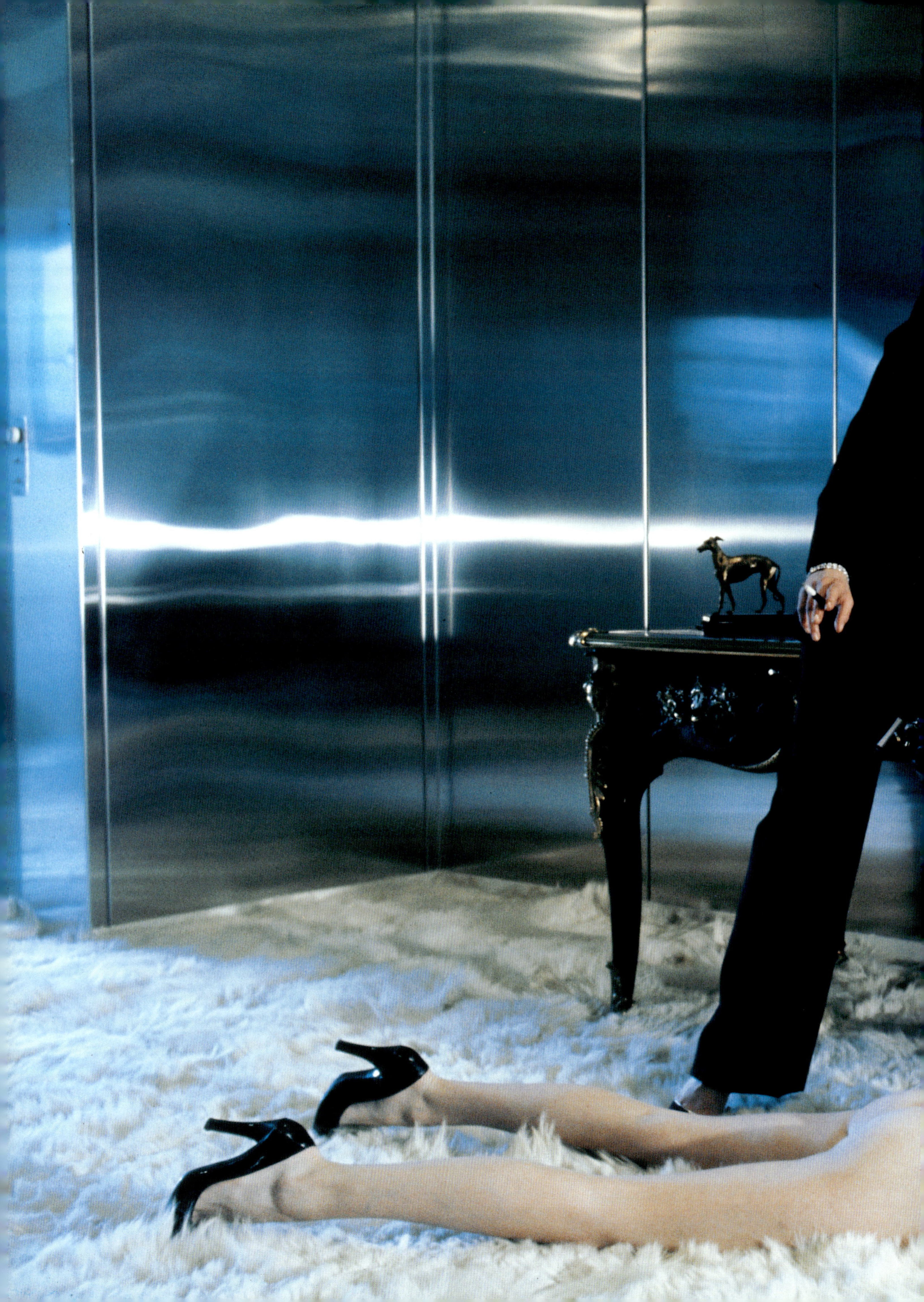

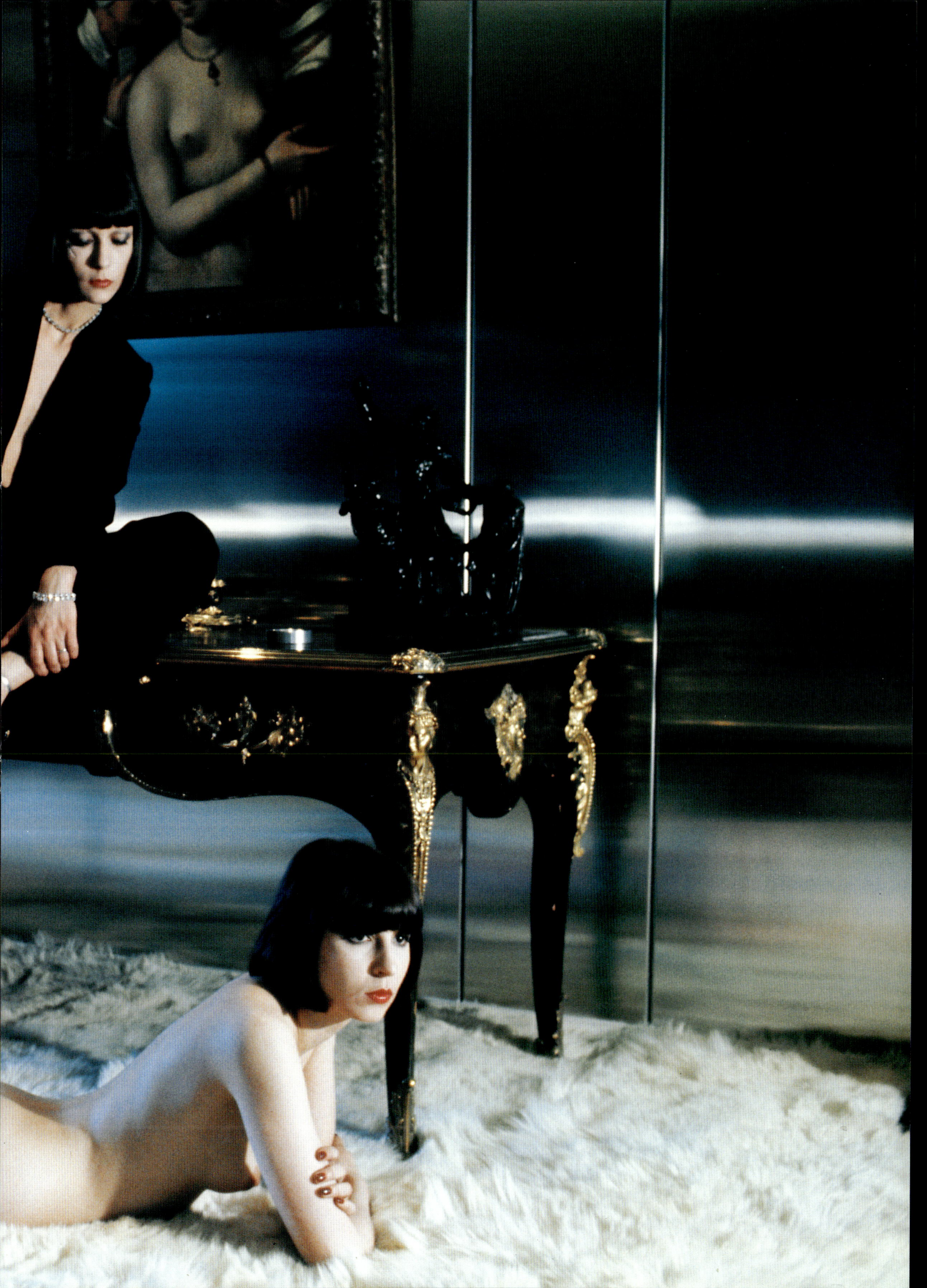

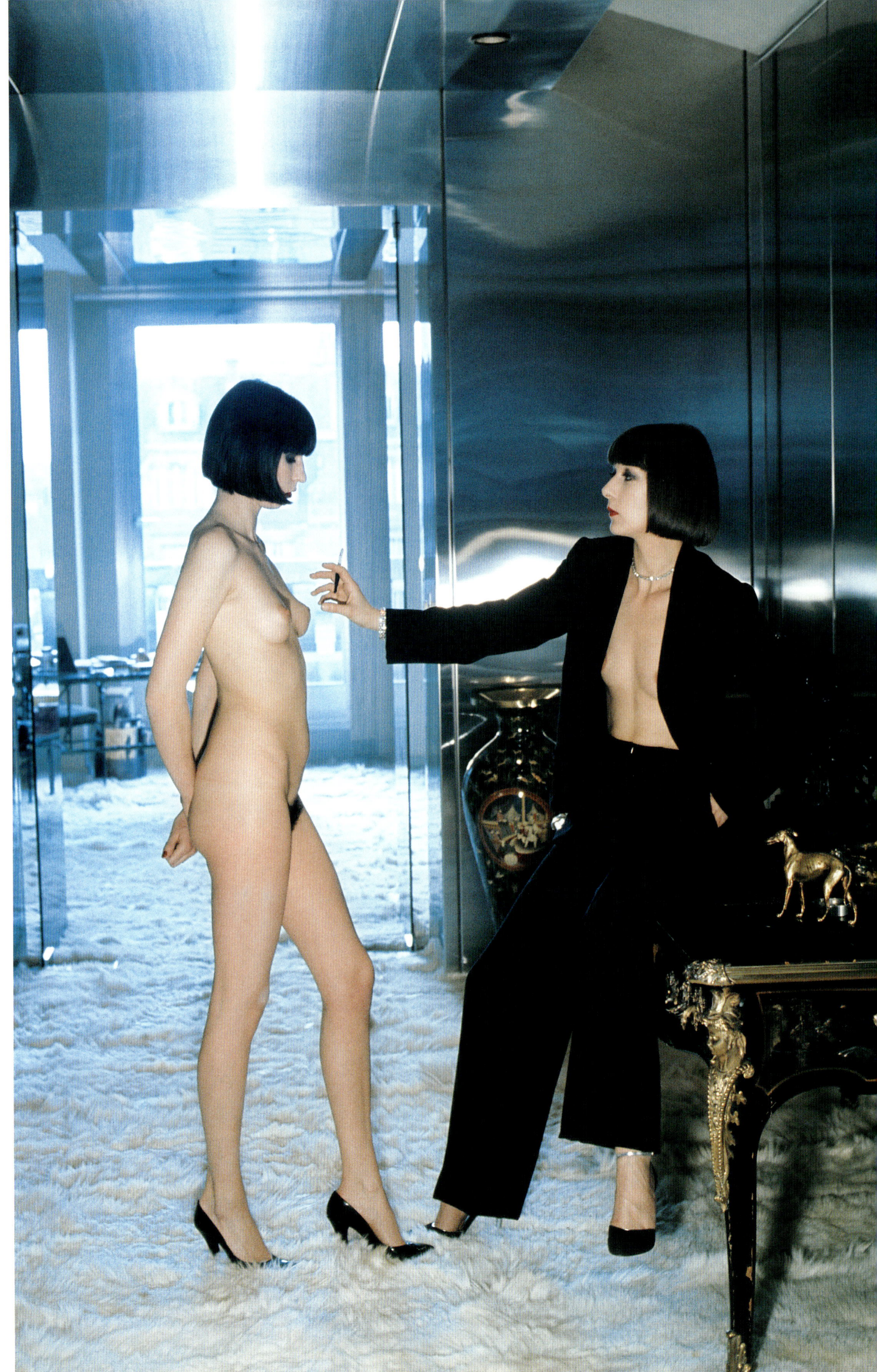

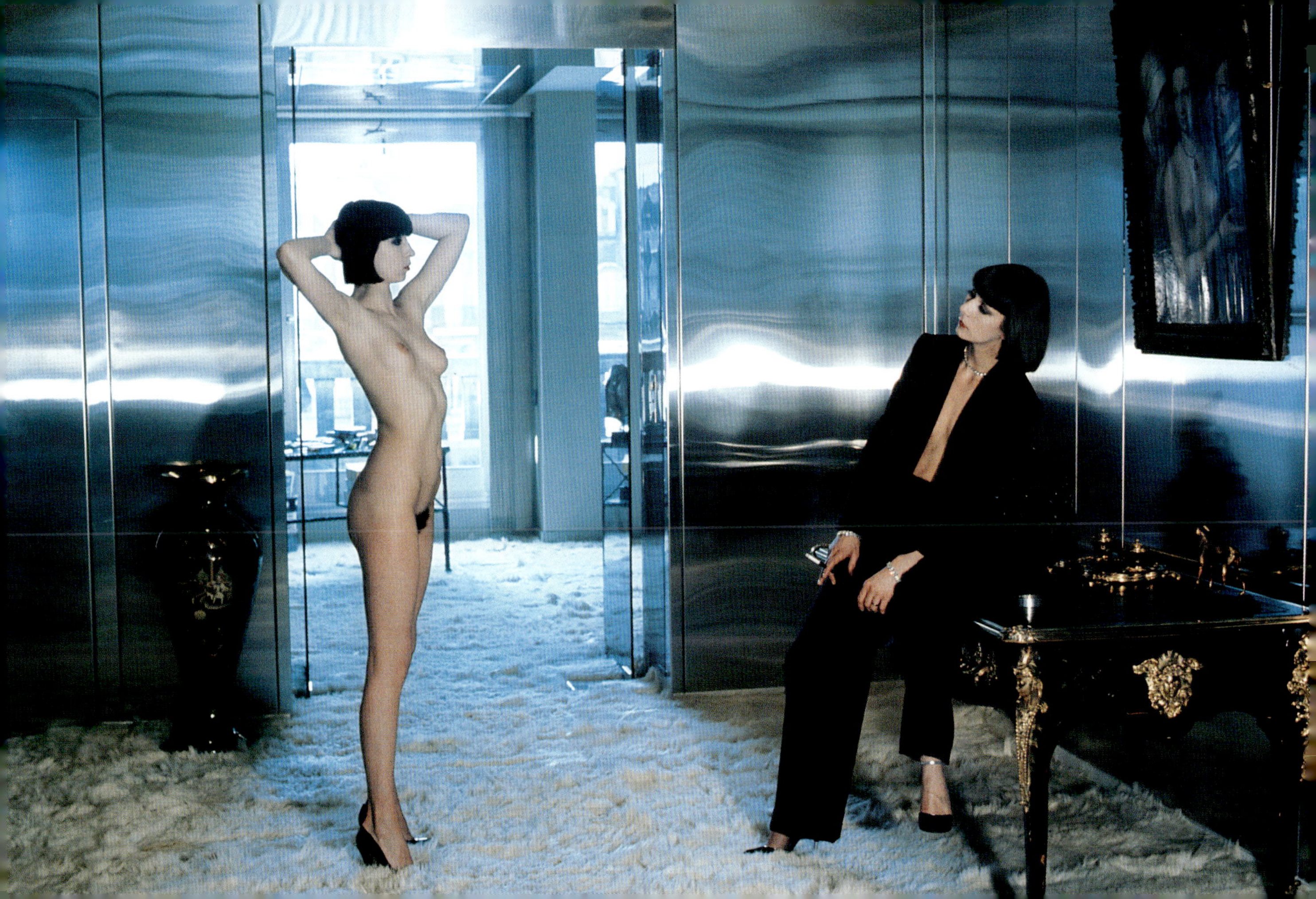

HELMUT NEWTON'S

PLAYMATES

FEATURING

Roberta Vasquez, Ava Fabian, Barbara Edwards, Cynthia Brimhall, Marianne Gravatte, Pamela Bryant, Christine Richters, Kimberly McArthur, Venice Kong, Rebecca Ferratti, Lynne Austin, Teri Weigel, Kathy Shower, and Lesa Ann Pedriana

September 1987

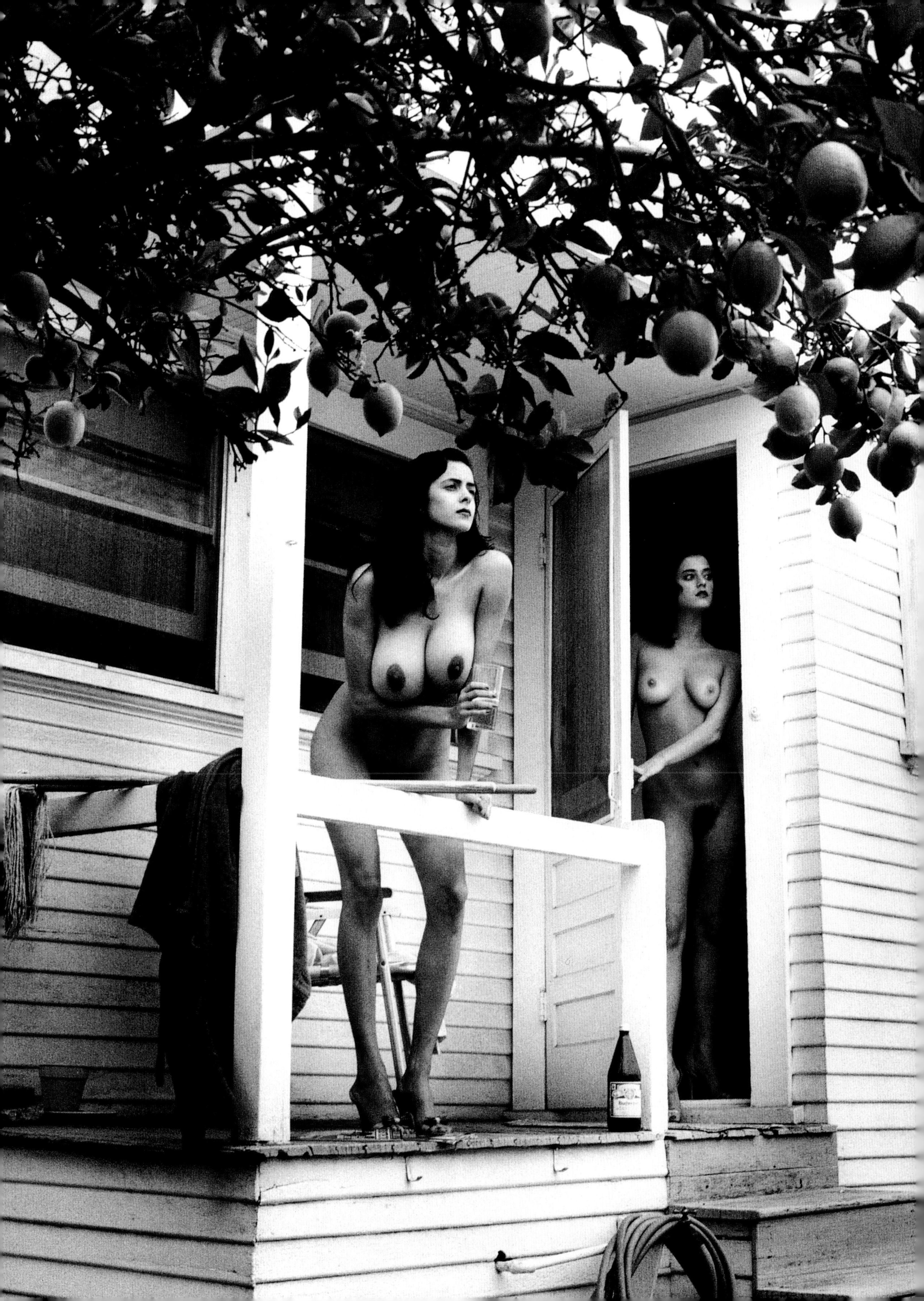

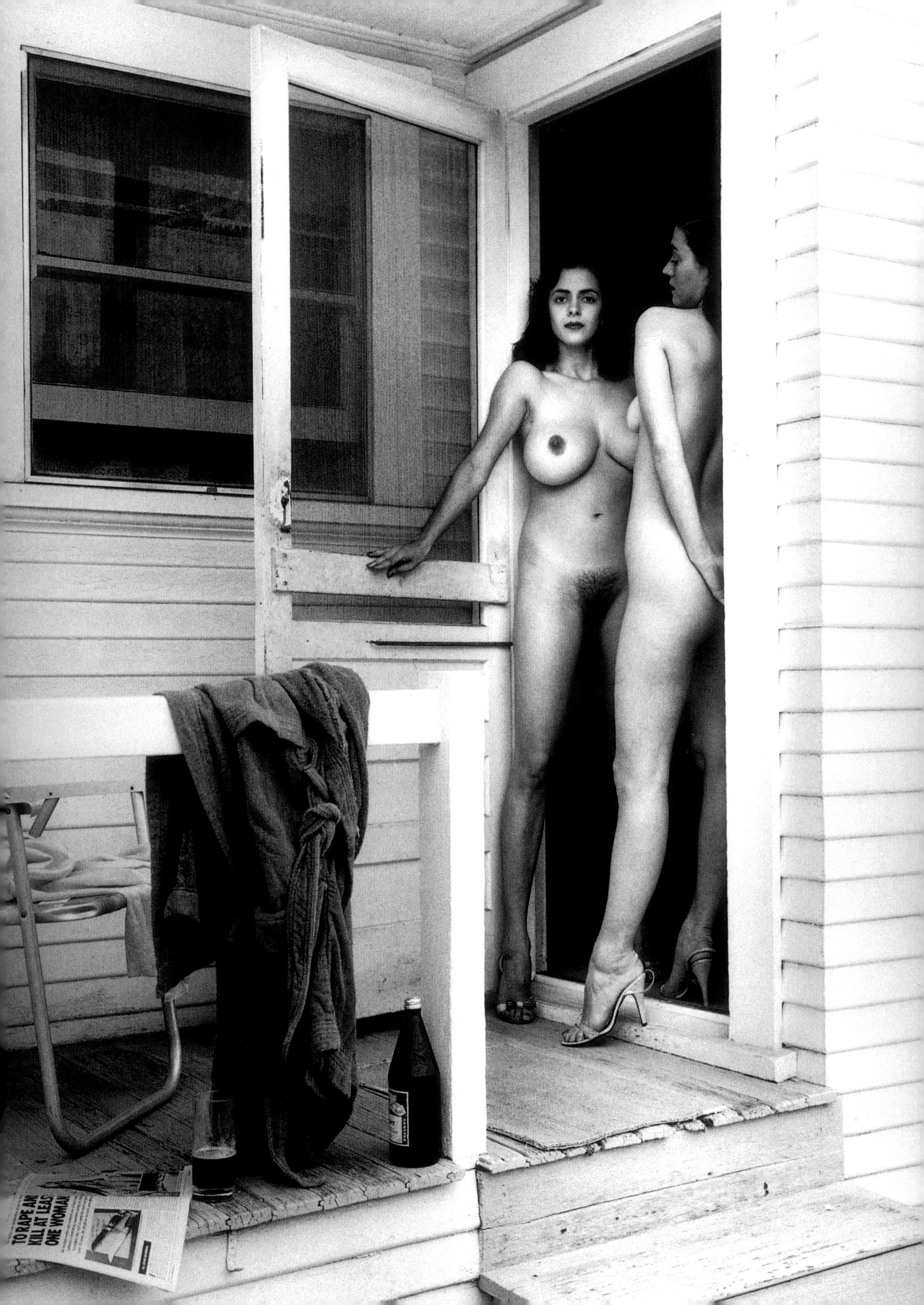
TO RAPE AN
KILL AT LEAS
ONE WOMAN

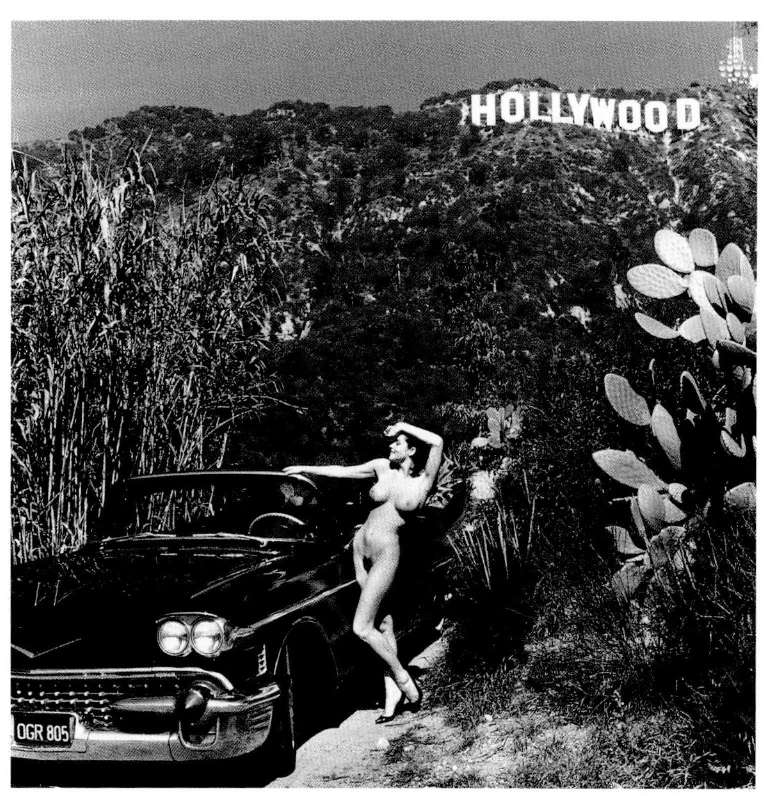
HOLLYWOOD
OGR 805

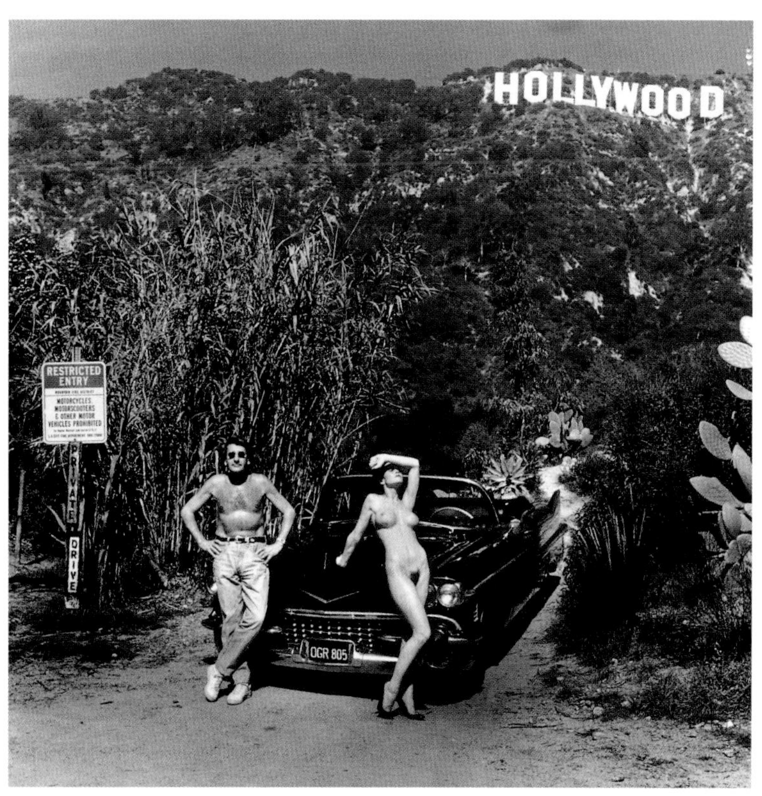
HOLLYWOOD
RESTRICTED ENTRY
MOTORCYCLES
MOTORSCOOTERS
& OTHER MOTOR
VEHICLES PROHIBITED
PRIVATE
DRIVE
OGR 805

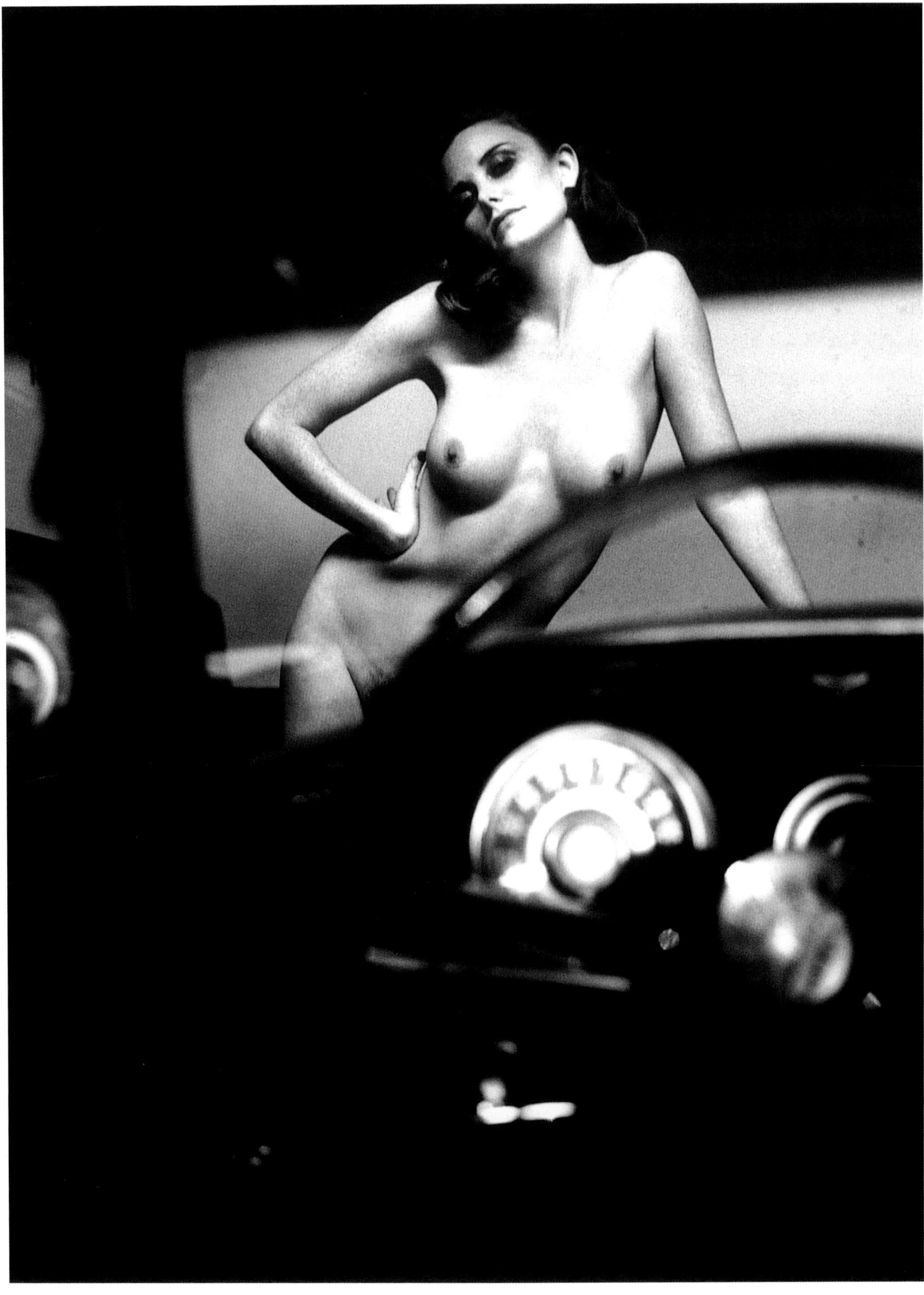

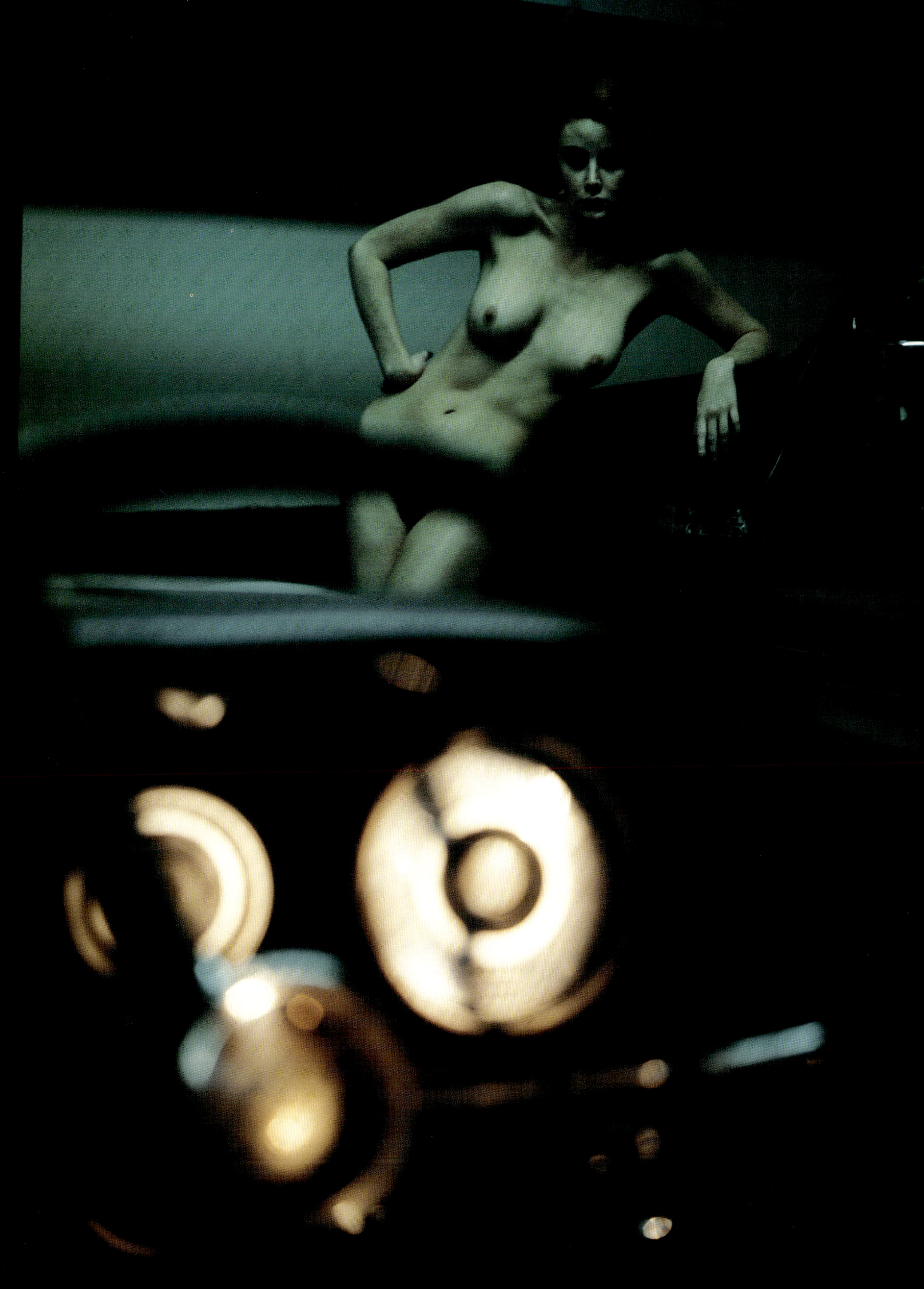

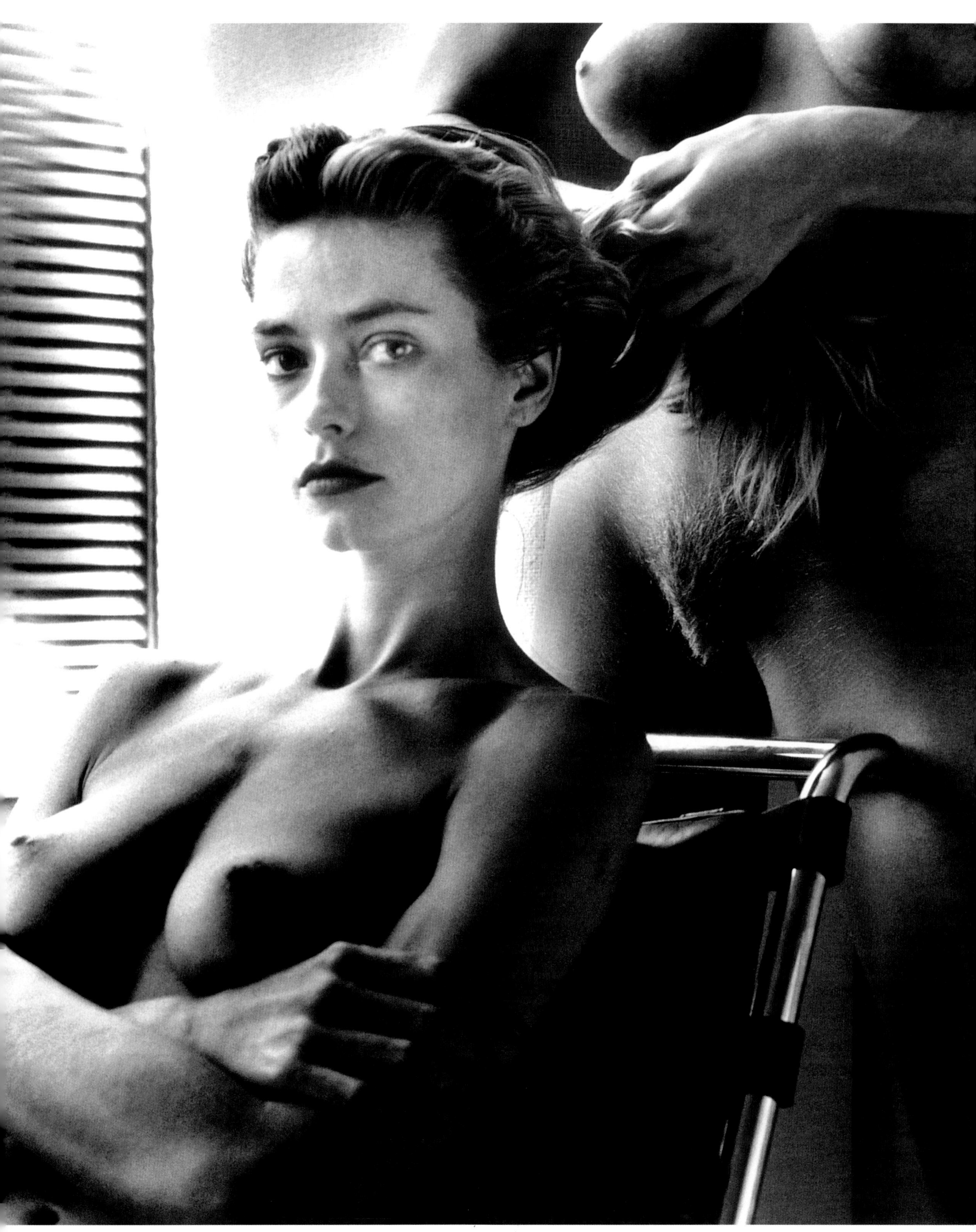

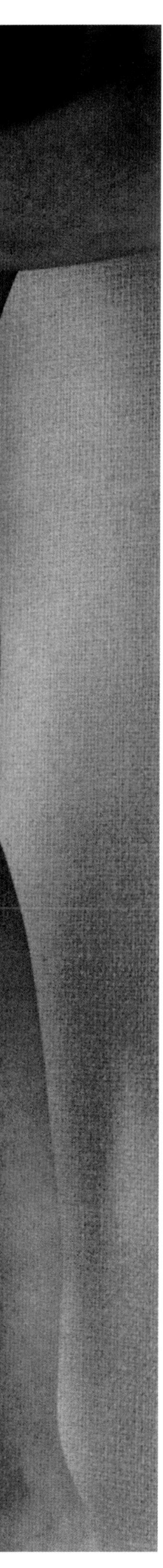

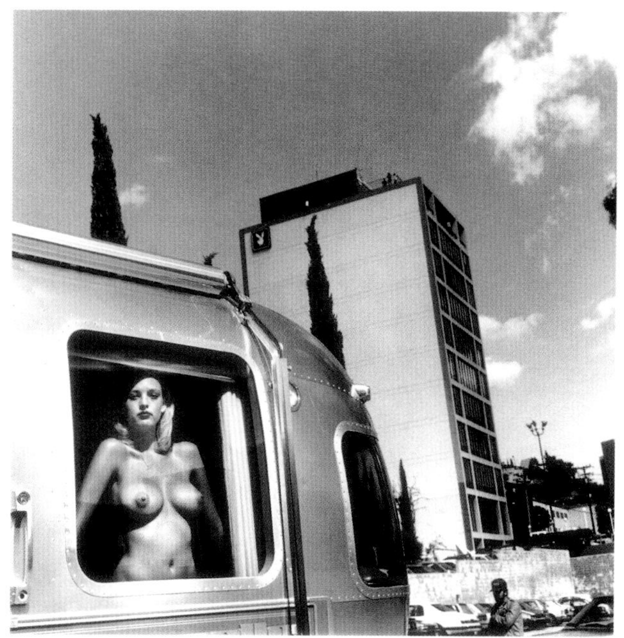

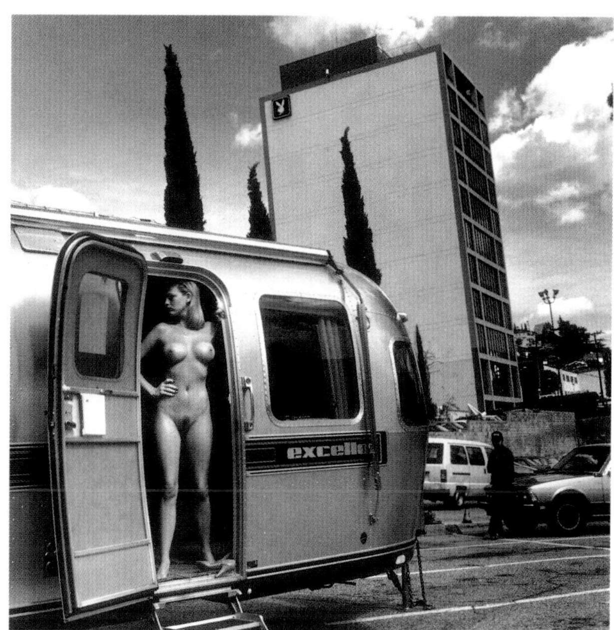

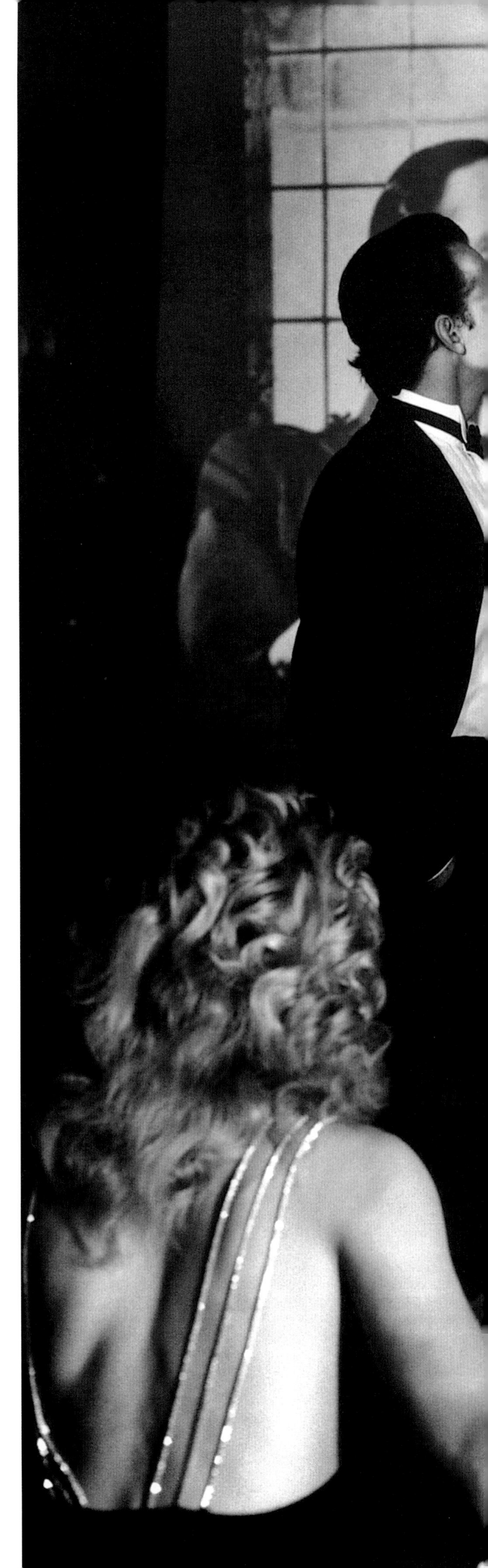

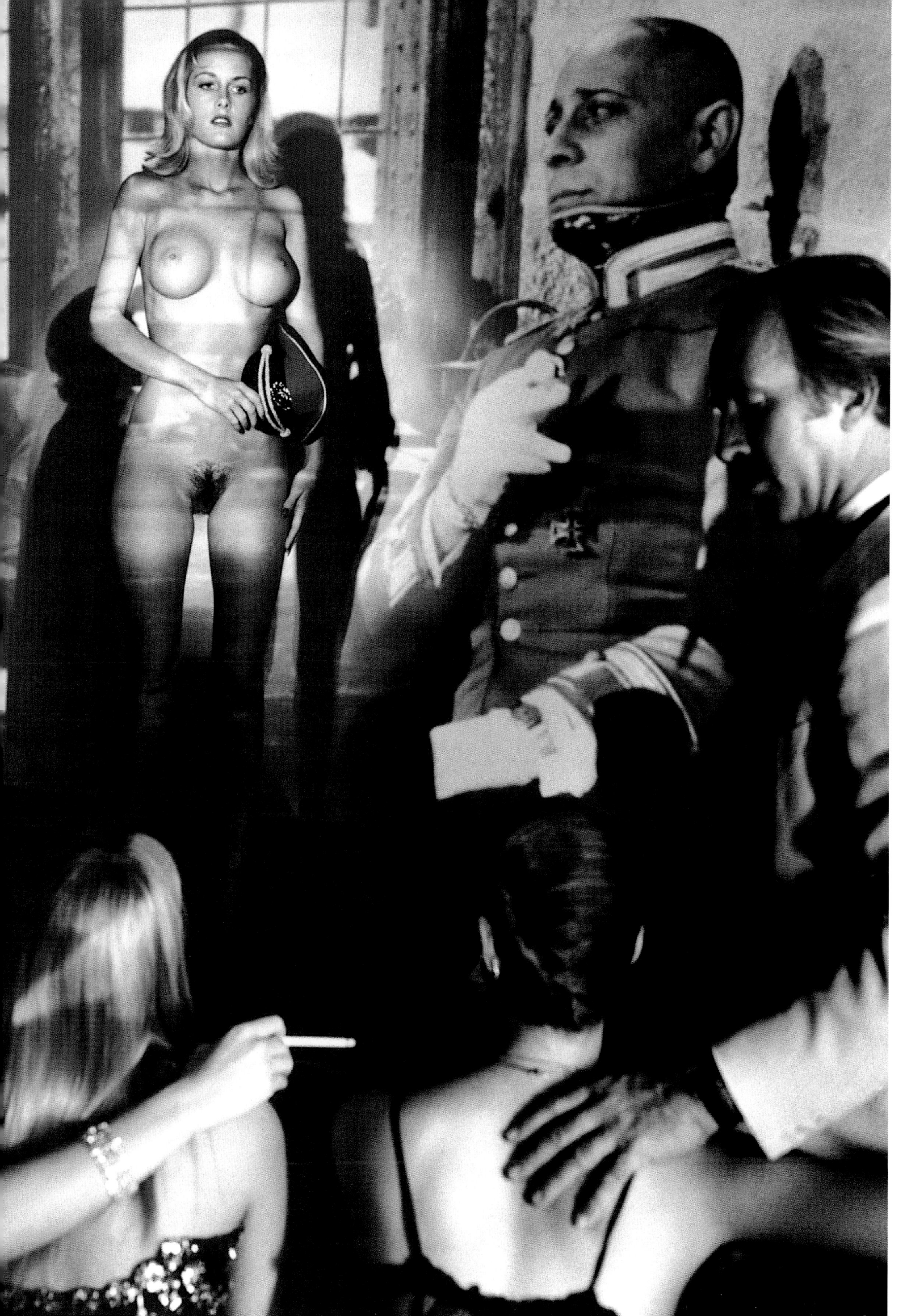

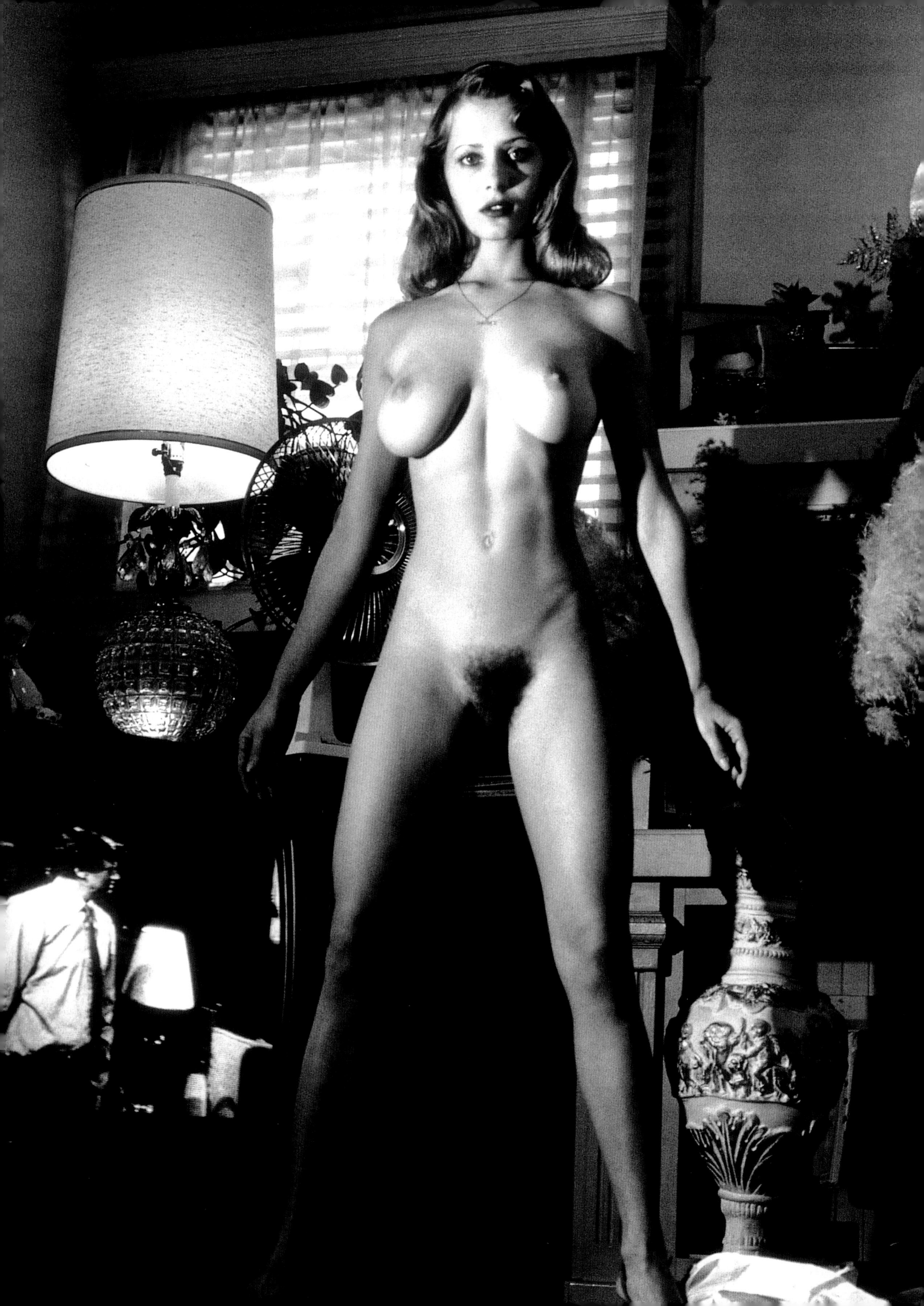

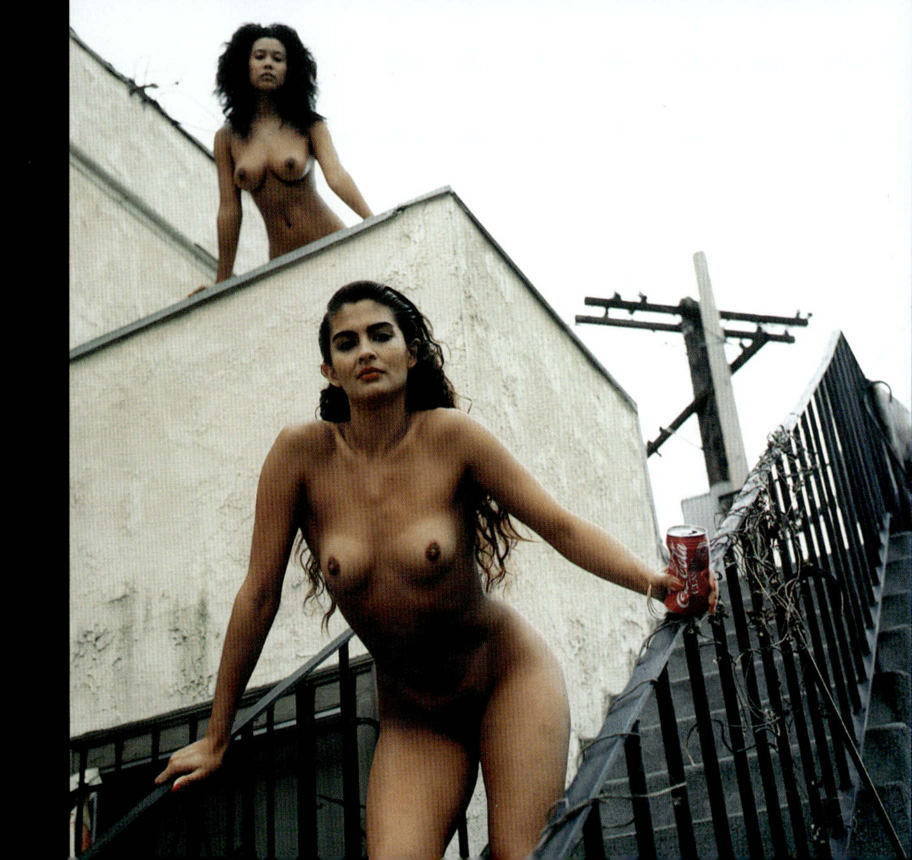

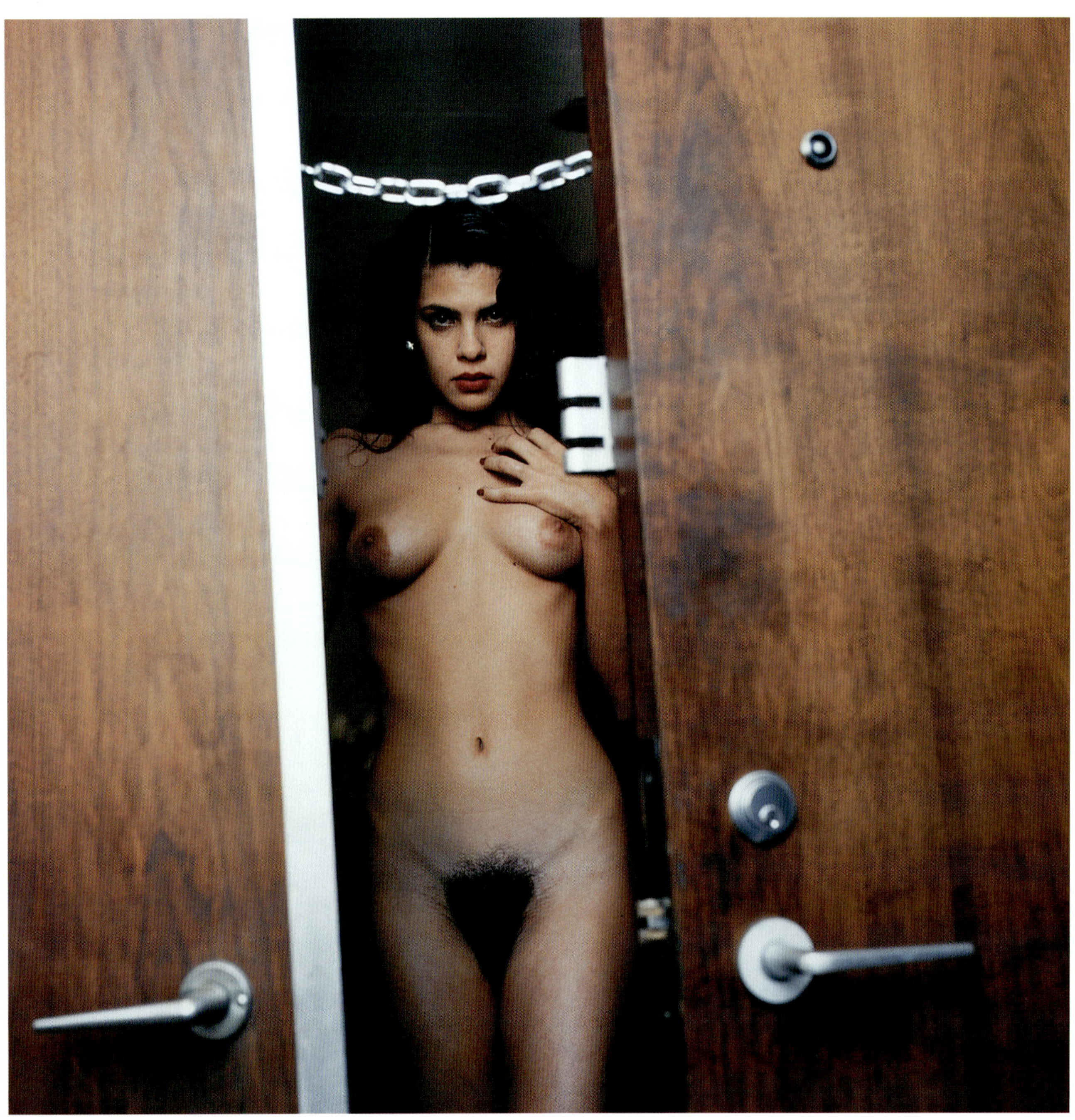

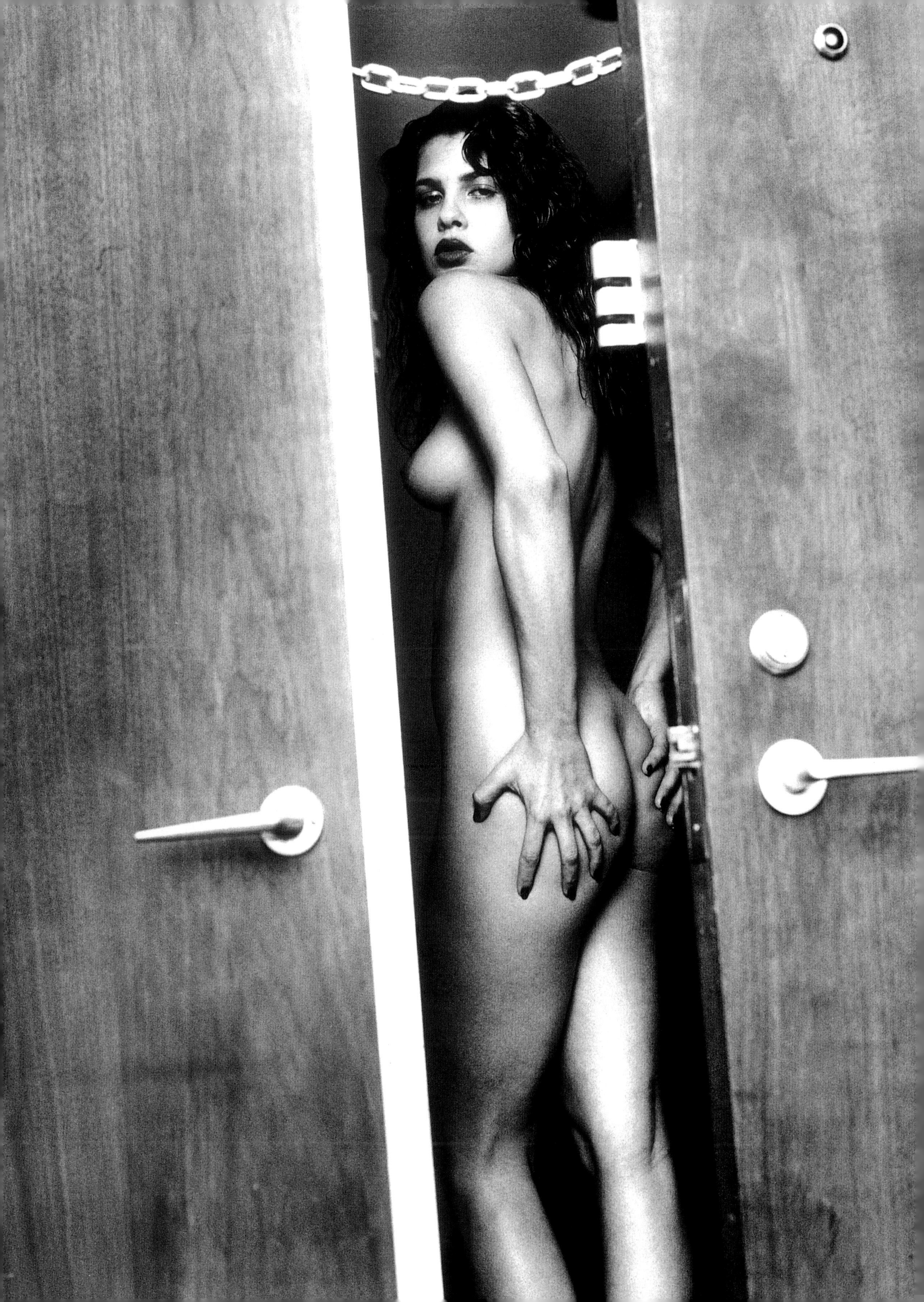

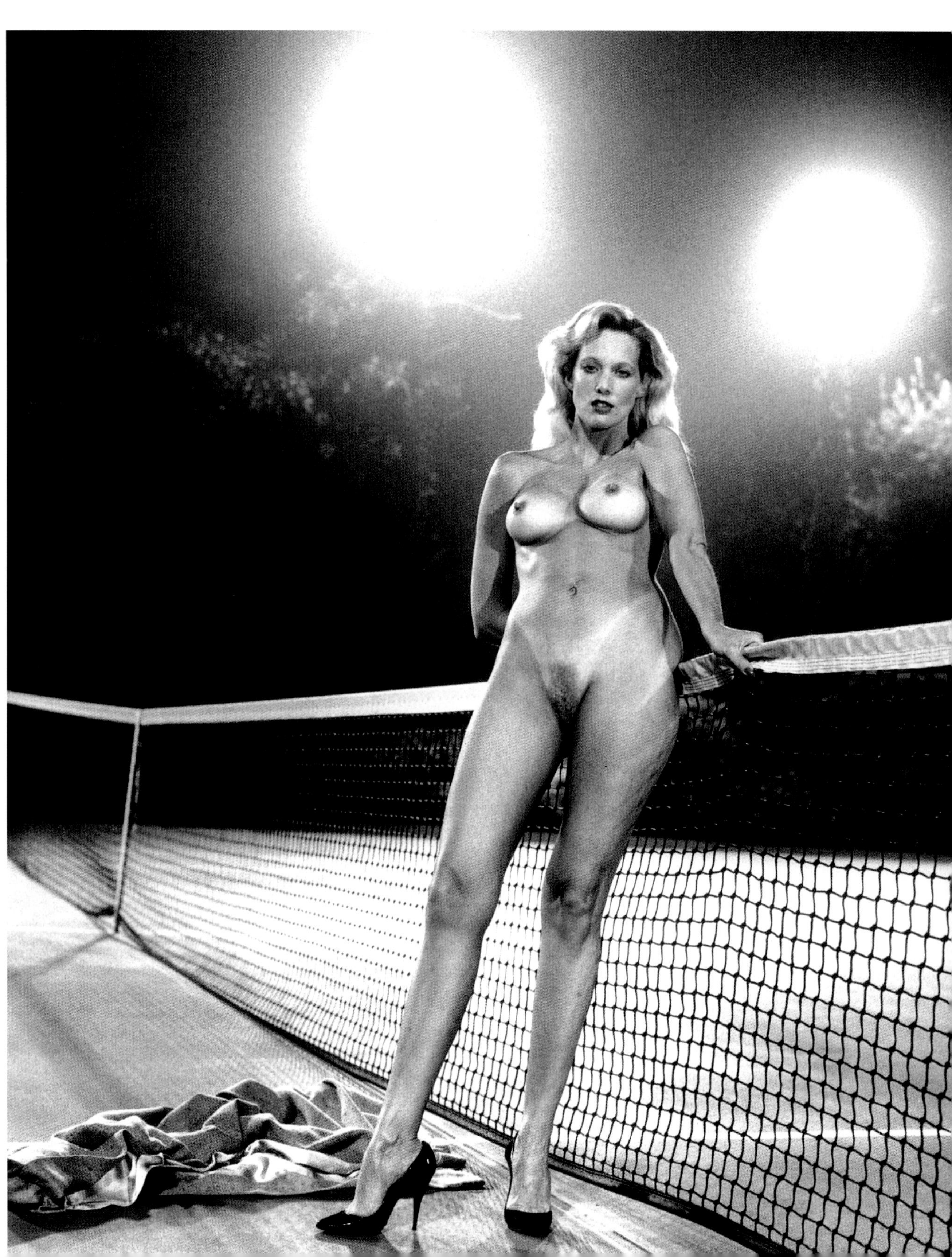

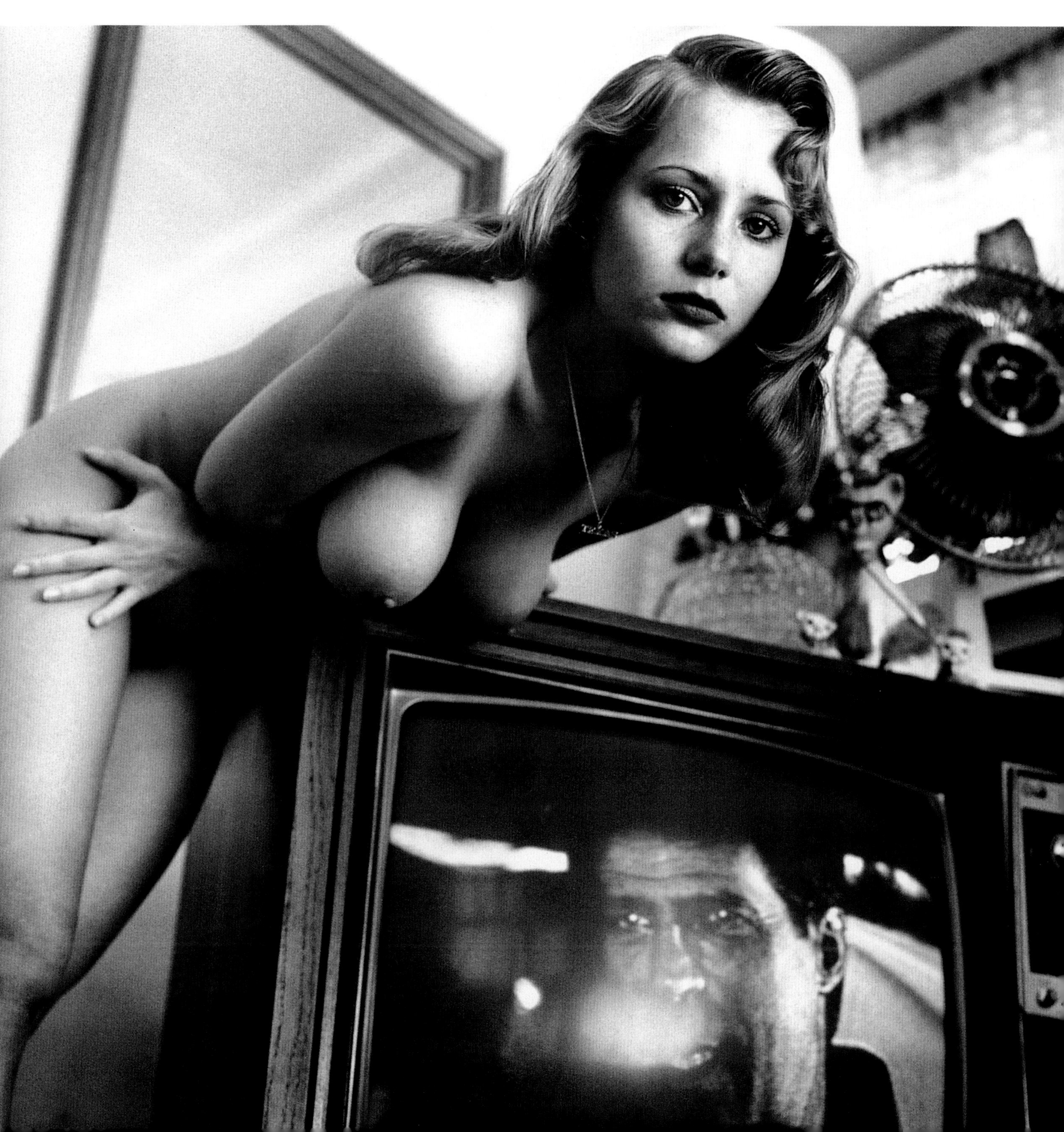

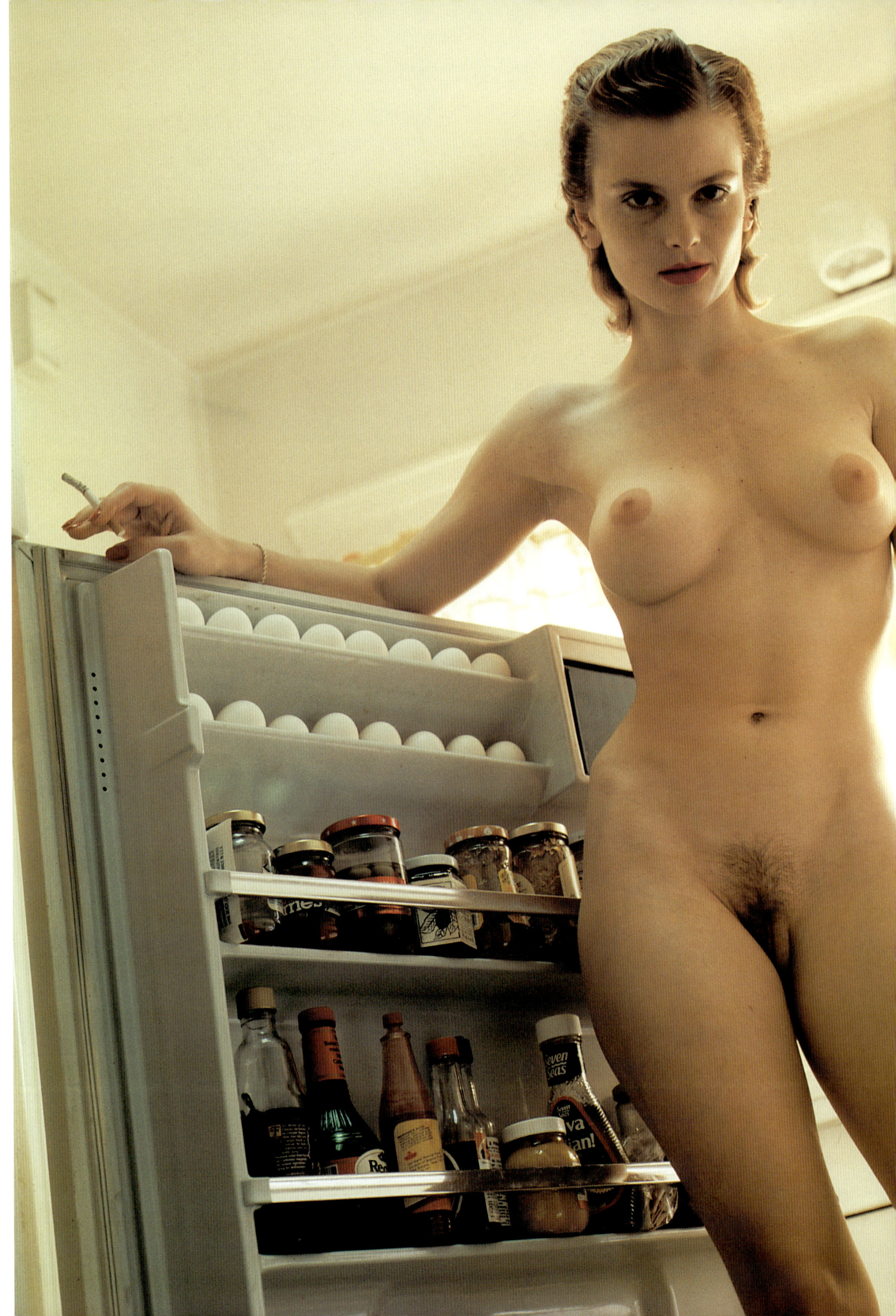
Seven Seas

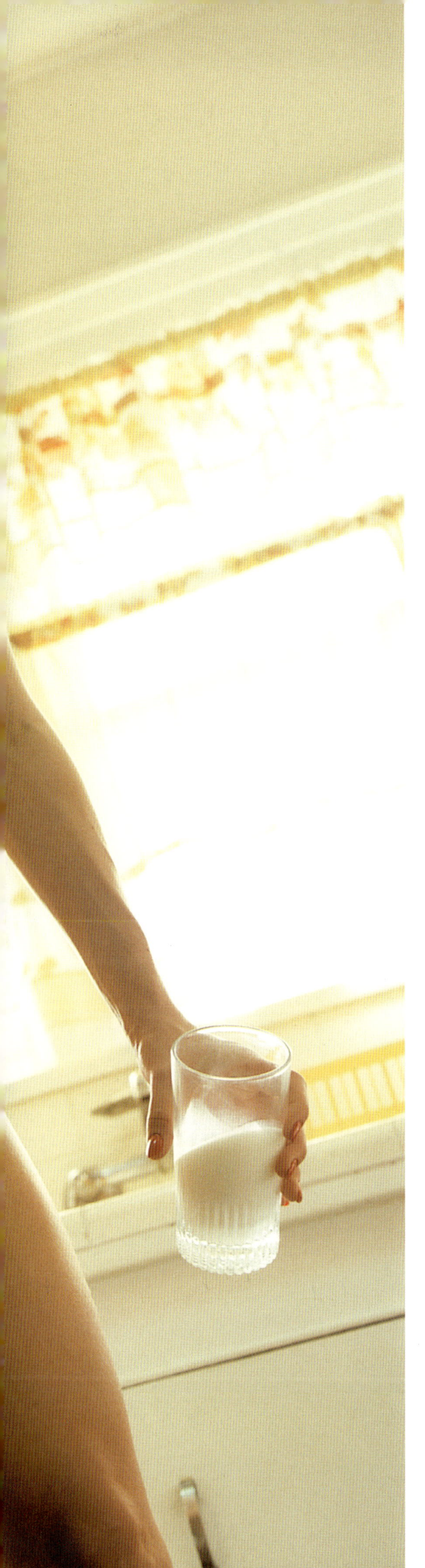

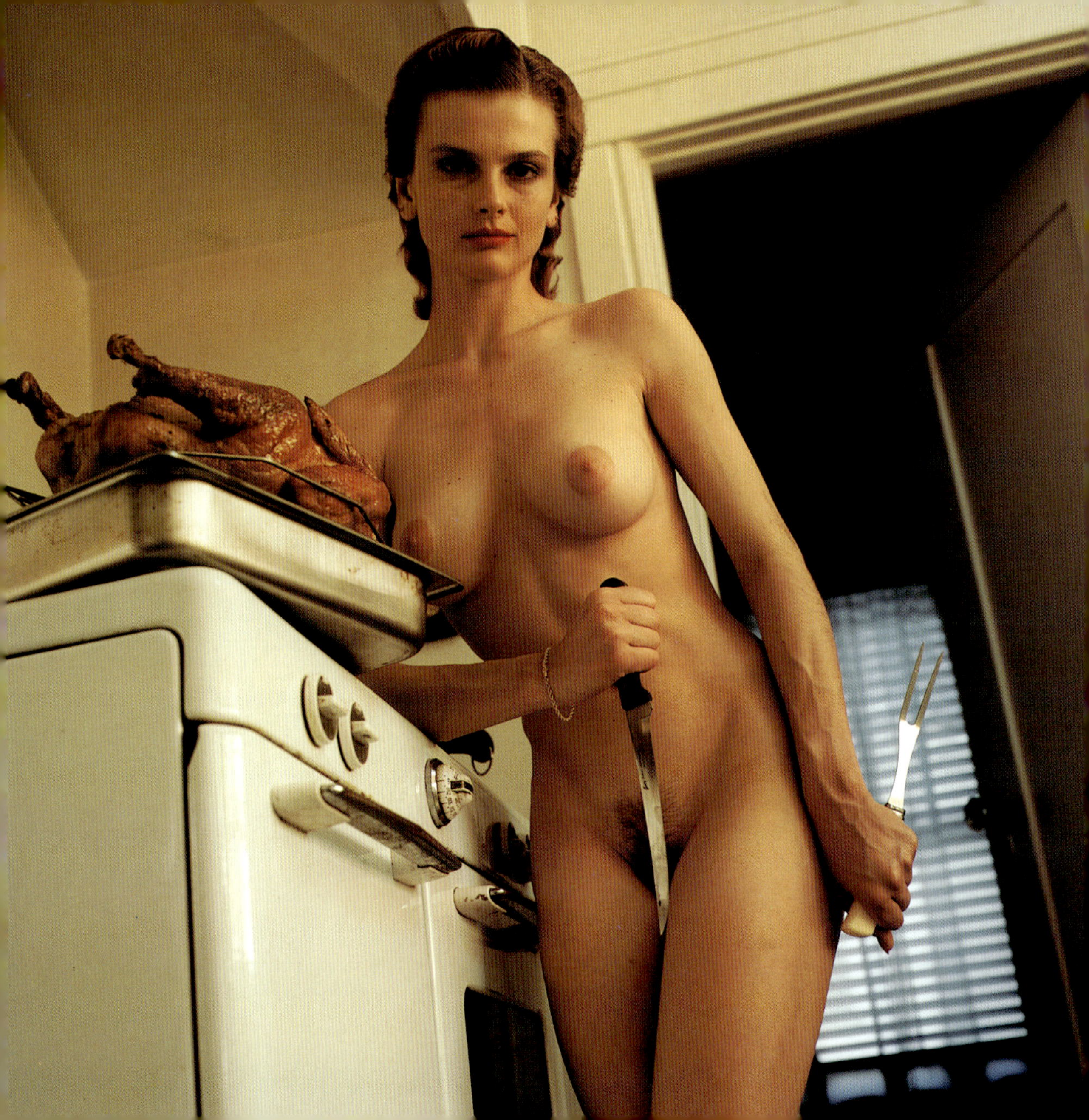

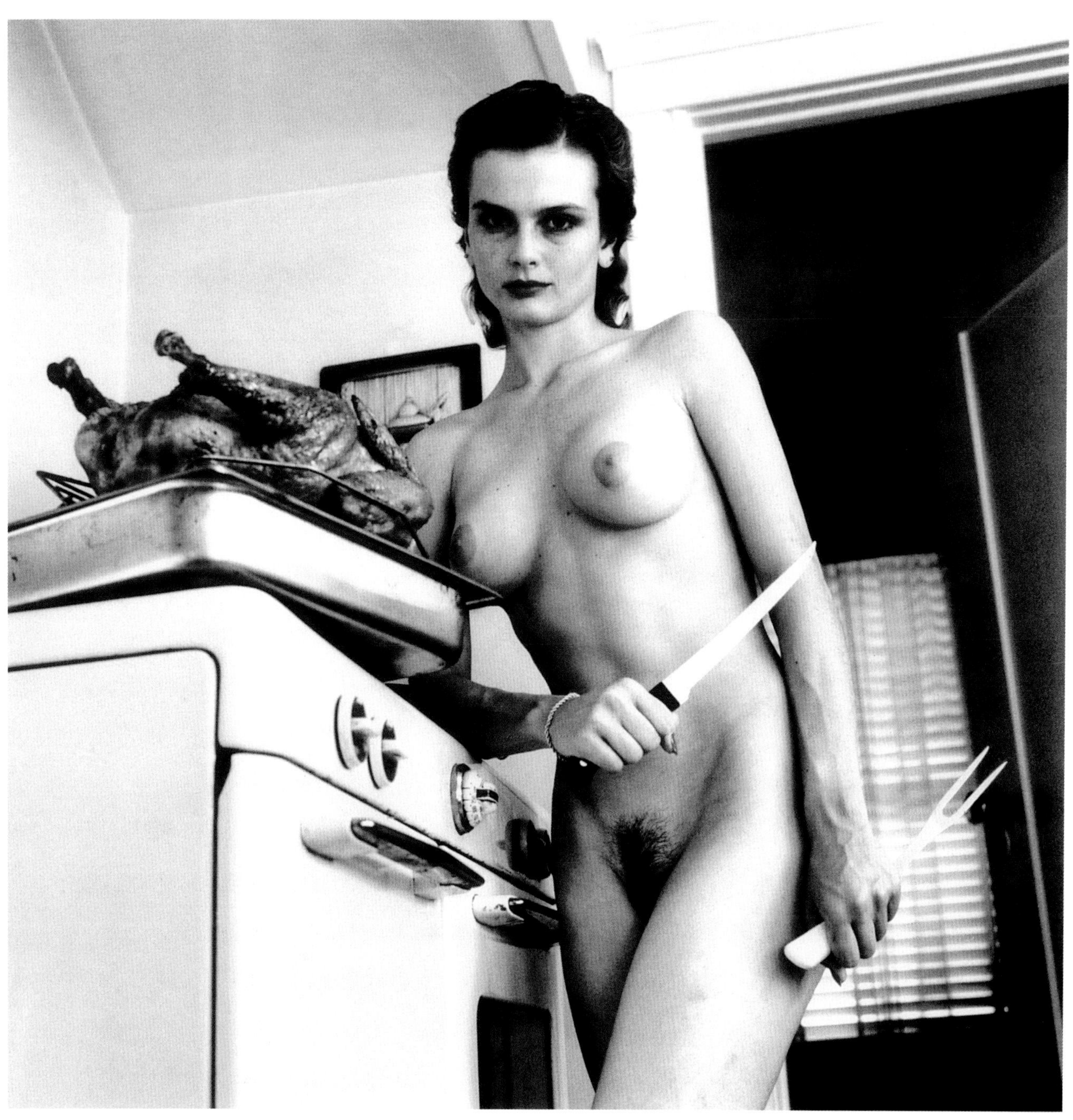

TOMORROW'S

TURN-ONS

FEATURING

Winnie Haller

January 1978

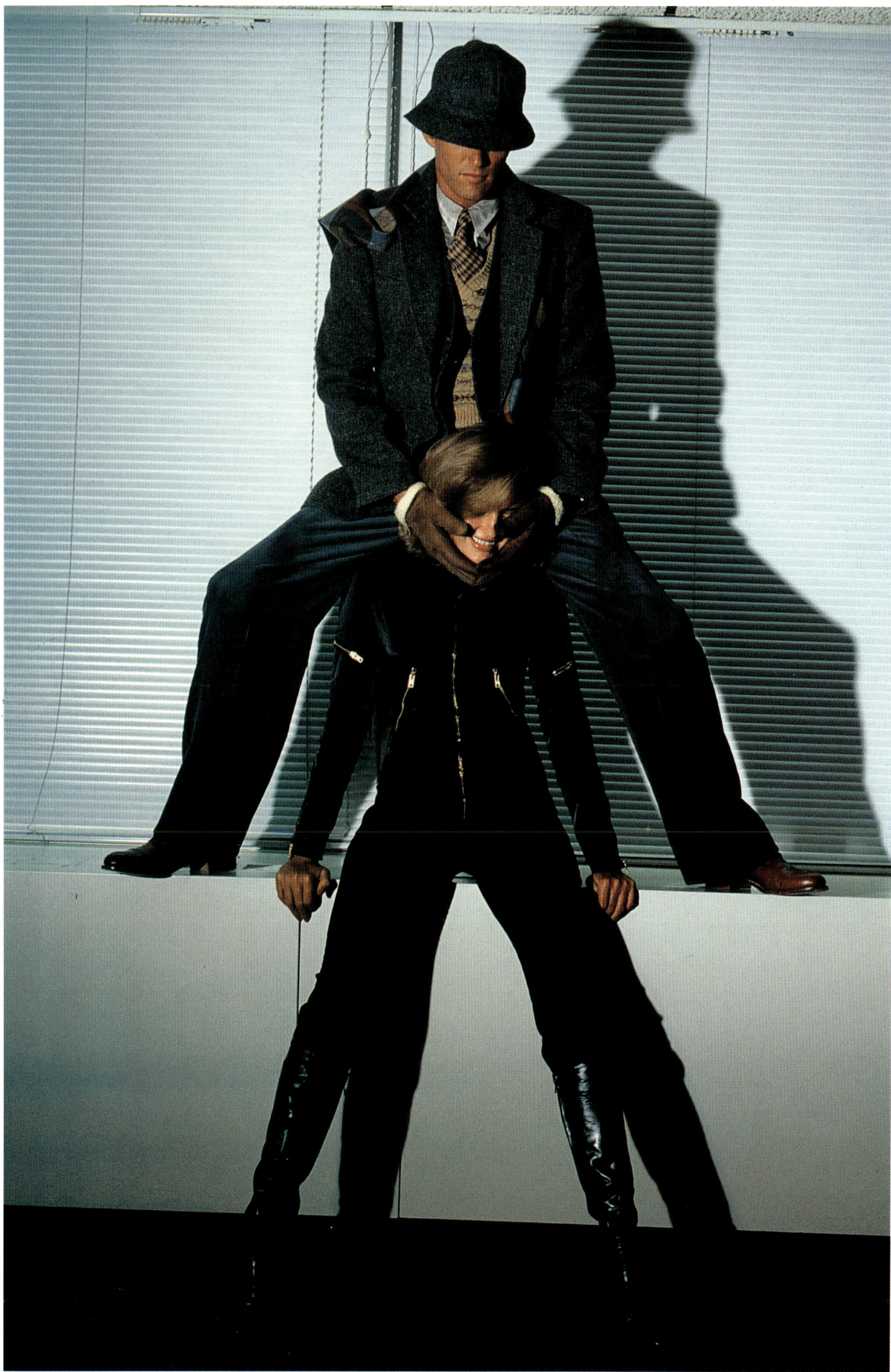

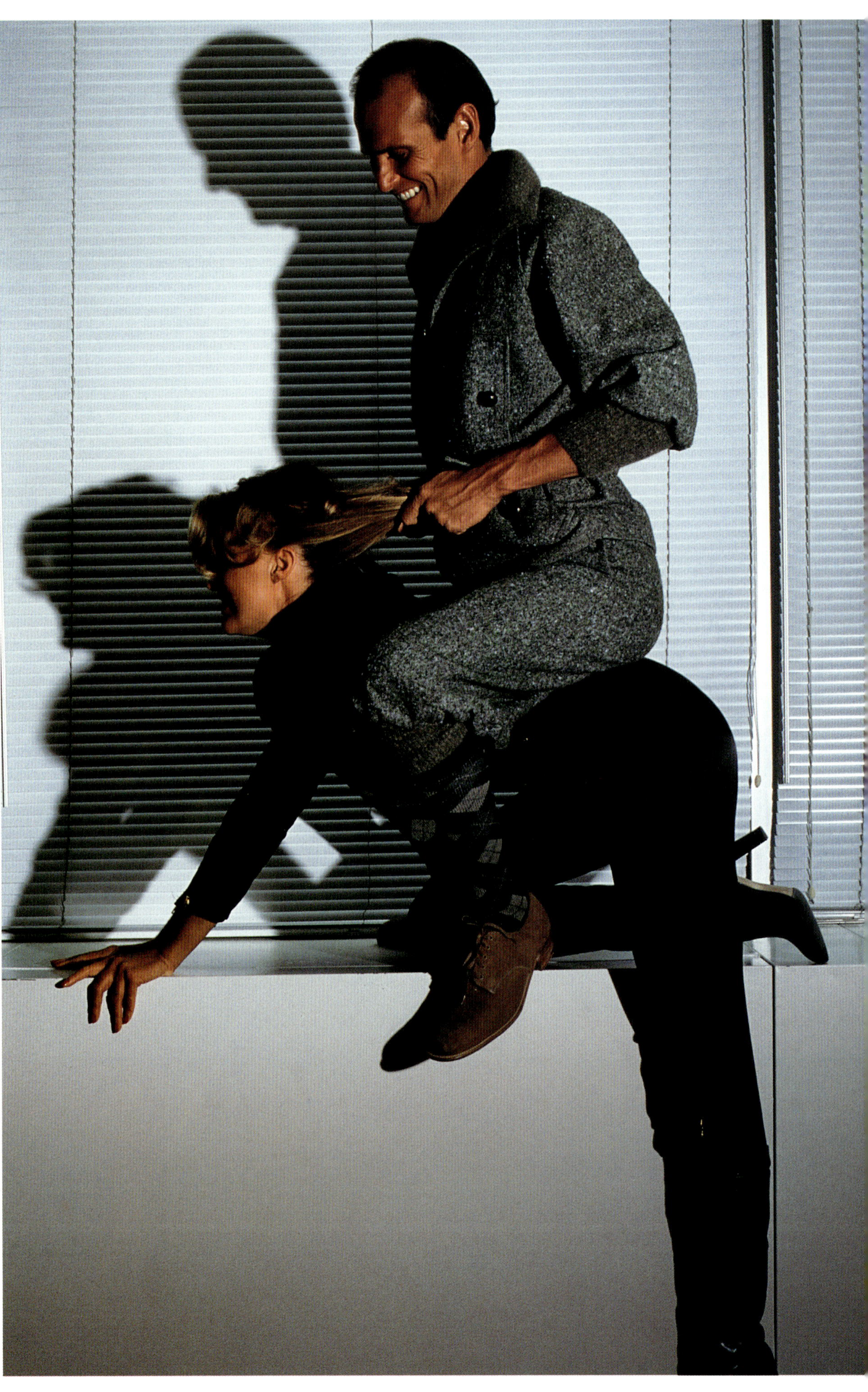

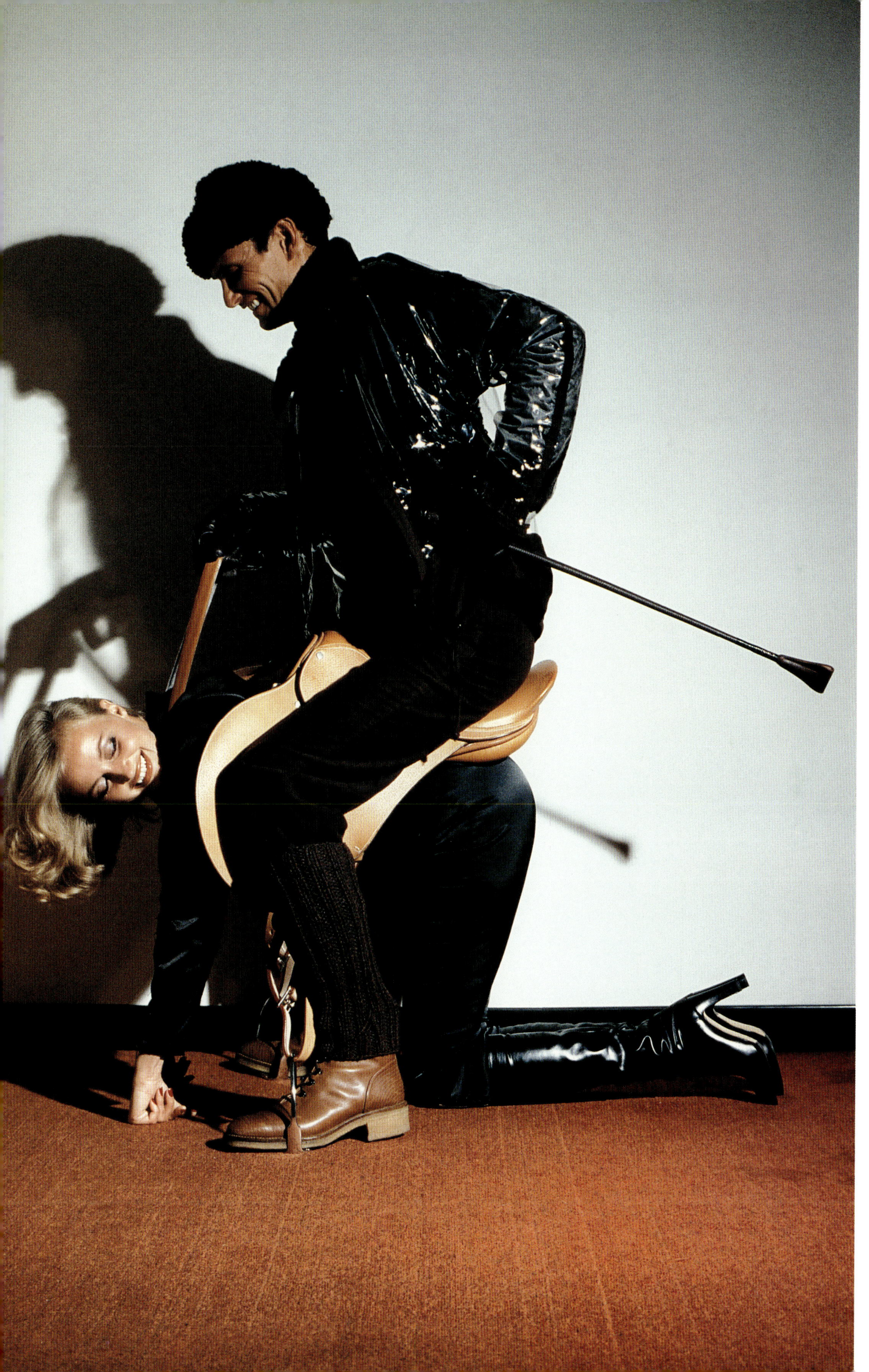

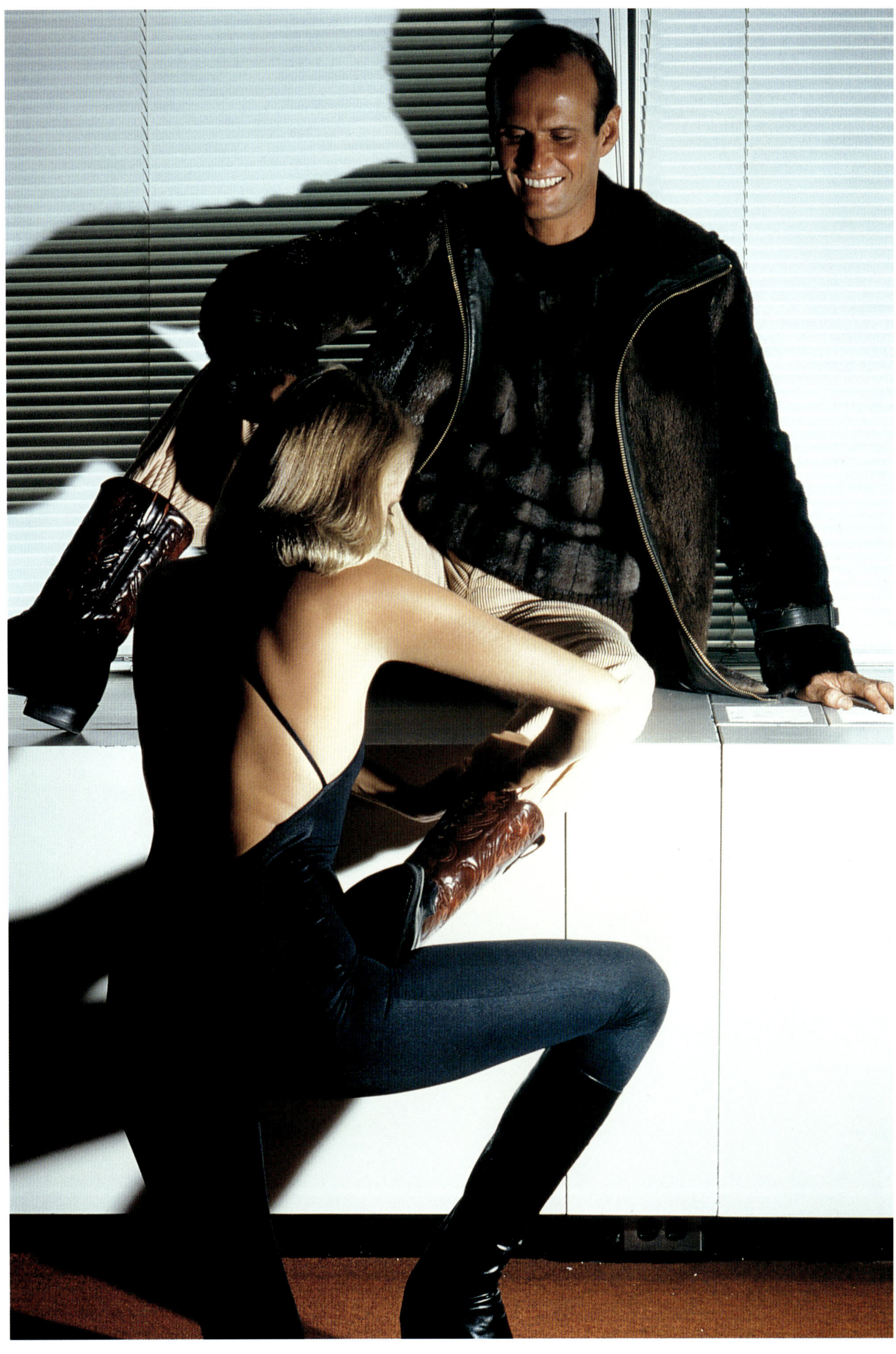

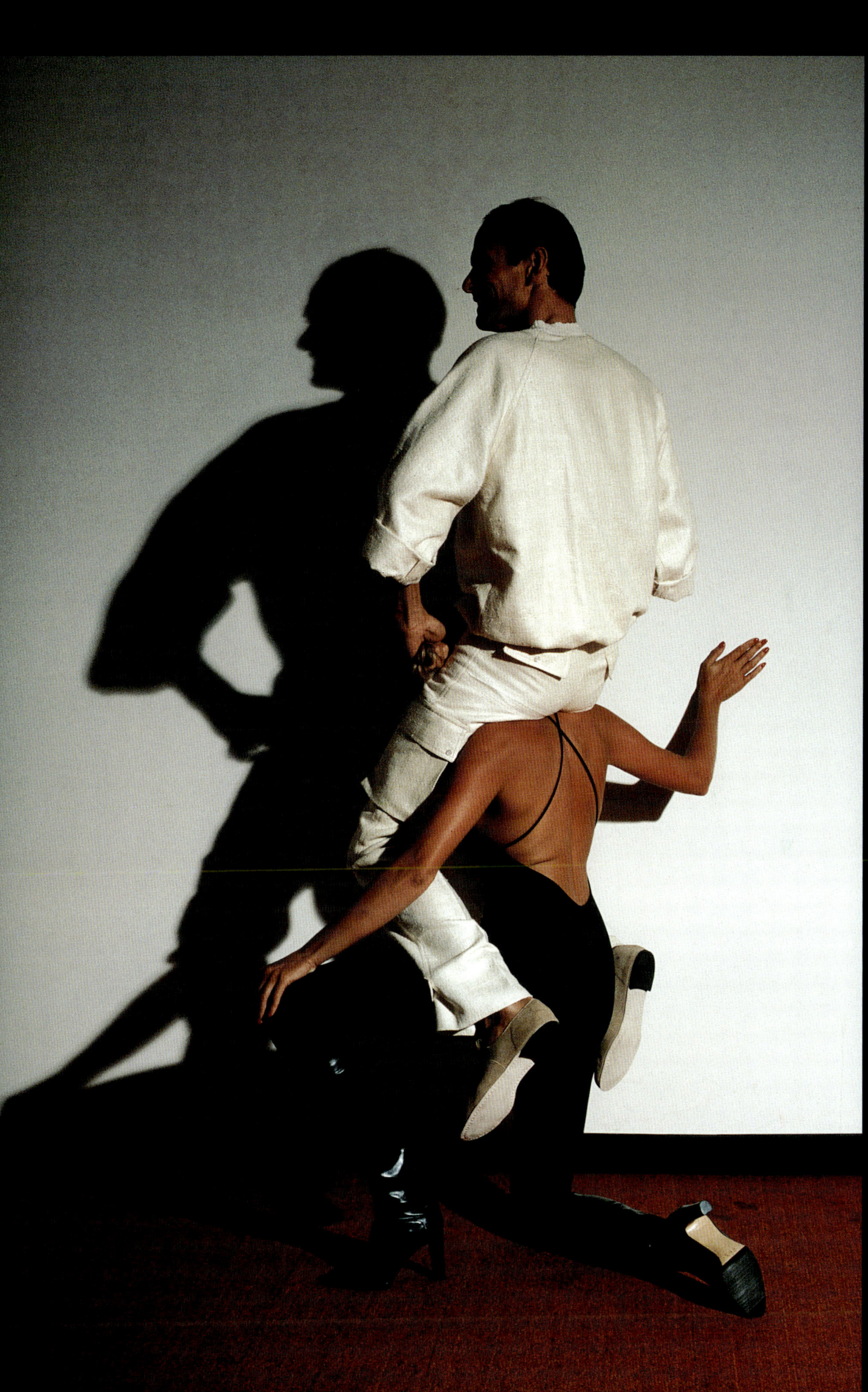

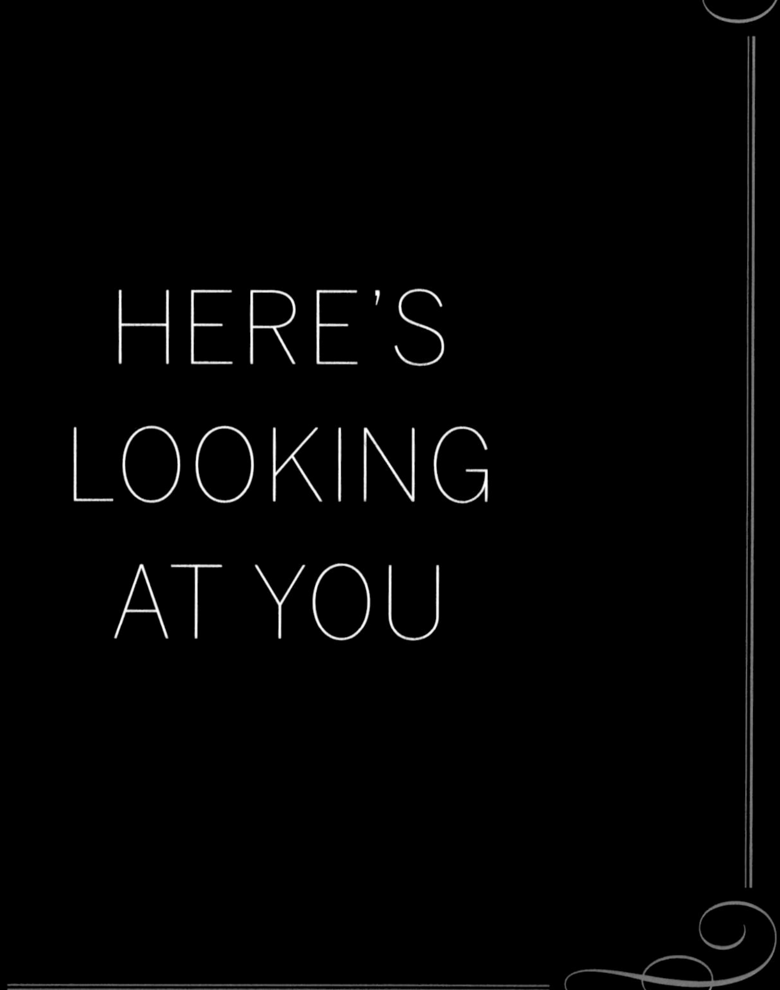

HERE'S LOOKING AT YOU

FEATURING

Hefner, Teri Weigel, Renee Griffin, Karen Foster, Kerri Kendall, Peggy McIntaggart, Barbara Leigh, Lisa Matthews, and Tawni Cable

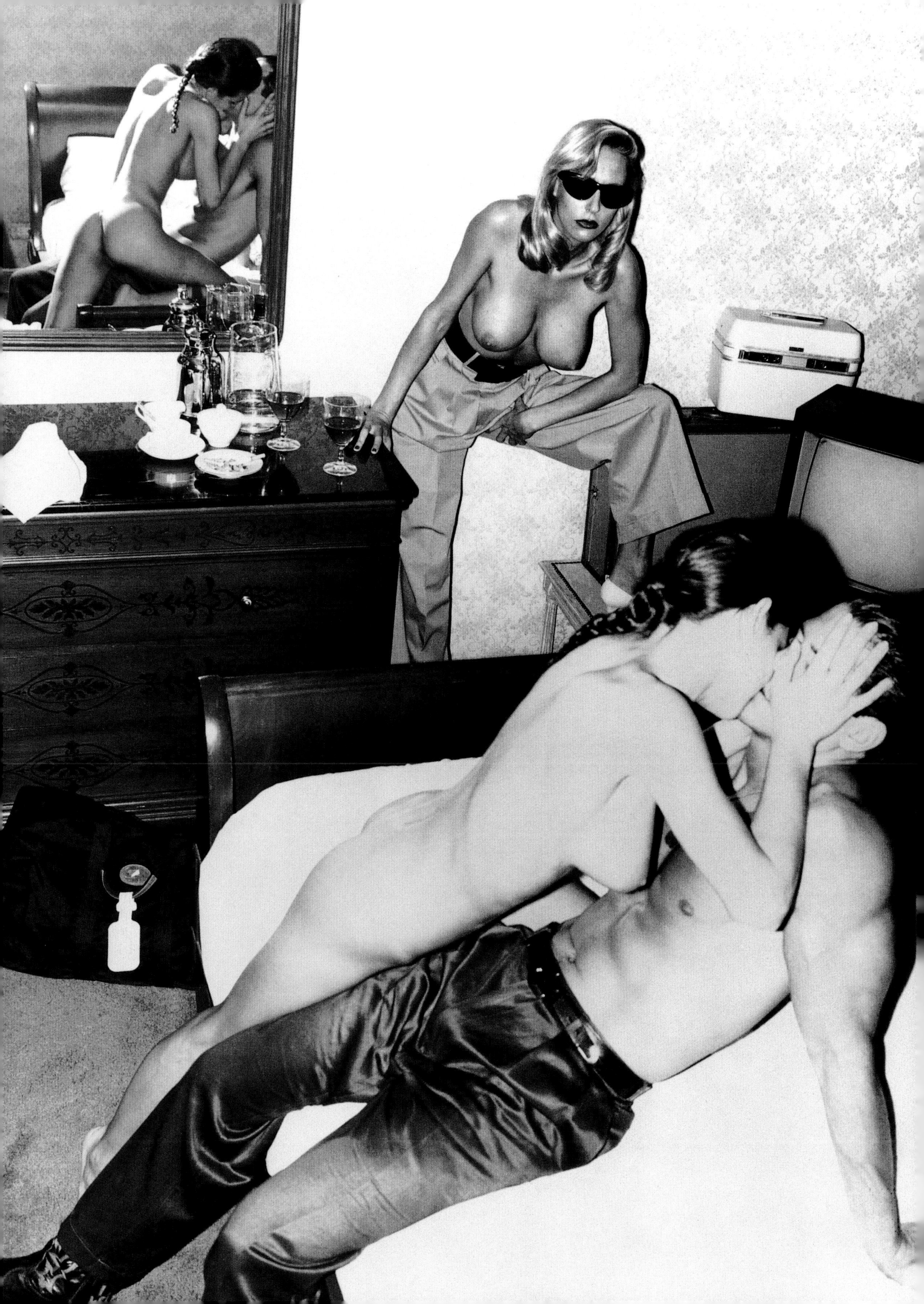

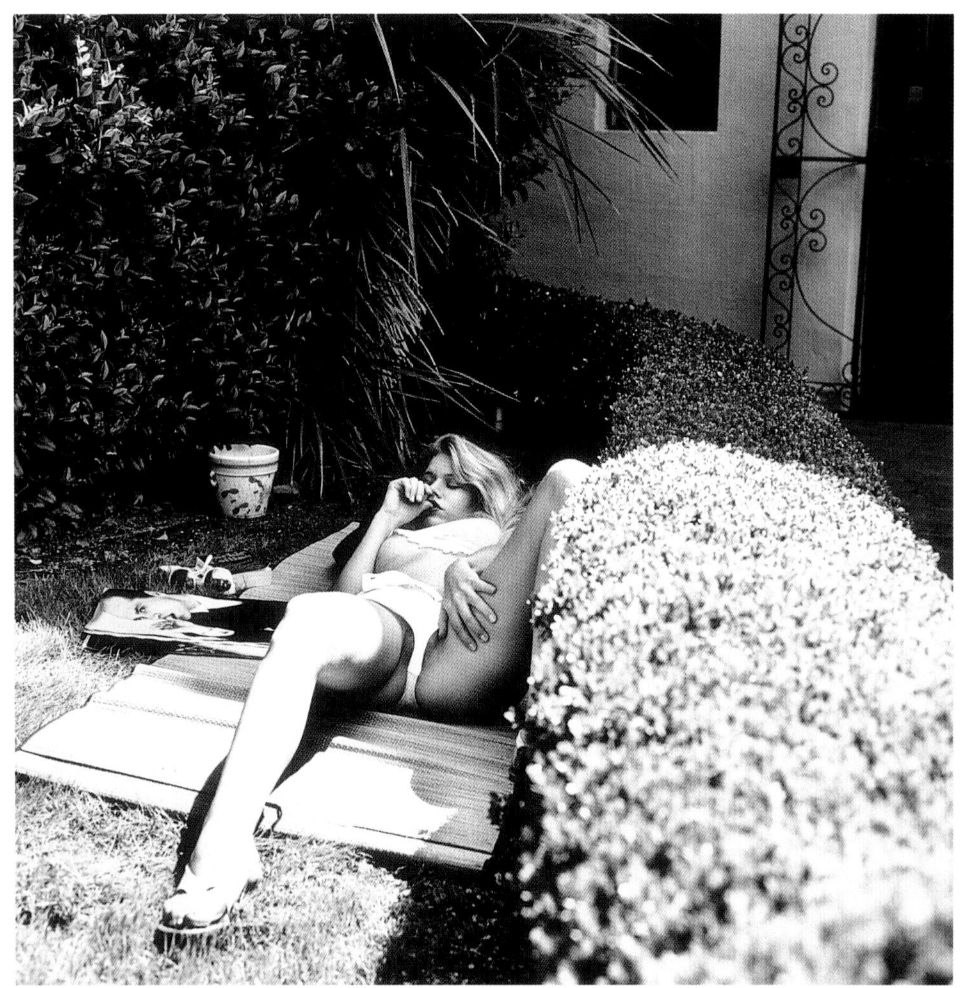

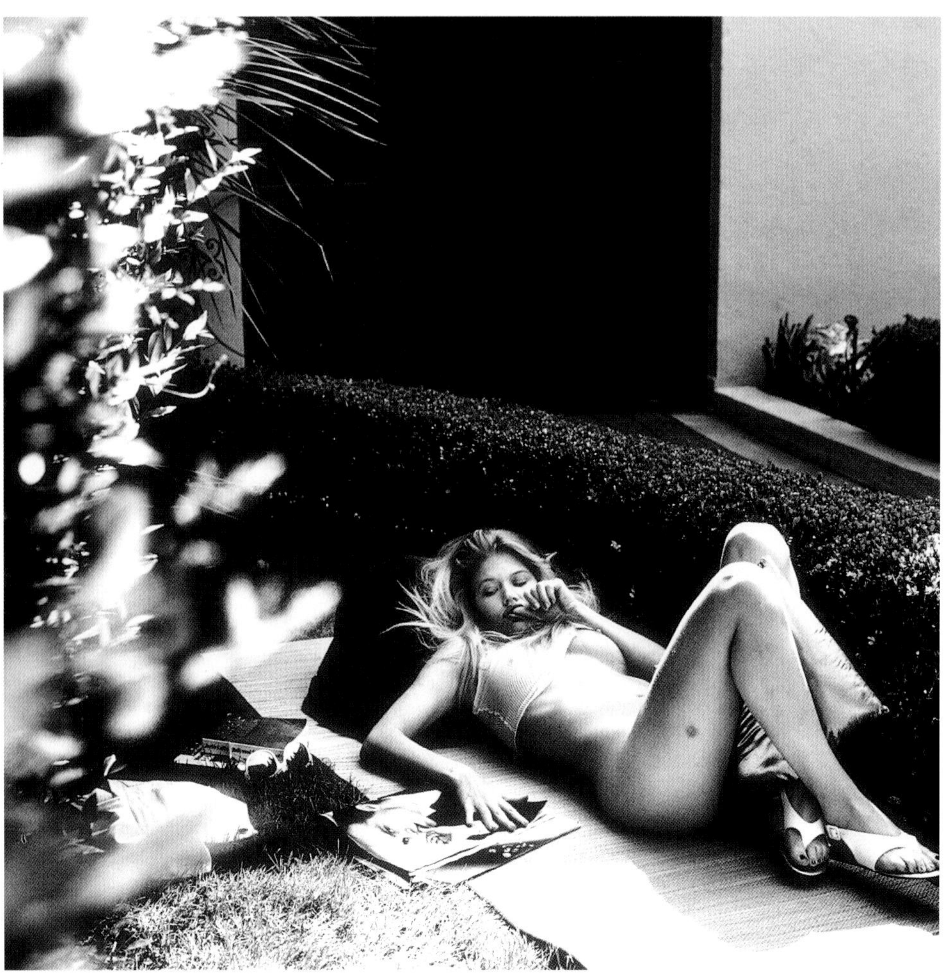

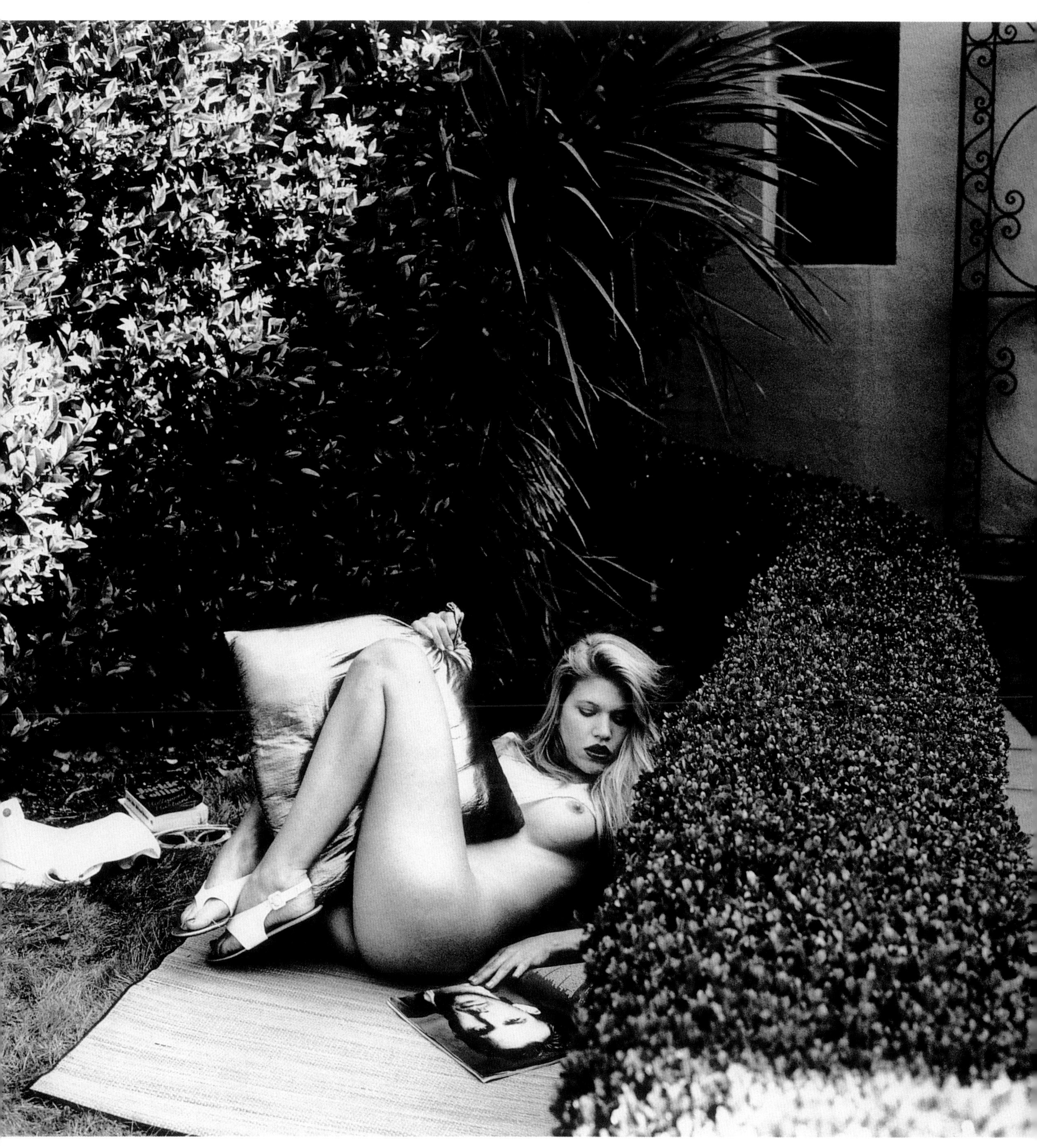

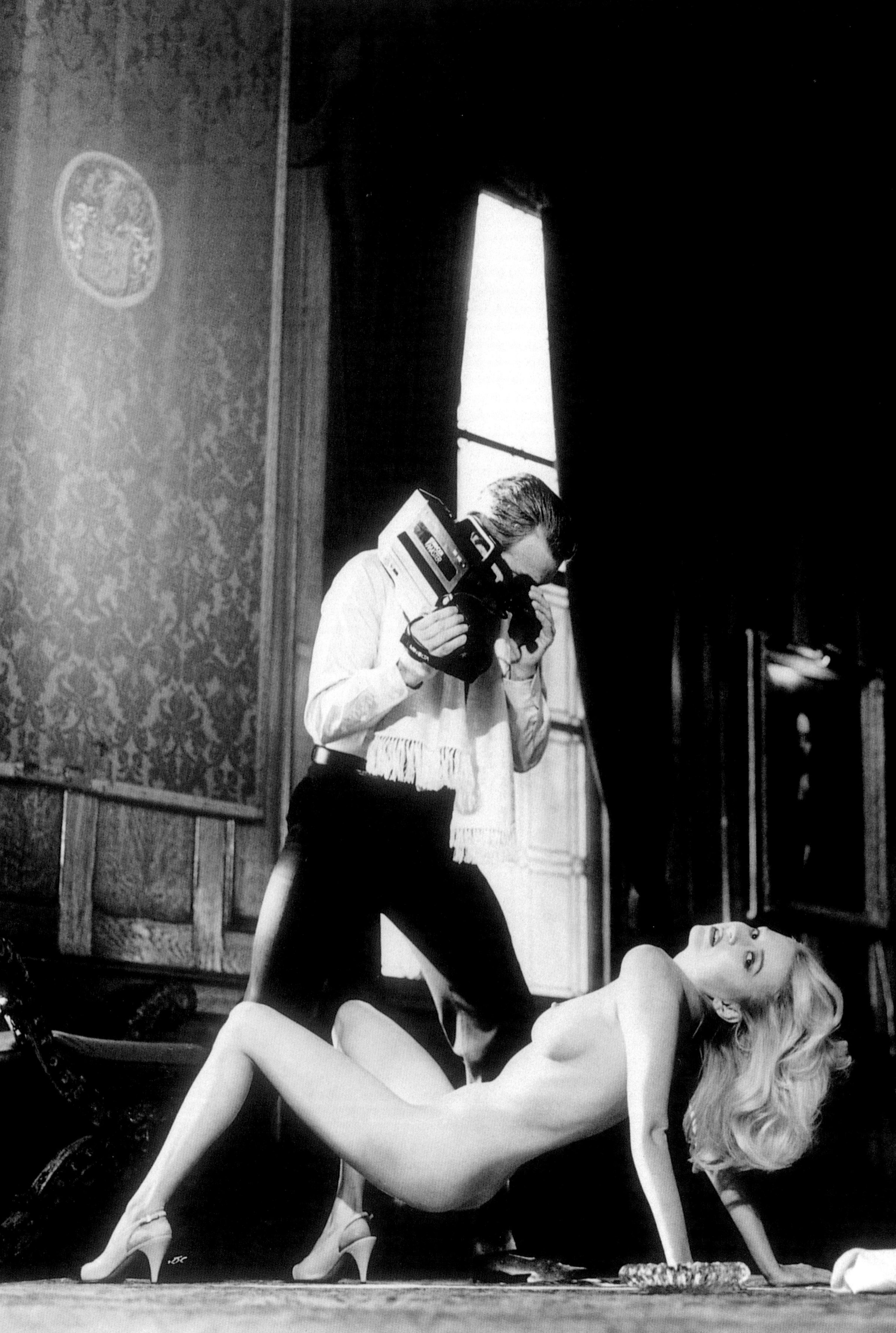

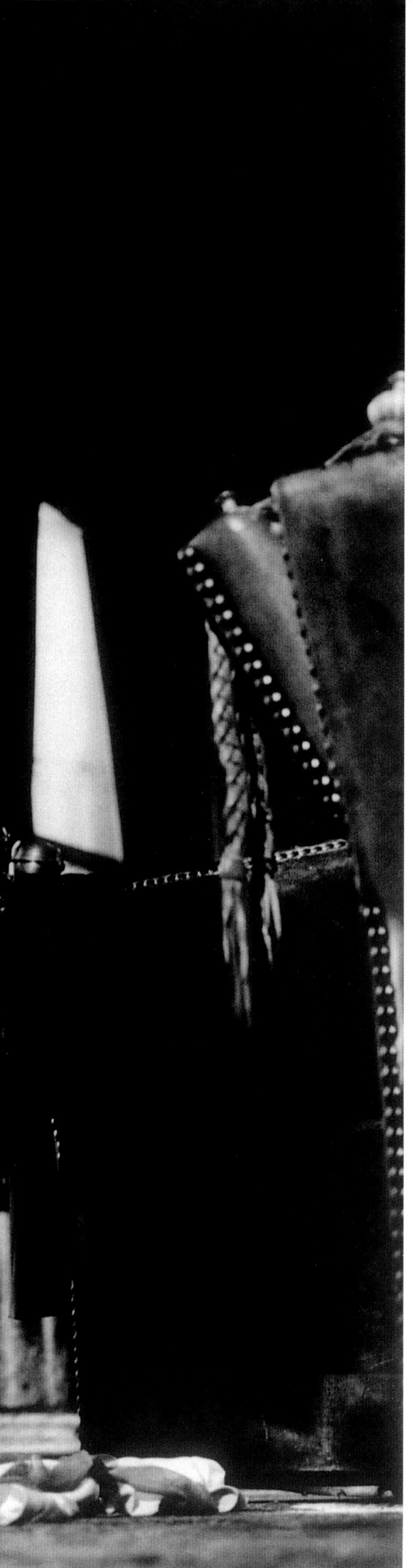

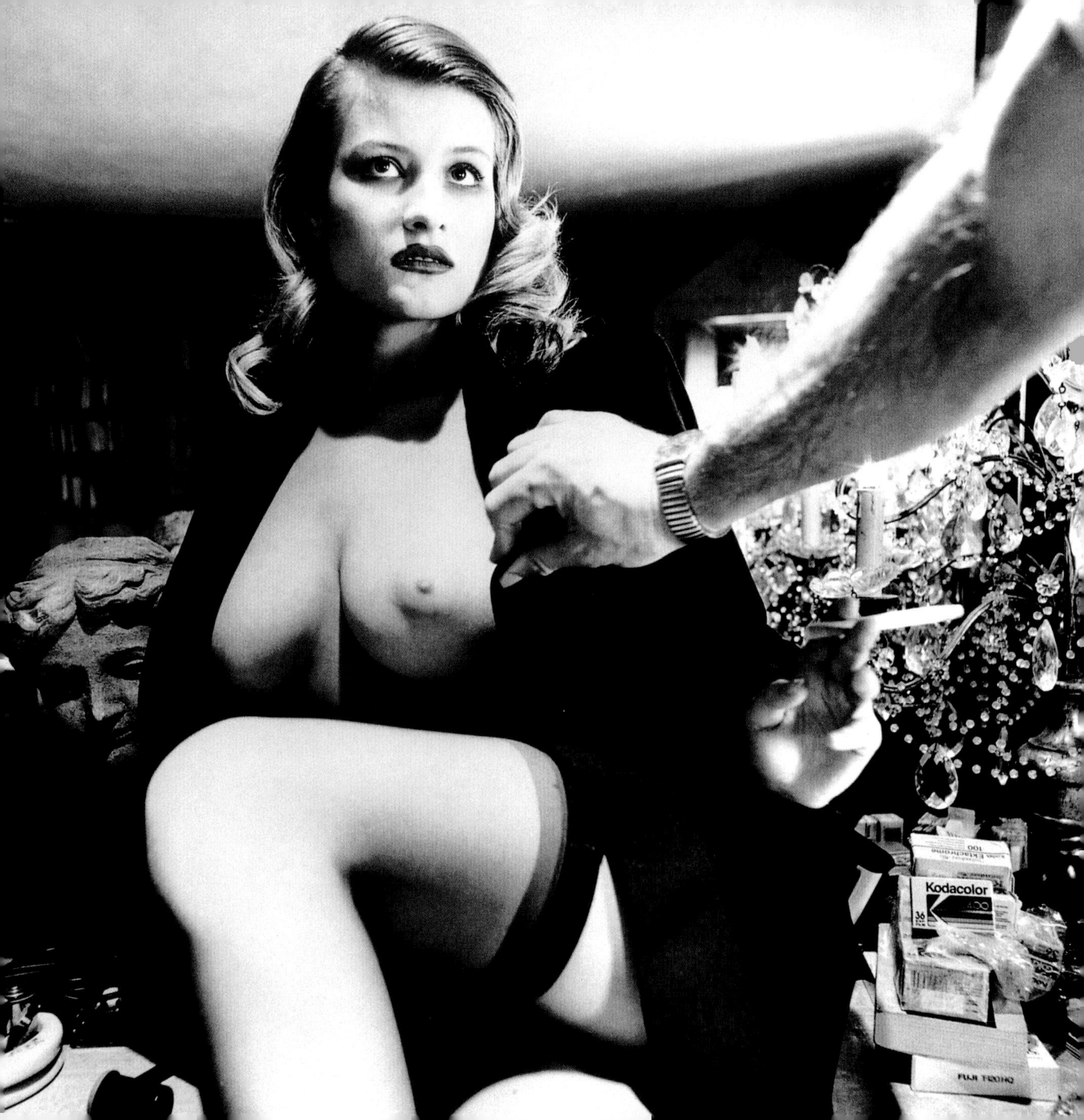
Kodacolor

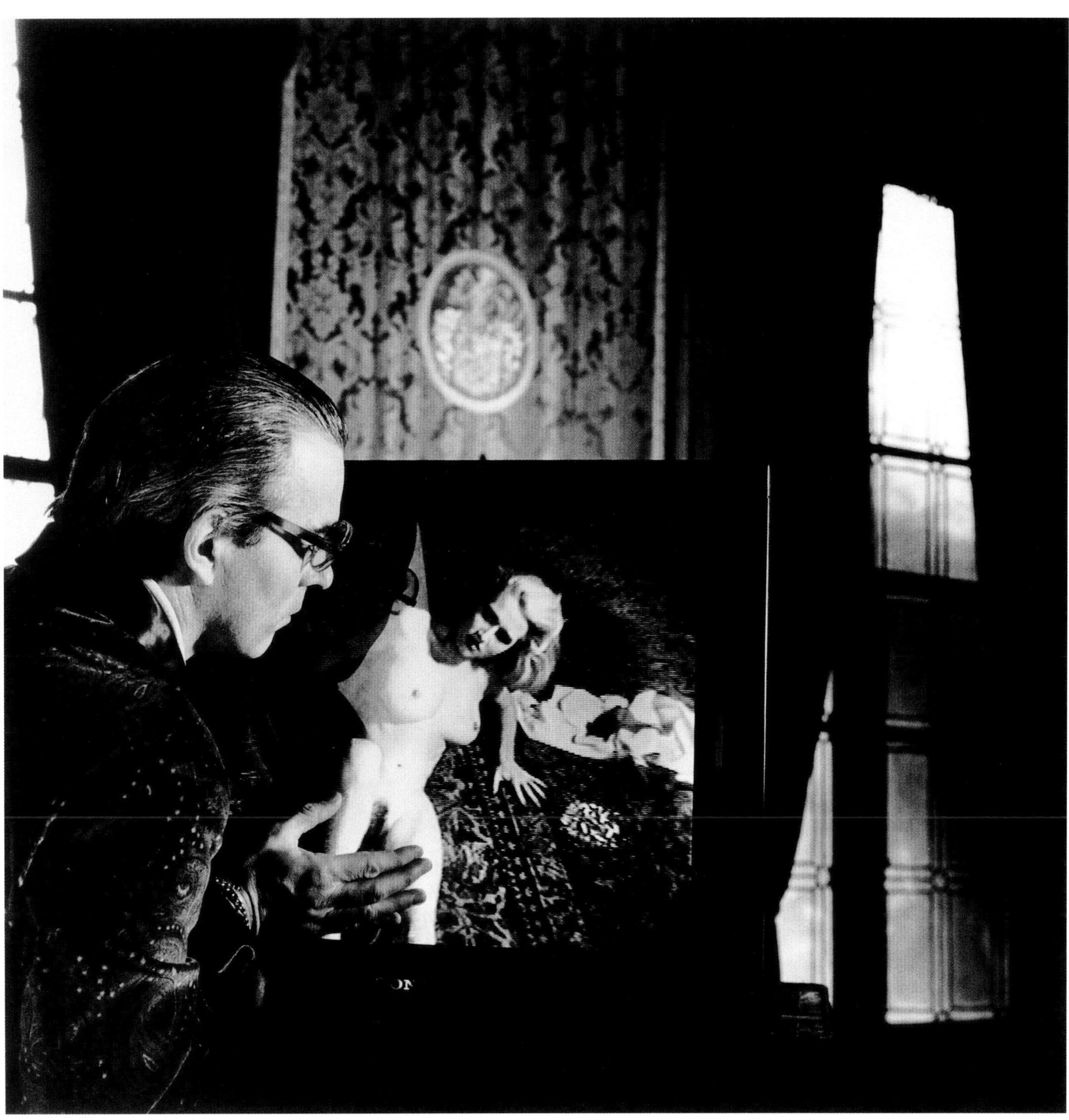

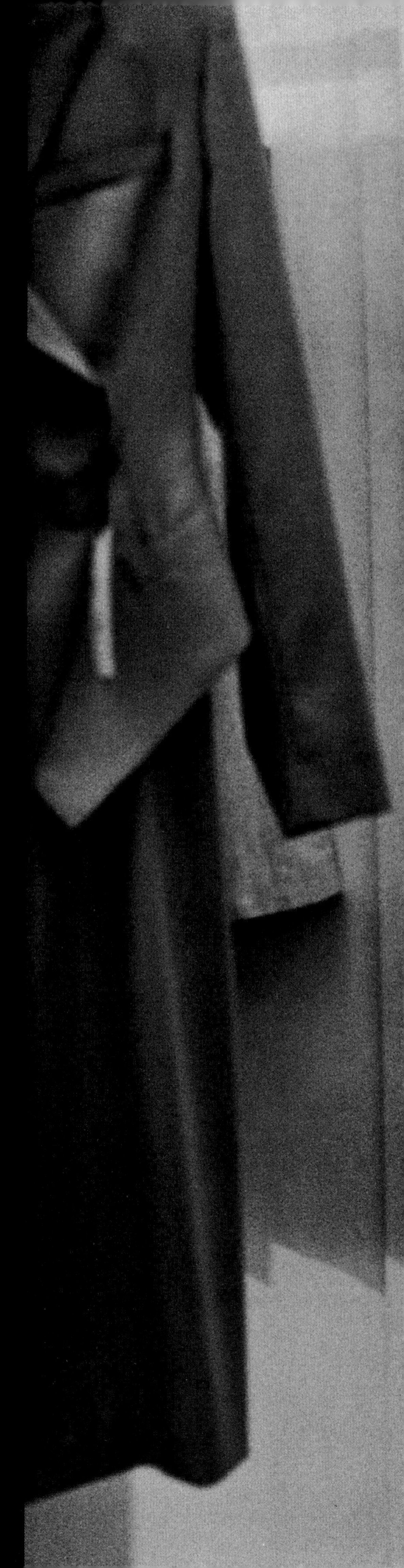

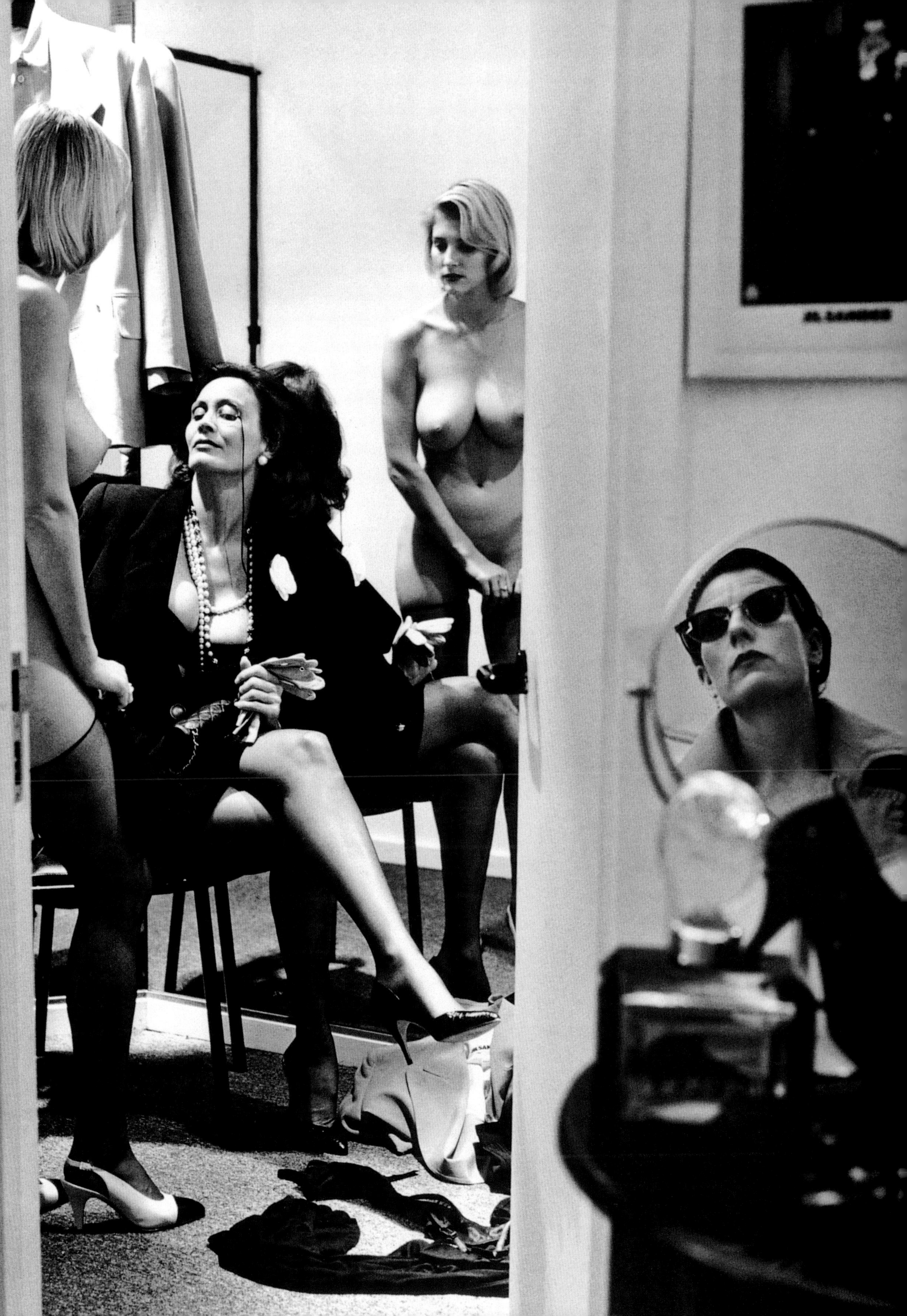

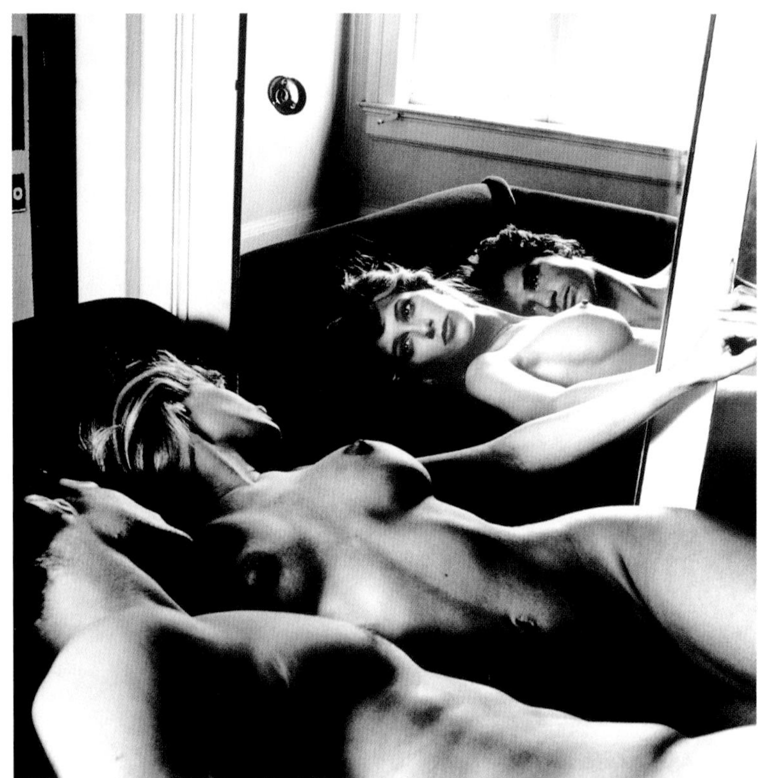

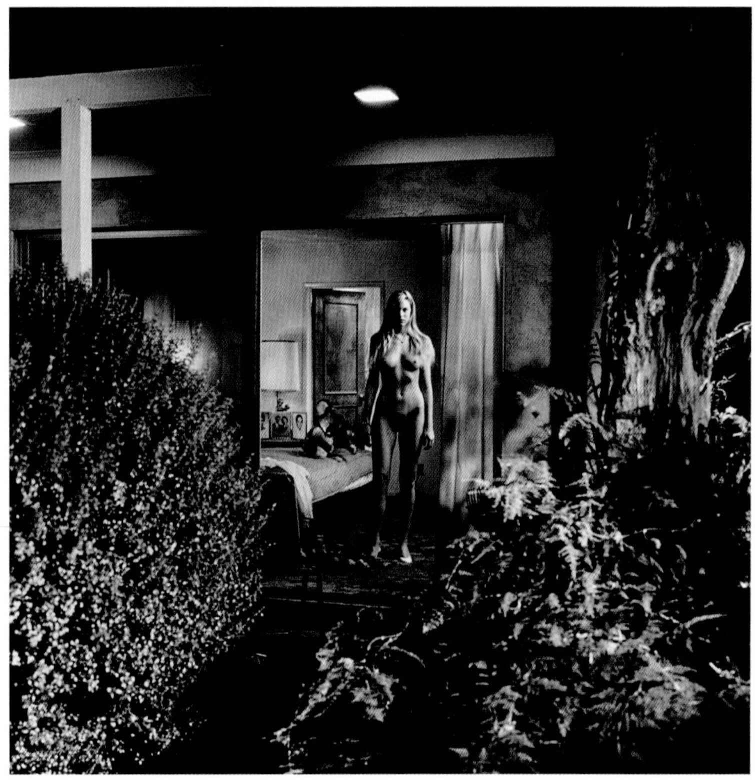

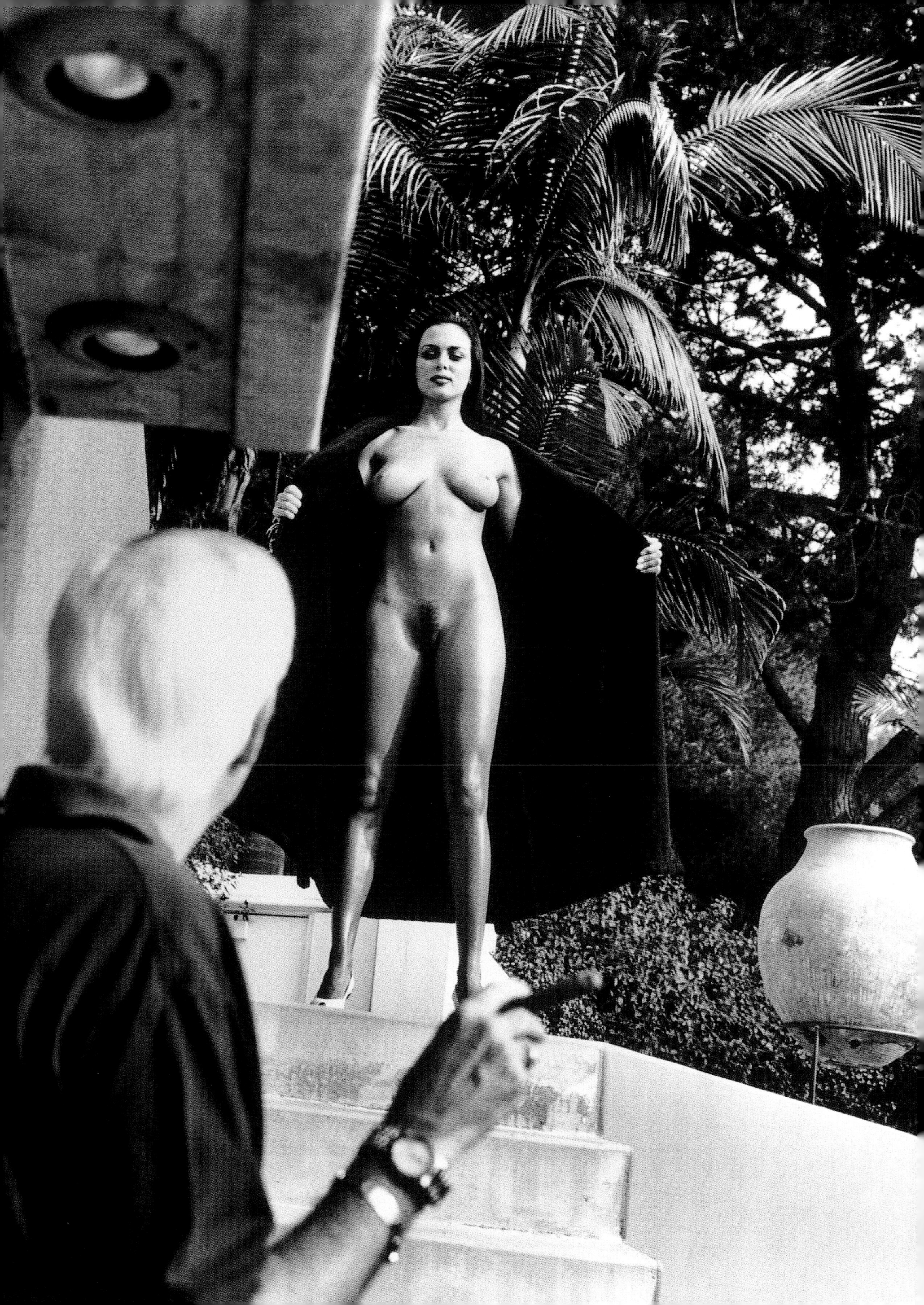

Newton's PHYSIQUES

FEATURING

Claudie Pellerin and Angeleen Gagliano

September 1976

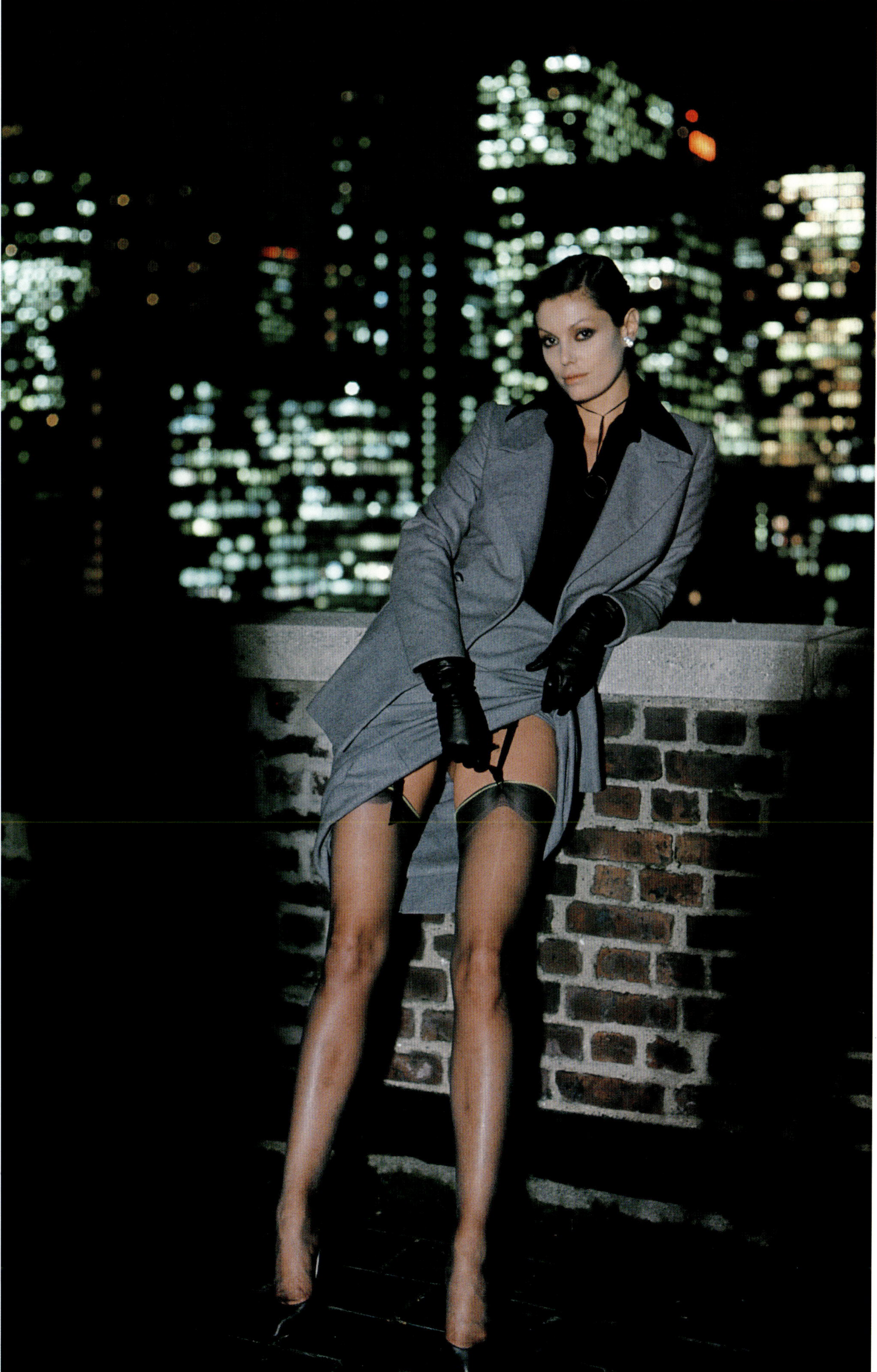

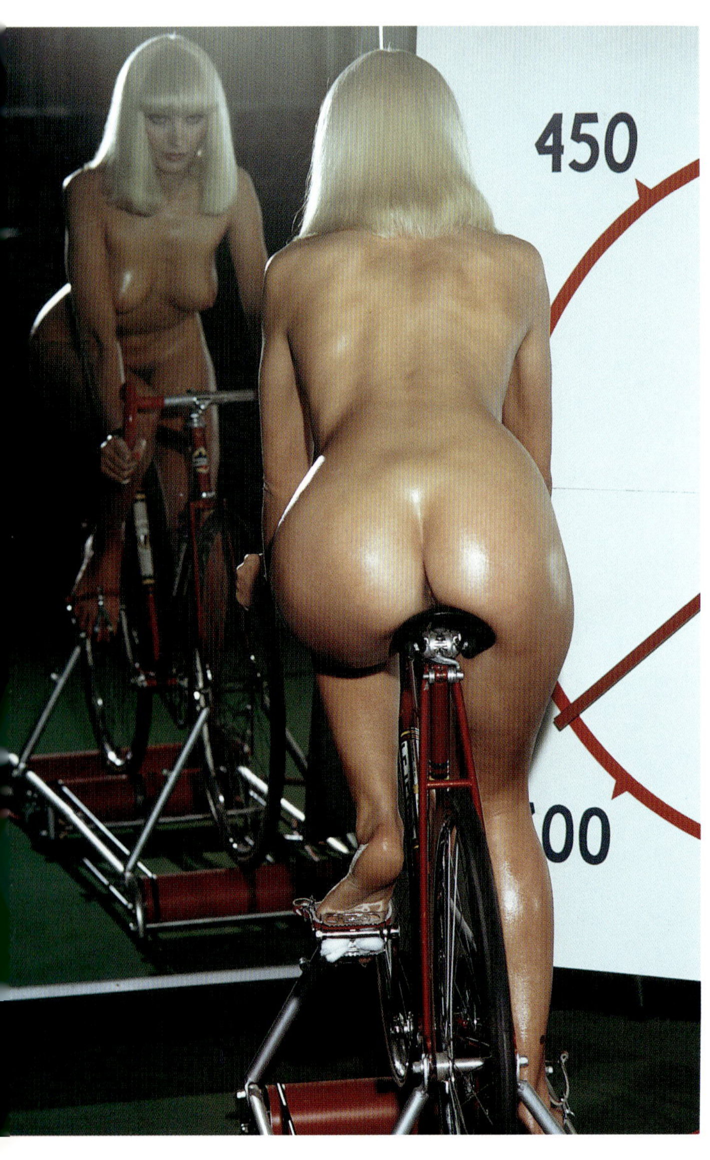
450

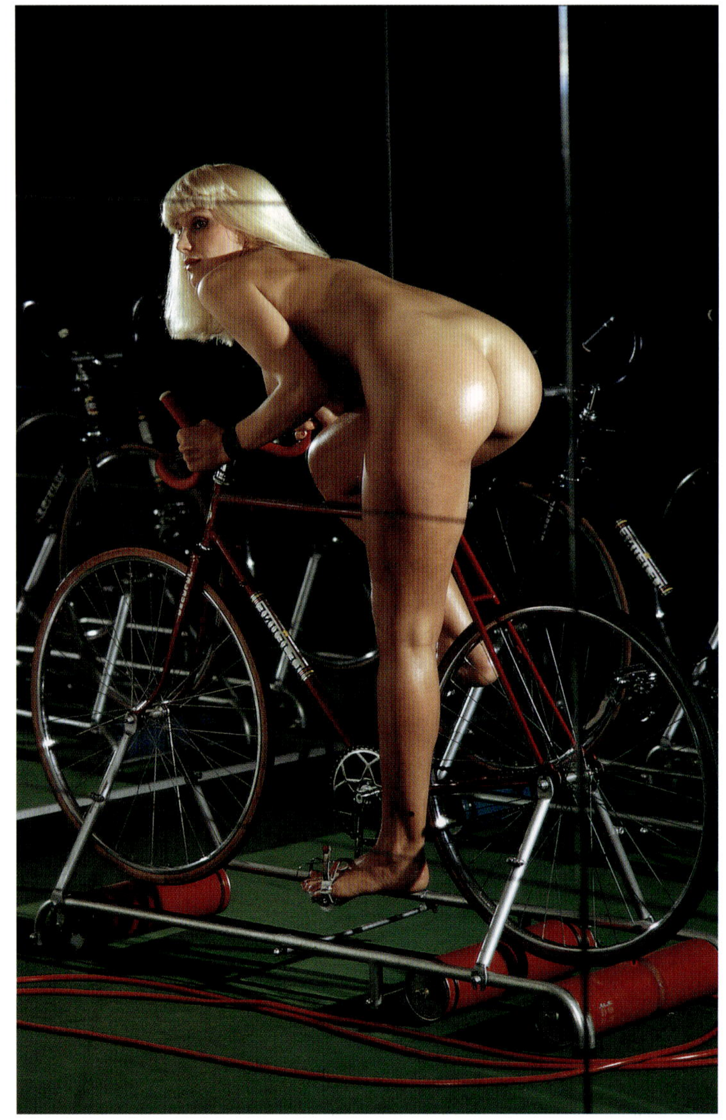

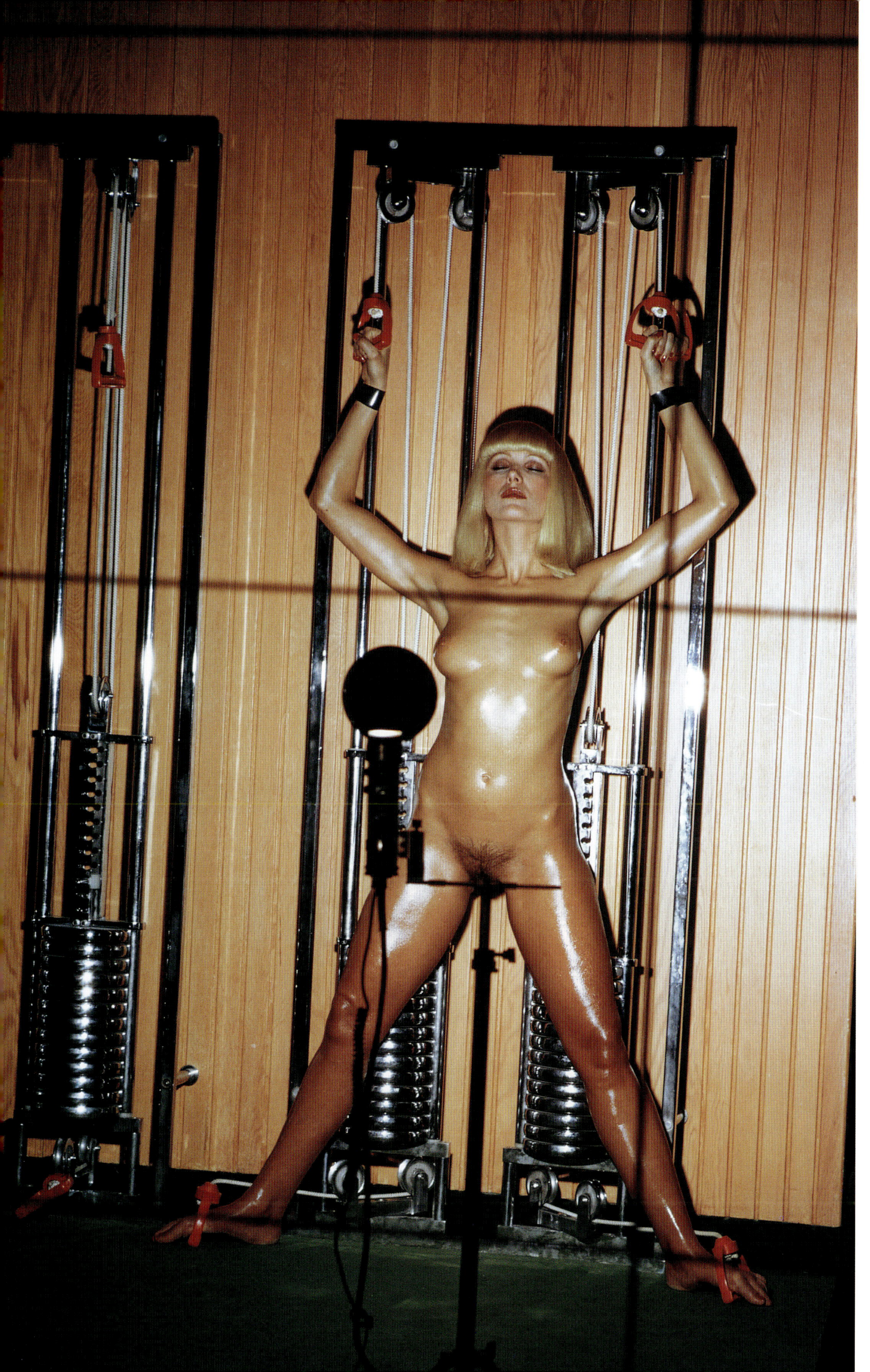

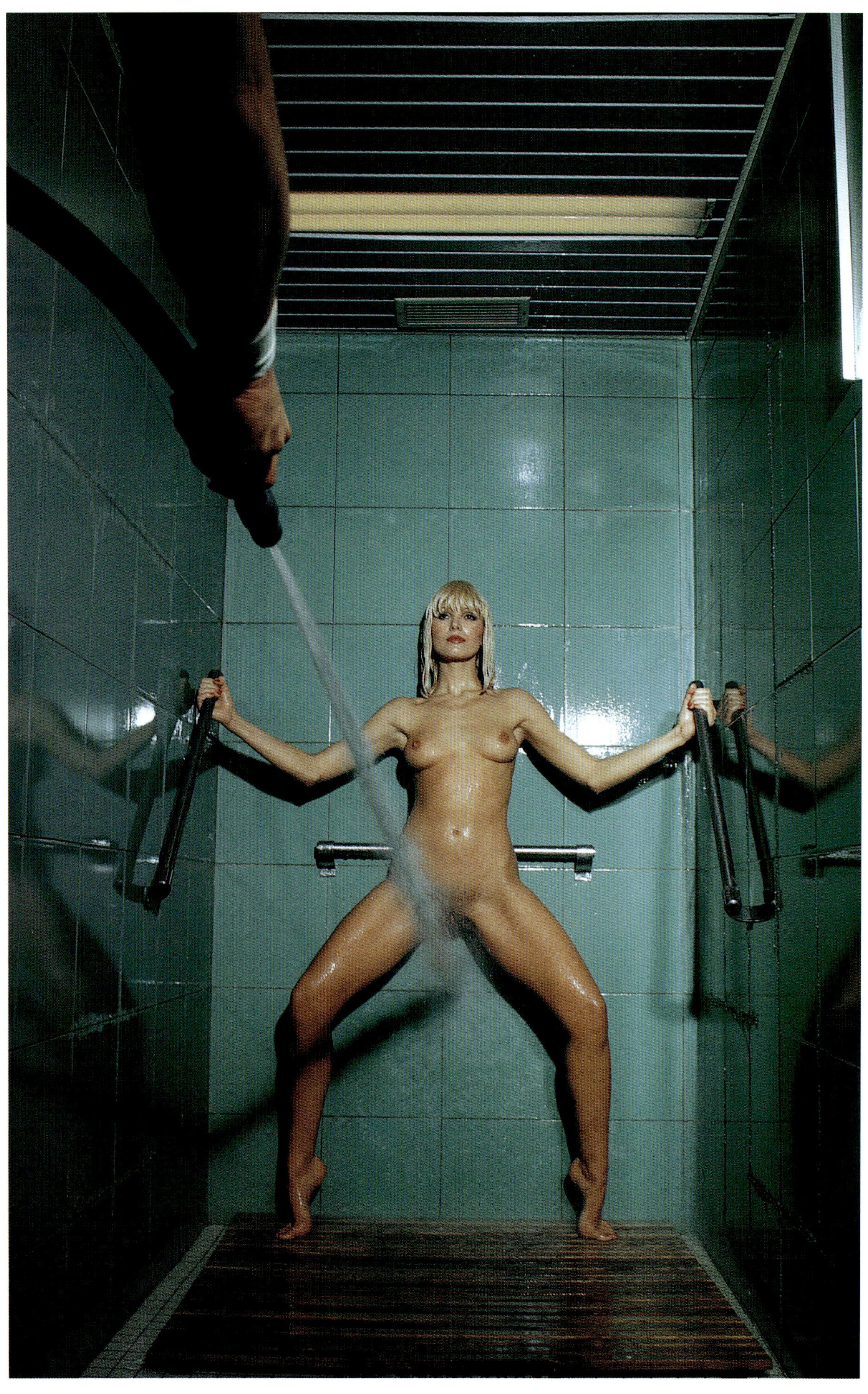

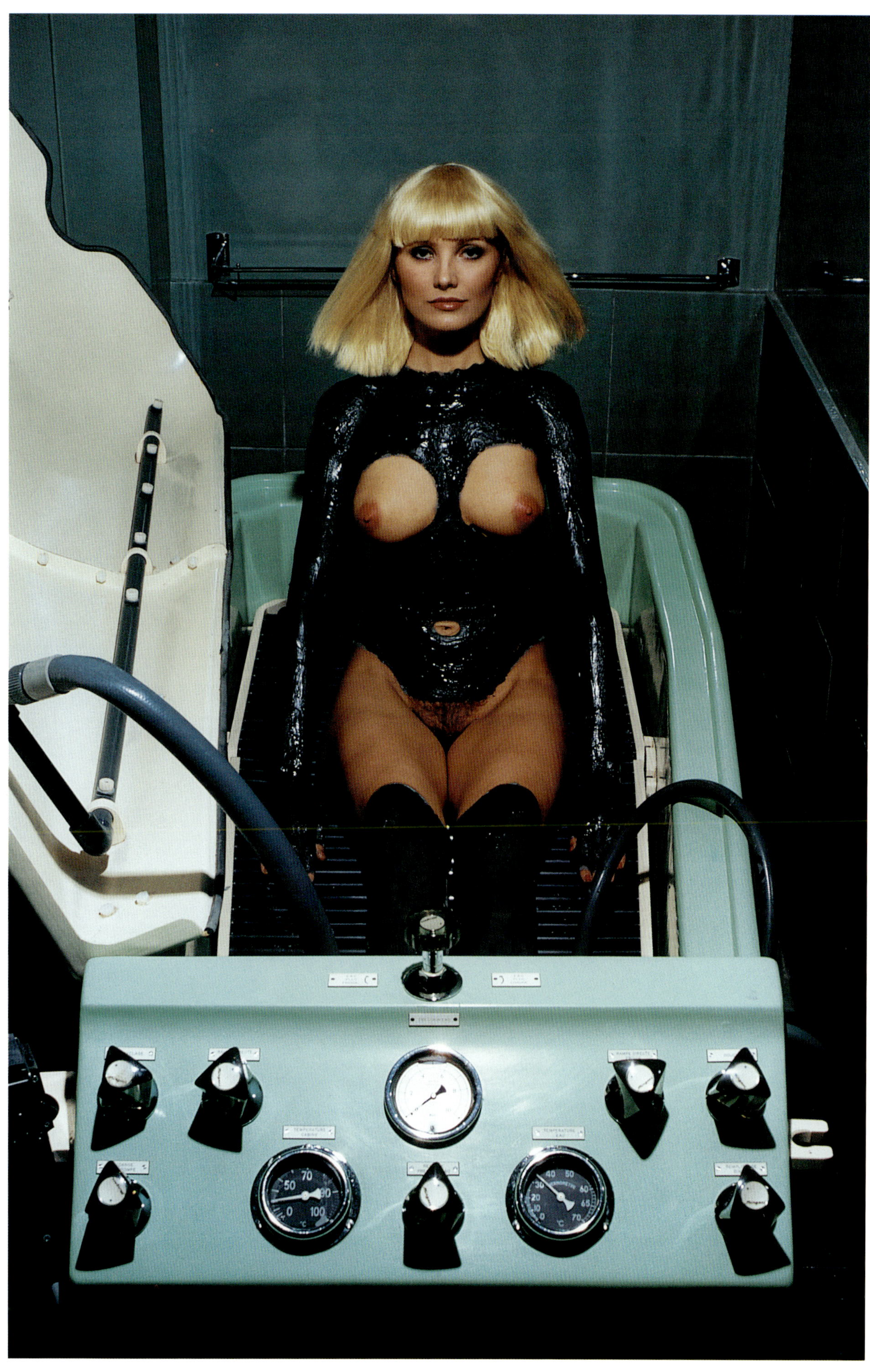

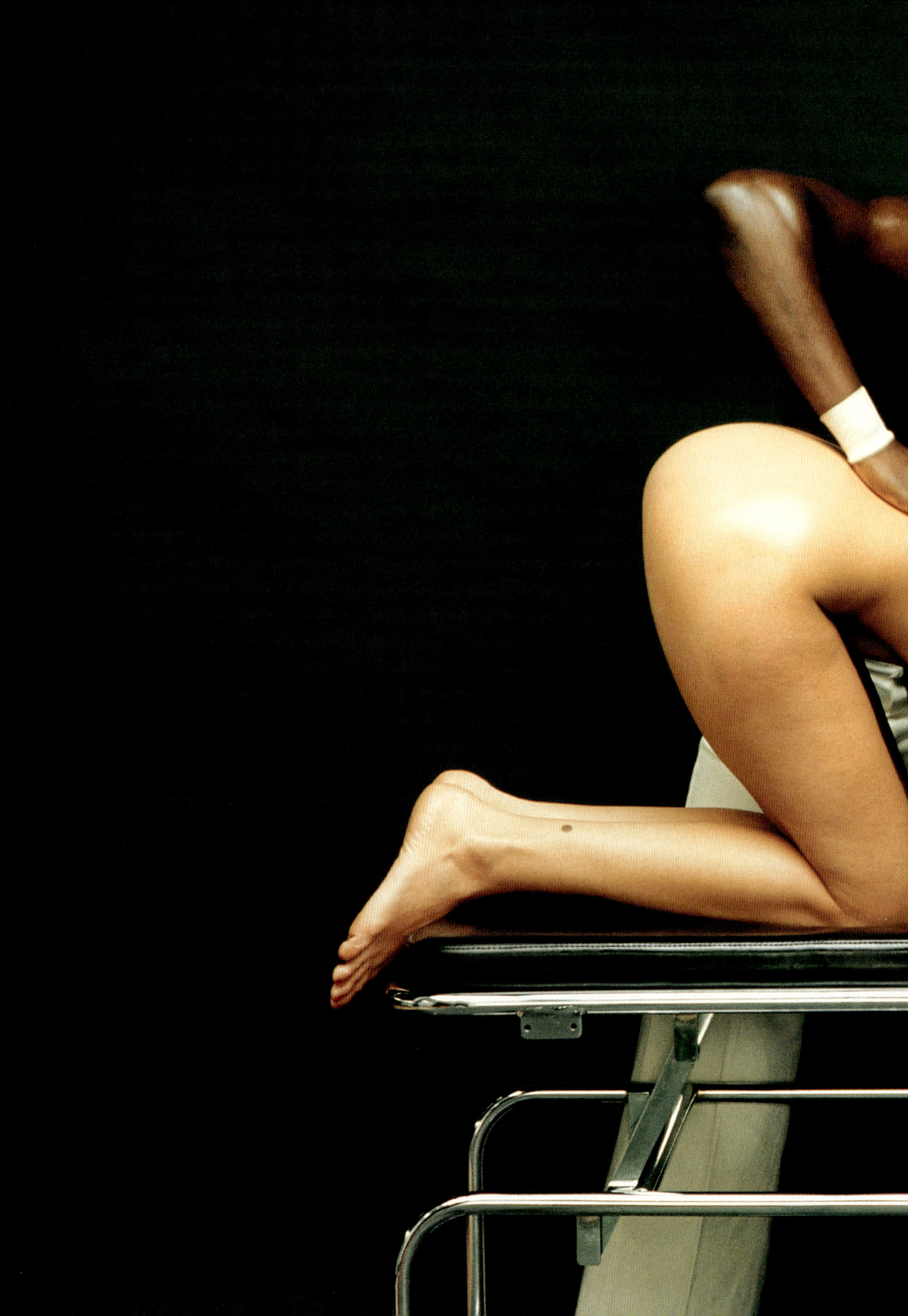

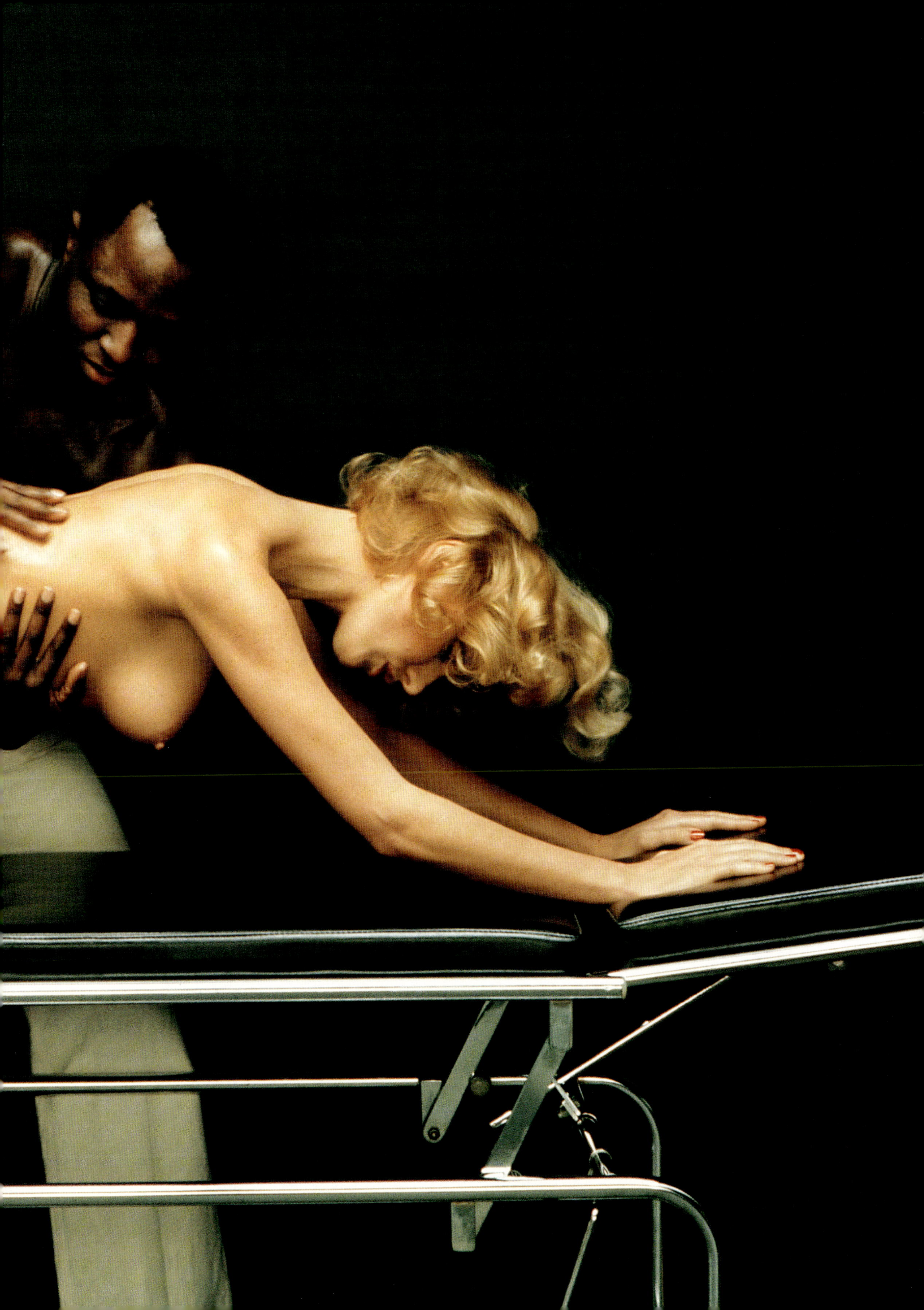

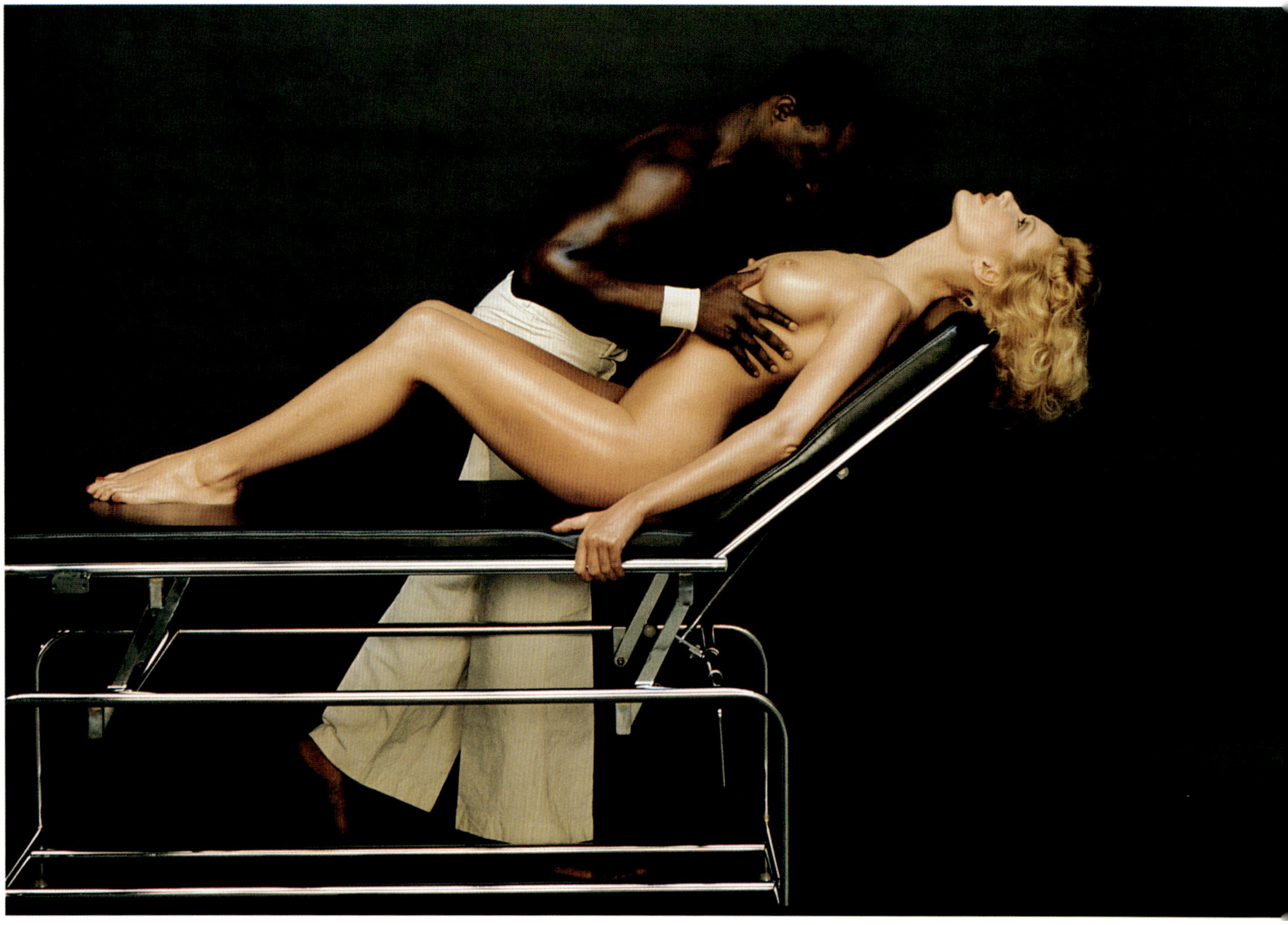

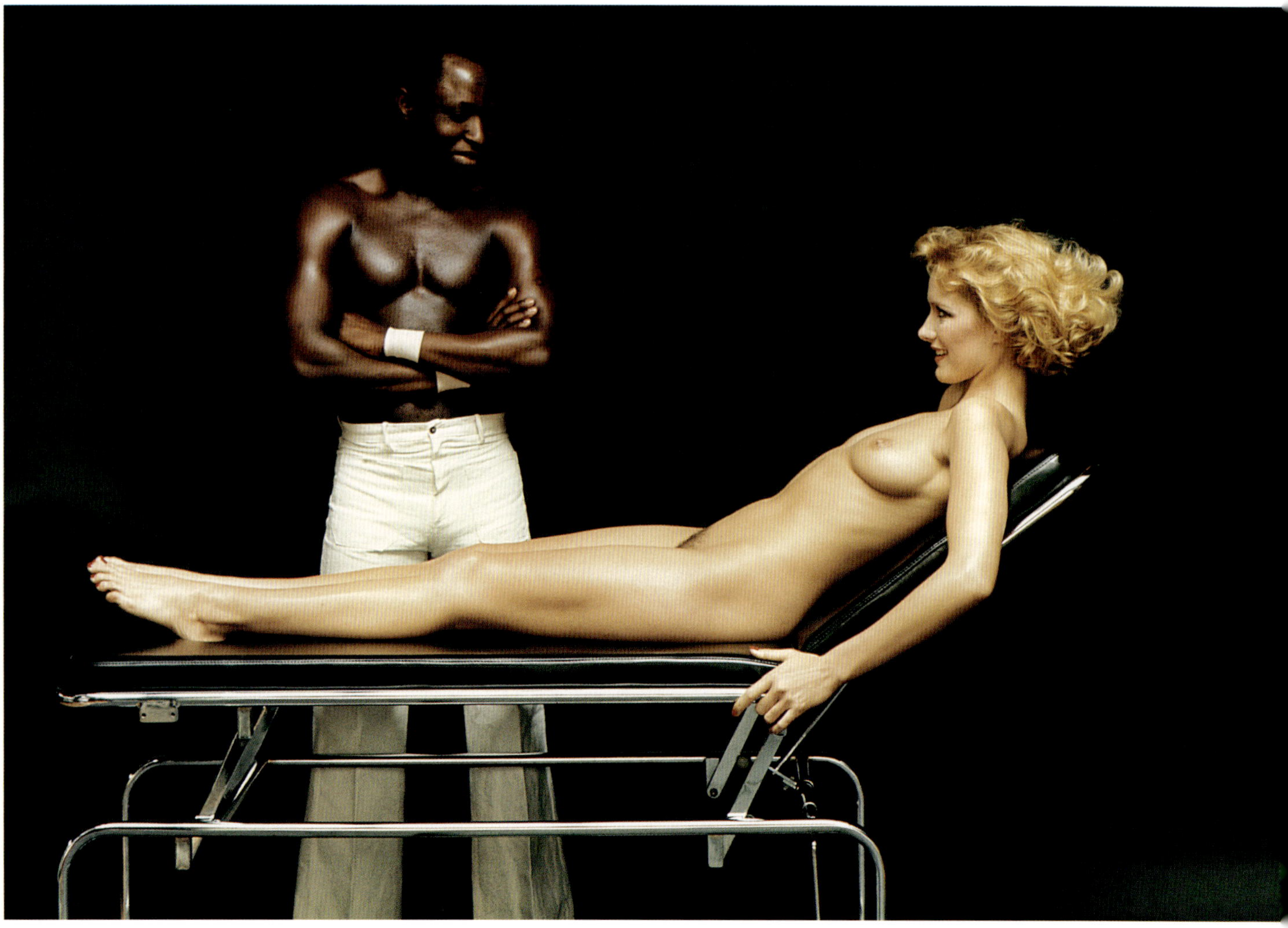

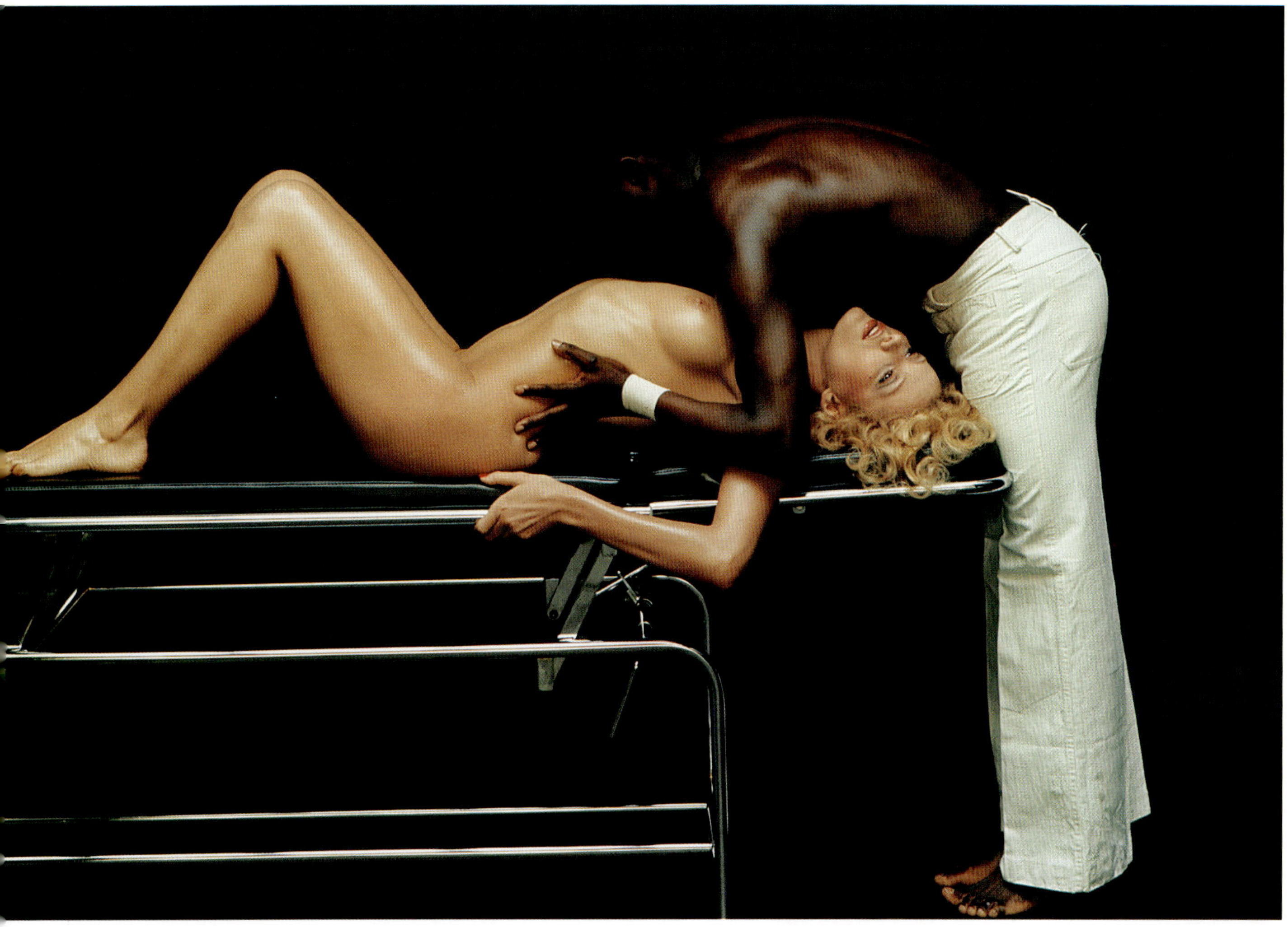

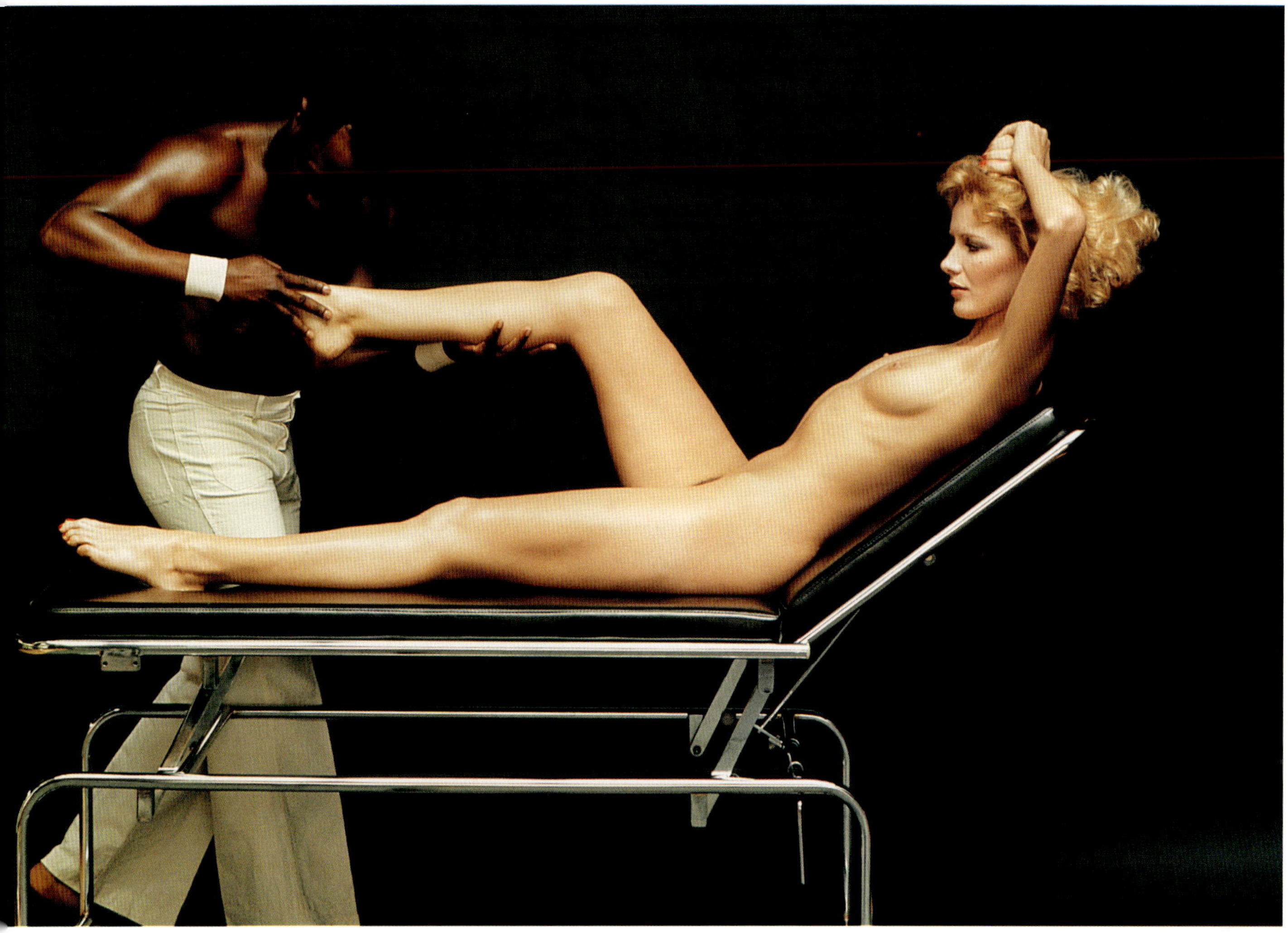

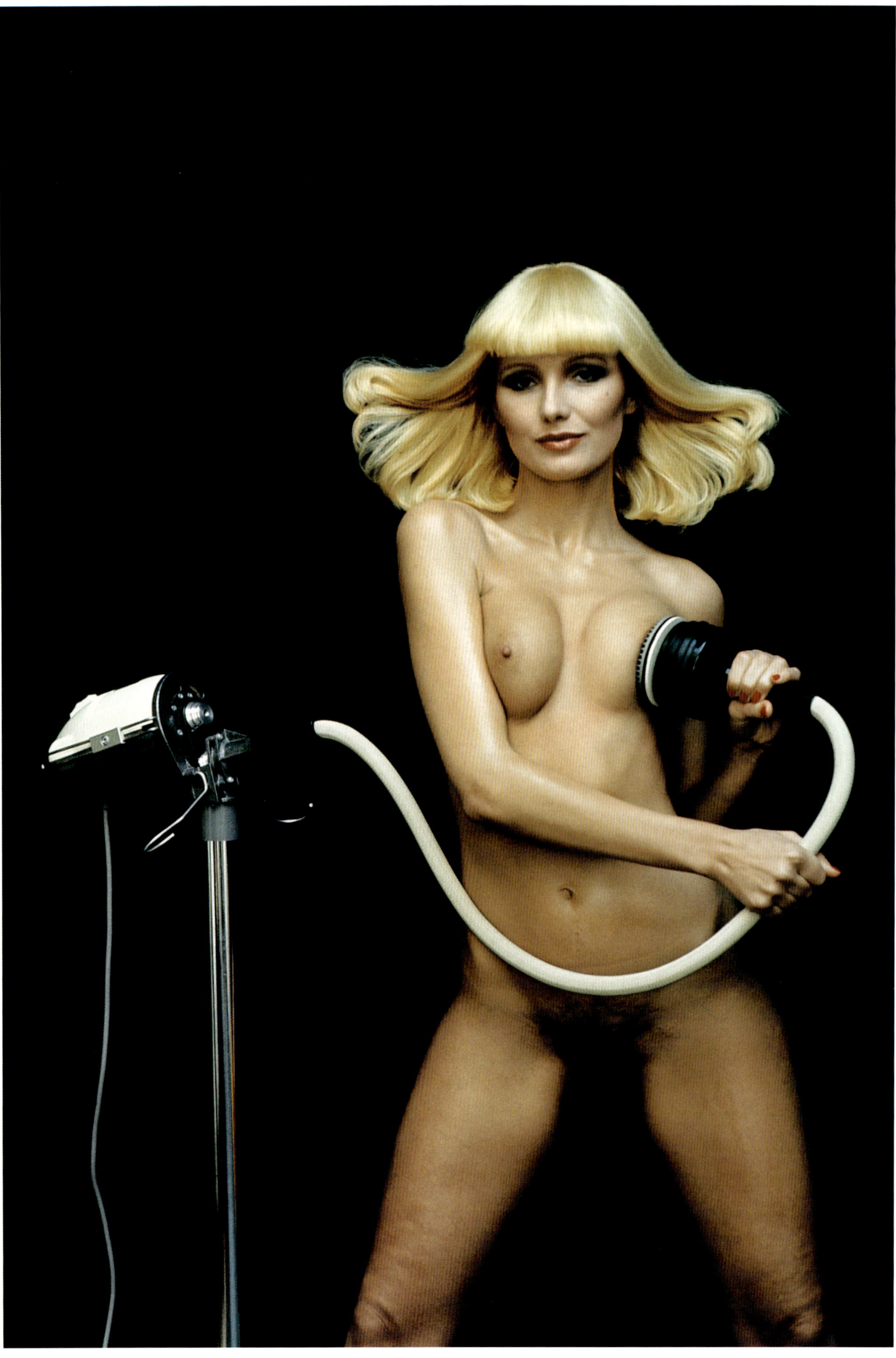

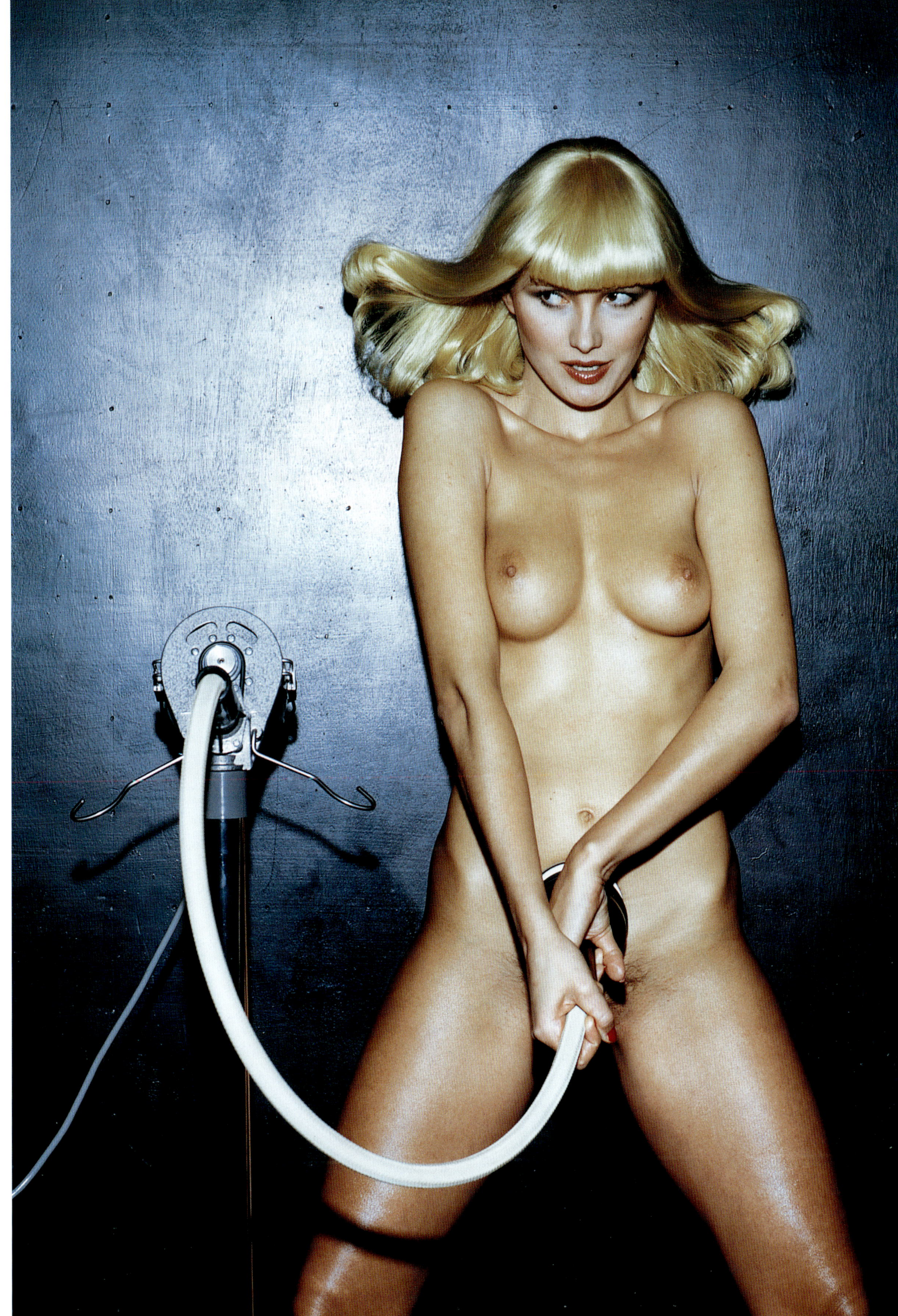

AFTERWORD

As you might expect from his work, Helmut Newton was a most interesting man. His death in a car accident in 2004 at the age of eighty-three represented the loss of one of the world's great visual stylists.

Helmut brought an overt sexuality to photography that simply hadn't been there before. It was bold and out of the context of what everyone else had been shooting. I'll always remember one of the first pictures of his I saw, in which a nude woman reclined next to a pool while a policeman looked at her. What did it mean? Perhaps nothing. But it had an edge. And it took us toward something dark and mysterious.

His photographs were not only edgy and unpredictable, they were uncompromisingly erotic. As Newton would often remark when he accepted an assignment, "Let's try something a little kinky this time." His fascination with photographing beautiful women naturally led him to *Playboy*, where his work first appeared in the mid-1970s. Debra Winger, Charlotte Rampling, and Grace Jones all posed for him. But his favorite *Playboy* subjects were Playmates, shot not in the typical Centerfold style but in unconventional, even dreamlike, settings.

We at *Playboy* became aware of him as a fashion photographer in his early days. He started with European *Vogue*, but he was in American *Vogue* soon thereafter. My predecessor at *Playboy*, Mark Kaufman, knew Helmut. Mark might have been *Playboy*'s first connection to Helmut when he assigned him to shoot Charlotte Rampling for the magazine. Helmut really liked *Playboy;* he loved working for the magazine. When he signed his contracts with Condé Nast, which would not allow him to work for other magazines, he always made a point of having an exclusion so he could continue to shoot for us.

During the 1970s and 1980s, actresses clamored to pose for him. They wanted to be part of his world of glamour and seduction. And his name on their photograph gave them instant credibility. To be shot by Helmut was to become a star.

Helmut's interest in celebrity photography began to wane in the 1980s as celebrities and their publicists insisted on more control over photographers. Helmut wanted to do his own thing, pursue his creative instincts without the intrusion of others. By the late 1980s, Helmut had passed the celebrity-photography torch to Herb Ritts, and he never looked back.

I first met Helmut in Chicago. Although he had done a number of fashion and celebrity assignments for us, it came as no surprise that he wanted to shoot nude pictorials. We arranged those first few assignments by phone, and he shot them in Paris or elsewhere in Europe. Helmut struck up a relationship with Marilyn Grabowski, *Playboy*'s West Coast photography editor. Marilyn's sense of style closely matched Helmut's, and together they produced many of Helmut's most memorable pictorials for the magazine.

To call Helmut fussy would be an understatement. We brought him to Chicago to do a shoot with exercise equipment, a combination service feature and nude pictorial. When he showed up at our offices he kept asking me, "Where are all the beautiful girls?" He had this fantasy that *Playboy*'s lobby and offices would be filled with tall young women walking around in five-inch heels and leather outfits. He was truly disappointed to learn that it wasn't so. We started casting girls for his shooting. We brought in every Playmate, every Playmate candidate, every model in the Midwest who would do nudity. We couldn't find one girl he was happy with. It wasn't that the girls weren't tall enough, that they weren't sexy enough. It was simply too structured a situation for Helmut.

Newton was so much more interested in what was in front of the camera than what was behind it. The equipment, the f-stops, didn't interest him. He was fascinated with women. He was always looking for models. He once called me from a hotel in Switzerland where he was staying, excited about a six-foot-tall waitress he had struck up a friendship with. He telephoned me and said, "Let me do this. She's fantastic. I have to shoot her." There was really no way to say no to Helmut once he latched onto an idea or a model.

Helmut always shot in the thirty-five-millimeter format for *Playboy*. He loved working in black-and-white and had his own darkroom guy in Paris; regardless of deadline, the prints always had to be made by his man. We had to persuade Helmut to shoot in color, because color is so central to the look of the magazine. Hef has a bias toward color. To Hef, black-and-white meant trying to save a buck. Plus, Hef loves the color of skin.

Helmut did almost all of his assignments for us on location. He loved ornately decadent settings. There were Paris hotels, and the mansions and estates of people he knew. He spent much of his time in Monte Carlo and often used its jet-set scenes as settings for his photographs. Although his photos often implied an Old World decadence, he also loved what he called American decadence. And the cities that best represented such decadence to him were Los Angeles and Las Vegas—L.A. with its veneer of glamour pasted over gas stations and car washes, Vegas for its twenty-four-hour underlayer of tawdriness. Tawdry excited Helmut.

For our "200 Motels" pictorial, he called me with an idea. He was in south Florida and wanted to do something in the seedy motels of Key West. We found an actress named Kristine De Bell, who had a young and innocent look. As a matter of fact, she had just been cast as Alice in an adult version of *Alice in Wonderland*. We sent her to Helmut, and the two of them traveled from motel to motel taking pictures. That was Helmut's idea of an erotic adventure. He was Humbert Humbert with a camera, and Kristine was his Lolita.

When we wanted to do a pictorial about voyeurism, Helmut was the perfect guy to shoot it. It was best not to give him any specific ideas for photos. If you gave him an idea, he'd always find a reason not to use it. And he would then bring back ideas that you'd never imagined. They were his visions, and they were always unique.

Sometimes Helmut's photography got too kinky for *Playboy*. The magazine doesn't publish bondage, and Helmut liked a good girl tied up now and then. I don't want to say he ever shot bestiality, but he had an inclination toward nudes and animals that made our legal department uncomfortable.

One of the last times I talked to Helmut, he called to say he had a chance to take pictures in a factory where they made high-priced, lifelike sex dolls, Rolls Royce versions of the blow-up doll. They cost $5,000 and up, and they could be custom-ordered as to expression, hair and eye color, breast size, and so on. Of course, that turned Helmut on to no end. "I have to do this shooting," he said. "Can I have an assignment?" We gave him the go-ahead. He shot it, but the magazine never published the feature. It was so odd that we couldn't find a place for it.

For fifty-six years Helmut was married to Alice Springs, a significant photographer in her own right. I always wondered what their private life was like. Photographically, she looked at things much the same way as he did. Helmut idolized his wife, and I think he considered her a greater creative talent than himself. It was odd but typical of the couple that she would take a photograph of the two of them as Helmut was dying on a table in the emergency room after his accident, his head cradled in her one hand, her camera in the other.

Helmut had suffered a serious heart attack years earlier and nearly died. He photographed himself throughout the entire ordeal, as he was being hooked up to monitors, having needles inserted in his arms. That kind of stuff fascinated him. Even in some of his fashion photography, he had tubes or surgical apparatuses attached to his models.

The man who saw the world through a lens darkly is now gone. But through his work, his vision continues to live.

GARY COLE

"You should feel that, under the right conditions, all women would be available."

HELMUT NEWTON